ICON READERS' GUIDES

Mary Shelley

Frankenstein

EDITED BY BERTHOLD SCHOENE-HARWOOD

Consultant editor: Nicolas Tredell

ICON BOOKS

Published in 2000 by Icon Books Ltd.,
Grange Road, Duxford, Cambridge CB2 4QF
e-mail: info@iconbooks.co.uk
www.iconbooks.co.uk

Distributed in the UK, Europe, Canada, South Africa and Asia by the
Penguin Group: Penguin Books Ltd., 27 Wrights Lane, London W8 5TZ

Published in Australia in 2000 by Allen & Unwin Pty. Ltd.,
PO Box 8500, 9 Atchison Street, St. Leonards, NSW 2065

Consultant editor: Nicolas Tredell
Managing editor: Duncan Heath
Series devised by: Christopher Cox
Cover design: Simon Flynn
Typesetting: Wayzgoose

ISBN 1 84046 134 9   823.8 SHE

Printed and bound in Great Britain by
Cox & Wyman Ltd., Reading

Contents

'I'll Be Back!': Reproducing *Frankenstein*

Looks at film adaptations of the Frankenstein theme, including James Whale's *Frankenstein*, Terence Fisher's *The Curse of Frankenstein*, Ridley Scott's *Blade Runner*, James Cameron's *The Terminator* and Sylvester Stallone's *Rocky IV*. Includes extracts from Paul O'Flinn's important analysis of the many transformations undergone by *Frankenstein* in the long history of its creative reproduction and Thomas S. Frentz and Janice H. Rushing's detailed work on the survival of the Frankenstein myth in contemporary cinema.

A NOTE ON REFERENCES AND QUOTATIONS

All references to *Frankenstein, or The Modern Prometheus* are given in brackets in the text of the Guide. All other references are given in the endnotes.

All quotations from Mary Shelley's novel have been amended to accord either with Marilyn Butler's edition of the 1818 text (OUP 1993) or with Maurice Hindle's edition of the 1831 text (Penguin 1985). These are the most recent and easily available paperback editions in the UK.

In the extracts in this Guide, insertions by the editor are in square brackets and standard type. Definitions of words, where provided in editorial insertions, have been taken from the *Collins Dictionary of the English Language* and *The New Shorter Oxford English Dictionary*, unless otherwise stated in the endnotes. Insertions in square brackets and bold type in the extracts are by the respective authors themselves.

In any quotation, a row of three dots indicates an editorial ellipsis within a sentence or paragraph, and a row of six dots (that is, two ellipses) indicates an editorial omission of a paragraph break, or of one or more paragraphs.

INTRODUCTION

F*RANKENSTEIN* IS without doubt Mary Shelley's most famous work. Even professional readers are unlikely to have heard of any of the novels Shelley wrote after the overwhelming success of her tale of artificial creation. Only very few people are familiar with the contents of *Valperga* (1823), *The Last Man* (1826), *The Fortunes of Perkin Warbeck* (1830), *Lodore* (1835) and *Falkner* (1837) or any of her shorter fiction, travel writing and biographical essays.[1] Similarly, her amply annotated edition of her late husband Percy's work, first published in 1839, is now almost exclusively reserved for the attention of scholars specialising in the critical appraisal of Romantic poetry.

This Guide is dedicated to an examination of *Frankenstein*'s unparalleled popularity, its enduring critical appeal, semi-mythical status and endless trail of creative remouldings, appropriations and reproductions. For over a hundred years after its first publication in 1818, Shelley's novel led a spectral existence in the shadow of 'high culture' and, as a monstrous oddity deemed unworthy of any closer scrutiny, found itself categorically ostracised from the realm of serious scholarly attention. This has changed dramatically since the late 1970s. Not only is Shelley now ranked amongst the best, most remarkably talented writers of her generation, but her first novel has also gained the status of a nineteenth-century classic whose meanings continue to proliferate beyond the symbolic fixity of any one definitive interpretation. Alan Rauch seems mistaken when he asserts that 'new perspectives on *Frankenstein* are hard to come by',[2] even though his statement is clearly not intended as a reference to the exhaustibility of *Frankenstein*'s repertoire of possible meanings, but rather as an admission of defeat in the face of the vast range of interpretations already facilitated by the novel. As Johanna Smith has demonstrated in her recent edition of *Frankenstein* as part of Bedford Books' series of case studies in contemporary criticism, the novel can be approached fruitfully from a multitude of different interpretive angles inspired by the reading practices of critical schools as discrete and often mutually incompatible as reader-response criticism, feminism, psychoanalysis, Marxism or cultural criticism. That there are absolutely no limits whatsoever to *Frankenstein*'s significatory spectrum is perhaps signalled most pertinently by the titles of two recent publications: Frann Michel's 'Lesbian Panic in Mary Shelley's *Frankenstein*' and Jay Clayton's 'Concealed Circuits: Frankenstein's Monster, the Medusa, and the Cyborg'. While Michel searches Shelley's 'apparently straight' text for 'subtextual and coded representations' of lesbian desire,[3] Clayton reads *Frankenstein* against an alleged 'similarity between Romantic and post-modern perspectives on reason, technology, and the environment'.[4]

As suggested by the great diversity of both critical and creative approaches to *Frankenstein* collected in this Guide, the enduring appeal of Shelley's novel is evidently to do with its radical indeterminacy and ambivalence, that is, its textual 'monstrosity' as a composition that amalgamates the oppositional and allegedly irreconcilable: the old and the new, life and death, maleness and femaleness, horror and enthusiasm, fantasy and the tragic inescapability of biographical fact. In her introduction to the revised 1831 edition, Shelley sets the tone for the novel as a whole when, divided emotionally between affectionate fondness and nauseous repulsion, she sees *Frankenstein* simultaneously as her 'hideous progeny' and 'the offspring of happy days' (*F* 1831, p. 10). This ambivalent attitude of the author towards her work mirrors the disastrous turmoil of Shelley's own experiences with procreation. Significantly, in both her life and her fiction, every birth manifests itself as a potential catastrophe, with the body of the newborn shockingly transmogrified into the monstrous corpse awaiting resuscitation in its mother's dream. Following the death of her first, prematurely born daughter in February 1815, Shelley notes in her journal: 'Dream that my little baby came to life again – that it had only been cold & that we rubbed it by the fire & it lived – I awake & find no baby – I think about the little thing all day.'[5] Given such documentary evidence, it is not difficult to detect a pertinent resemblance between the story of *Frankenstein* on the one hand and Shelley's biography on the other. Haunted by her baby's death and vainly conjuring possibilities of reviving her, Shelley was also deeply traumatised by the knowledge of her own mother's death in giving birth to her. It seems important to note here that all her life Shelley felt responsible for causing the demise of her mother, Mary Wollstonecraft Godwin, who was a woman of strong political convictions and the author of *A Vindication of the Rights of Woman* (1792), which became the conceptual cornerstone of the nineteenth-century British feminist movement.

Frankenstein's central vision of an artificial reanimation of the dead may well find its roots in the author's painful loss of her mother and first-born child, which may also explain her novel's intensity of feeling as well as its sudden mood swings from parental love to guilt and disgust and from filial subservience to anger and resentment. However, it took a casual story-writing competition between Mary, her husband Percy, Lord Byron and Byron's friend John Polidori for Shelley's wishful fantasy to surface and take narrative shape. In the summer of 1816, kept indoors by inclement weather, the Shelleys spent much time at their neighbour Byron's Villa Diodati at Cologny on Lake Léman in Switzerland, where the friends kept themselves amused by reading ghost stories to each other and discussing the political and scientific topics of the day. Percy Shelley and Lord Byron were particularly intrigued by the possibility of 'ensouling' lifeless matter by means of electricity, which was widely regarded as the force most likely to generate and sustain life. When finally the friends decided to write a ghost story each and see whose was the most chilling and terrifying, Mary came up with *Frankenstein*, a tale that owed as much to her own life story as to the scientific queries and fanciful ideas entertained by the men closest to her. However, not only the scientific themes and pressing emotional issues that inform *Frankenstein* are inspired by the author's real-life experiences and circumstances. According to Chris Baldick in *In Frankenstein's Shadow: Myth, Monstrosity, and Nineteenth-Century Writing*, the autobiographical dimension of *Frankenstein* is perhaps most conspicuous in the novel's manifold references to Shelley's immediate family and friends. Pointing out that 'the names and status of some of the novel's characters are drawn from Mary Shelley's acquaintance', Baldick writes:

■ Elizabeth was the name of Percy Shelley's sister and his mother, and Victor was a name adopted in boyhood by Percy himself – a fact which has encouraged some commentators to identify him too hastily with Victor Frankenstein, when his portrait is given more clearly in the character of Henry Clerval. William was the name not just of Mary Shelley's father but also of her half-brother and of the son she was raising while writing the novel.[6] □

According to the majority of critics cited in this Guide, Shelley's greatest achievement resides in her novel's allegorical multi-facetedness which renders references of an intimately personal nature part of a larger historical metaphor that accentuates the universal applicability of *Frankenstein* as a moral fable. Thus, an investigation into the author's character and the circumstances surrounding the genesis of her tale opens up to a general problematisation of the nineteenth-century woman writer's irresolvable division between her masculine aspirations on the one hand and feminine duties on the other. Also, as the product of a writing competition between three men and one woman, *Frankenstein* takes shape under constant male probing or, to put it more acutely, barely tolerable patriarchal pressure. '"Have you thought of a story?" I was asked each morning', Shelley writes, 'and each morning I was forced to reply with a mortifying negative' (*F* 1831, p. 8). Invariably, it seems, in *Frankenstein* the personal becomes political while the biographical subsumes history and fantasy feeds on the hypotheses of contemporary scientific conjecture.

The first chapter of this Guide begins with a discussion of the early reviews of *Frankenstein*. About half of these condemn the novel as both formally and thematically offensive because of its Gothic style, anarchic attitudes and blasphemous disposition, which identify it clearly as a text that not only advertises but flaunts the political legacy of the French Revolution. Even those reviews that initially appear to propagate a more balanced assessment with regard to the author's talent, vision and skill are dismissive and unsympathetic in their response to *Frankenstein* as the herald of a new age that threatens to destabilise the ideological foundations of society's status quo. Clearly, while the central imagery and motifs of Shelley's novel could not fail to capture and intrigue the popular imagination, the self-professed guardians of cultural propriety found *Frankenstein* severely lacking in the kind of morally edifying instruction that was thought to characterise a genuinely 'good' read. Only in the second half of the twentieth century was *Frankenstein* rehabilitated as a profoundly moral text whose sources of inspiration encompassed the whole western tradition from the Bible to Edmund Burke's highly influential eighteenth-century aesthetics of the sublime. In this respect, M. A. Goldberg's seminal essay on morality and myth in *Frankenstein*, first published in the late 1950s, must be seen as an important precursor to George Levine and U. C. Knoepflmacher's *The Endurance of Frankenstein*, which has come to stand as an index of the critical diversification of Shelley's novel in the 1970s and its belated canonisation as a kind of missing link in the evolution of British fiction.

Chapter two contextualises Shelley's achievement within a complex web of intertextual relations that range from the work of her immediate family – her mother, father and husband – to that of her Romantic peers and from classical mythology to the philosophy of the Enlightenment. As this chapter also shows, there is a widespread critical tendency to pathologise Shelley as a badly traumatised female who, debilitated by biographical and historical circumstance, appears to write exclusively for therapeutic reasons. According to this view, perhaps most strikingly epitomised by Elisabeth Bronfen and Mary Poovey's readings, Shelley must be regarded as a painfully self-conscious victim of familial strife compounded by patriarchal coercion. Alternatively, so James Carson and James O'Rourke suggest in their essays, Shelley can be seen as a defiant and remarkably independent mind who forges a representational aesthetics of her own beyond, and in pronounced opposition to, her fellow Romantics' masculinist cult of the self and obsessive celebration of creative originality. This latter view concurs with Theodore Ziolkowski's perception of *Frankenstein* as modernity's most poignant and topical myth, which it took a genius like Shelley to craft, more or less single-

handedly, out of an inspired aggregation of different, mutually contra-
dictory western traditions.

The third chapter combines an examination of psychoanalytic
approaches to *Frankenstein* with a more general investigation into the
legitimacy and truth-claim of a variety of different strategies of critical
meaning-making. Thus, Paul Sherwin's formidable apologia of Freudian
thought both celebrates psychoanalytic criticism's challenging experi-
mentality and strongly repudiates its interpretive practice of construing
definitive meanings from a text's 'hidden' deep structure of authorial
trauma and repression. Fred Botting is equally protective of the novel's
fundamental ambivalence. Intriguingly, he shows how *Frankenstein* can
be read allegorically as a critique of a certain type of reading process
within which the critic assumes the position of the male overreacher
who, by violating the original authenticity of the female-authored text,
creates a monster that represents not the desired integrity of a single
meaning but, on the contrary, reveals the composite, intrinsically chaotic
nature of signification itself. Criticism invariably aims to unriddle literature's potentially subversive obscurity by making sense of its
inconsistencies, flaws, and general significatory deviance. Hence, so
Devon Hodges suggests, literary criticism is perhaps best apprehended
analogically as a 'masculine' assertion of power that, with patriarchal
sanction, perpetrates a symbolic colonisation of the 'feminine' text. Of
course, such an analogy would gain particular significance within the
context of a critical assessment of women's writing, whose textual 'monstrosity' – defined by its technical unconventionality and apparent
imperviousness to interpretation – constitutes an intransigent gesture of
female resistance in a masculinist world of symbolic perfection.

Feminist criticism has had an enormous impact on the critical revaluation of *Frankenstein* over the last two decades. In fact, in many respects
it could be said that it was literary women's studies which initiated the
process of scholarly reassessment that eventually resulted in the canonisation of Shelley's novel. It was primarily the publication of three
important feminist re-readings in the late 1970s and early 1980s that
induced academia to reconsider the status and significance of *Frankenstein*.
These were Ellen Moers's reading of the novel as a 'birth myth', Sandra
Gilbert and Susan Gubar's provocative analysis of *Frankenstein* as a
'daughterly rewrite' of John Milton's *Paradise Lost* and, finally, Barbara
Johnson's suggestion that it may well have been Shelley's female 'pen
envy' as a categorically marginalised woman writer that prompted her to
portray a group of men as corrupted and crazed by 'womb envy'. The
fourth chapter of this Guide is concerned with an examination of some
of the critical offspring of these early feminist repositionings, most especially Anne Mellor's illuminating, but reductive reading of *Frankenstein* as
a feminist indictment of men as compulsive and emotionally unbalanced

rapists of Mother Nature, and Burton Hatlen's extremely sophisticated interpretation of the novel as an attempt to dismantle 'the patriarchal mythos of creation' and replace it with a less hierarchised system of values and qualities traditionally owned by the feminine gender. The chapter concludes by looking at the recent trend among feminist critics to concern themselves more sympathetically with Shelley's representation of men. Both Bette London and Colleen Hobbs read the novel as a critique of patriarchal processes of man-making that often lead not to the desired creation of superhuman heroes but instead spawn monsters running amok in the grip of hysterical paranoia. As the texts collected in chapter five indicate, this is only one possible aspect of the great diversity of both cultural and political discourses of monstrosity that one finds encapsulated in the imagery and other representational techniques of *Frankenstein*. Lee Sterrenburg, for example, reads Shelley's novel against the background of late eighteenth- and early nineteenth-century reactionary literature, which is full of strategic devices designed to demonise the revolutionary project. Choosing an entirely different point of departure, Alan Bewell discusses *Frankenstein*'s apparent preoccupation with obstetrical explanations of monstrosity and Alan Rauch reflects on the novel as a commentary on the pre-programmed terror that invariably inhabits new scientific discoveries in general. Finally, in chapter six, the Guide ventures briefly into an examination of creative re-interpretations of *Frankenstein*'s monstrosity. The changing configurations of meaning inspired by the prototypal quandary of Victor Frankenstein's relationship with his monster are traced from their original composition to James Whale and Terence Fisher's highly successful film adaptations as well as more recent cinematic reproductions of the Frankenstein theme, such as *Blade Runner, The Terminator* and *Rocky IV*.

Frankenstein has maintained its imaginative appeal and socio-political relevance for almost 200 years and at present there seem no limits to its ongoing popularity. Still very much alive, there can be no doubt that it will continue to celebrate triumphant comebacks. Therefore, rather than opting for the spurious linearity of a chronological narrative, this guided tour through the secondary literature on *Frankenstein* has chosen to follow as closely as possible the intricate structure of Shelley's novel. Comprising an elaborate patchwork of different critical perspectives, the Guide allows itself to come full circle from *Frankenstein*'s original production to its multifarious appropriations, all the time revolving concentrically around one single purpose, which is the acknowledgement of Shelley's creative genius and the eventual release of her reputation from 'the caricature which has plagued her since 1818 – that she was an inept neophyte who chanced upon a myth'.[7]

CHAPTER ONE

'It's Alive!': The Reception and Endurance of *Frankenstein*

THE CONTEMPORARY reviews responding to the first publication of *Frankenstein* in 1818 fall roughly into two oppositional groups: those quick to voice their moral outrage and indignant disapproval, and those guardedly expressing a sense of intrigue, fascination and respect. In order to make sense of this apparent rift between conservative and cautiously progressive reactions to Mary Shelley's novel, it seems essential to understand the early nineteenth century as an age of transition during which Britain struggled to emerge from the cataclysmic aftermath of the French Revolution in 1789 and began to brace itself, if still quite reluctantly, for desperately needed societal reform. Against this background the tale of Victor Frankenstein assumes epochal significance. The theme of the monstrous *doppelgänger* metaphorically encapsulates a schismatic present that is at once discursively constituted and tragically torn by the ideologically irreconcilable demands of a despotic past on the one hand and an increasingly democratic future on the other. Mixing fantastic irrationality with scientific speculation, *Frankenstein* embodies a patchwork of different traditions that are about to converge into something unprecedented and new. The fanciful tale of Frankenstein's creation is backed up by the most recent developments in early nineteenth-century science.[1] Significantly, according to the 'Author's Introduction' of 1831, the nightmare that allegedly inspired the novel was fuelled by Shelley's silent attendance at her husband and Lord Byron's nocturnal discussions of 'various philosophical doctrines . . . and among others the nature of the principle of life, and whether there was any probability of its ever being discovered and communicated' (*F* 1831, p. 8). However, most strikingly symptomatic of *Frankenstein*'s oscillation between scientific fact and individual fantasy seems the circumstance that, although it clearly represents the prototype of a new literary genre – that of science fiction,[2] it continues to employ the rather worn-out, sensationalist devices of the Gothic novel, which reached its peak of popularity in 1794 with the publication of Ann Radcliffe's *The Mysteries of Udolpho* but, by the early 1810s, had entered on a course of rapidly accelerating decline.

Essentially a missing link between the eighteenth and nineteenth centuries, *Frankenstein* incorporates both romantic and realist qualities. For example, it features solitary, larger-than-life characters of a Gothic mould yet eschews the introduction of clear-cut contrasts between villainous and heroic figures. Instead of providing unequivocal moral reassurance by confirming and thus reconsolidating orthodox beliefs and attitudes, in *Frankenstein* the good and the evil are often presented provocatively as virtually indistinguishable from each other – be it in the dualism of Victor and his monster or, by implication, in the relationship between Satan and God. However, while Shelley skilfully exploits the allegorical potentialities of the Gothic – especially its dream-like atmosphere and archetypal encounters that set the scene for a haunting literary enactment of general human fears and desires – her novel also contains many long treatise-like passages exhibiting and elaborating on philosophical arguments characteristic of the Enlightenment period. In retrospect, then, contemporary reviewers may seem quite justified to have regarded *Frankenstein* either as a belated, hopelessly anachronistic spin-off from the Gothic or as a forward-looking, even prophetic work of genius containing a hitherto unheard-of, boldly visionary problematisation of scientific progress. It seems vital in this context also to remind oneself of the rigid generic rules and inflexible critical parameters that governed both the production and evaluation of literature in the early nineteenth century. Longer prose texts were categorically divided into 'novels' on the one hand and 'romances' on the other. Hence, the main criterion in the original assessment of *Frankenstein* concerned the question if it could justifiably be described as a 'novel'. Was it 'realistic' in its rendition of a fictional world, that is, did it faithfully subscribe to ordinary notions of morality and comply with a 'proper', commonsensical understanding of social life? Or was *Frankenstein* better described as a 'romance', that is, as a narrative inspired by wild flights of fancy resulting in a subjective and hence potentially subversive representation of the human condition? This classification of *Frankenstein* as either a 'novel' or a 'romance' was crucial. In the early nineteenth century, critics were inclined to read improbable, 'romantic' plot developments as indicative of the author's decadence and moral depravity. Literary deviancy was widely suspected to be expressive of political deviousness and dissent.

Conflating the narrative genres of 'novel' and 'romance', *Frankenstein* represents an example of literature in transition. Marked by passionate outbursts of unruly and excessive feelings of love, hatred, revenge and guilt, it inevitably strikes most readers as a typical offshoot of the 'Gothic craze' that dominated literary expression in the late eighteenth century. At a second glance, however, it might just as legitimately be described as a precursor of realism – soon to become the new century's most popular and dominant mode of narration. Pertinently, according to George Levine, *Frankenstein* displays a religious scepticism and obsessive preoccupation with the material world that are typical of almost all major achievements in nineteenth-century creative, philosophical and scientific thought:

■ In writers as central and various as [Ludwig] Feuerbach [1804–1872, German philosopher], [Auguste] Comte [1798–1857, French mathematician and philosopher], [Charles] Darwin [1809–1882, English naturalist], [Karl] Marx [1818–1883, German founder of modern communism], and [Sigmund] Freud [1856–1939, Austrian originator of psychoanalysis] we can find Victor Frankenstein's activity: the attempt to discover in matter what we had previously attributed to spirit, the bestowing *on* matter (or history, or society, or nature) the values once given to God.[3] □

The ambiguous, hybrid nature of *Frankenstein* as a Gothic novel with realist tendencies or, alternatively, as an early realist novel firmly rooted in the Gothic tradition, is interestingly addressed in Percy Shelley's originally anonymous 'Preface', in which he poses as the novel's author. In anticipation of Victorian values and ideals, Percy describes *Frankenstein* as devoid of 'the enervating effects of the novels of the present day' and chiefly interested in 'the exhibition of the amiableness of domestic affection, and the excellence of universal virtue' (*F* 1831, p. 12). *Frankenstein* is claimed to be quite evidently *not* a Gothic novel since 'the event on which the interest of the story depends is exempt from the disadvantages of a mere tale of spectres or enchantment'. At the same time, Percy resolutely defends *Frankenstein*'s tendency to imagine rather than simply represent reality. Instead of condemning authorial innovation and creativity as gratuitous manifestations of a poetic licence better declined than made use of, Percy hails them as all truly great literature's most indispensable assets. Accordingly, the fanciful improbabilities of *Frankenstein*'s plot ought not to be criticised but appreciated as opening up 'a point of view . . . more comprehensive and commending than any which the ordinary relations of existing events can yield' (*F* 1831, p. 11).

Ironically, it is Mary Shelley herself who in her introduction to the edition of 1831 self-consciously detracts from *Frankenstein*'s realist implications. Ultimately effecting a deplorable diffusion of *Frankenstein*'s profoundly political impact and significance, she refers to the novel as a mere 'ghost story' motivated by little more than her own whimsical passion for 'the formation of castles in the air – the indulging in waking dreams – the following up trains of thought, which had for their subject the formation of a succession of imaginary incidents' (*F* 1831, p. 5). Thirteen years after her novel's first publication, Shelley seems ready to abandon her youthful commitment to radical politics and adapt to the new *zeitgeist* of reactionary consolidation. As Fred Botting argues, Shelley's introduction represents far more than 'an appendage' (*F* 1831, p. 5); it constitutes 'a new frame' that transforms the novel by recontextualising it.[4] Shelley displays an acute awareness of the problems her early nineteenth-century readers confronted in their encounter with her 'hideous progeny' (*F* 1831, p. 10), problems that invariably culminated in the question if *Frankenstein* made proper, respectable reading material. In *Ariel Like a Harpy*, the first monograph on *Frankenstein*, Christopher Small draws attention to the contradiction that, although the novel was officially branded as 'disgusting and horrifying . . . it has continued, with these qualifications, to be read ever since'.[5] Shelley's re-presentation of *Frankenstein* as an 'occasional' tale certainly helped popularise the novel by making it a more acceptable read. However, published just one year before the first Reform Bill (which began the gradual legislative process of extending the franchise in Britain), Shelley's introduction may also signal how sensitive the author had become to her novel's explosive potential as an upsetting reminder of the horrors of the French Revolution as well as the possibility of those horrors returning. It seems worth remembering that *Frankenstein*'s original publication in 1818 must have seemed like a major affront to all those who, after Napoleon's defeat at Waterloo in 1815, had reason to believe that the age of revolutionary chaos and real-life Gothic terror had at long last come to an end. In contrast, by the time *Frankenstein* went into its third edition in 1831, Britain seemed to have overcome the traumatic upheavals of the past and found itself at the beginning of an era of reform and political renewal. Shelley's introduction appears to reflect her consciousness of this promising development as well as her utterly erroneous assumption that real-life reforms had begun to outdate the spectacular topicality of her monster, reducing it to little more than an obsolete, if historically interesting, gesture of defiance.

One is tempted to speculate that if the original edition of *Frankenstein* had been furnished with an explanatory author's note similar in tone and content to the 1831 introduction, the novel would have been unlikely to attract reviews as vituperative and frenetic as John Croker's, which appeared in the *Quarterly Review* in 1818. Rather than incensed by the novel's actual content, Croker's relentless disparagement of *Frankenstein* seems primarily motivated by the work's anonymous dedication to William Godwin, Mary Shelley's father, who was loathed by the conservatives as a Jacobin anarchist and notorious supporter of the French Revolution. For this reason, Croker's review must first and foremost be read as part of a reactionary backlash against radicalism and the general popular hope for societal change. Within the framework of Croker's diatribe, *Frankenstein* is treated not exclusively as a work of literature but moreover as the manifestation of an impending political catastrophe. Looking back on the many negative responses to the first publication of *Frankenstein*, Christopher Small explains:

■ For *Frankenstein* and works like it are not read, any more than they are written, as deliberate allegories whose moral may be approved or disapproved, but as events in themselves, and it was from the book as an event, a summing-up of the actual processes and forces of disturbance and change, that those frightened by change in general involuntarily recoiled. Such a reaction was, one may say, instinctive, and reasons were found for it later or remained unspoken.[6] □

Most of Croker's review consists of a sarcastic plot summary aimed at denigrating the intellect, imagination and craftsmanship of the novel's author. The creation of Frankenstein's monster, for example, is ridiculed as a moment of farcical vacuity: 'The creator, terrified at his own work, flies into one wood, and the work, terrified at itself, flies into another.'[7] Presenting William Godwin as 'the patriarch of a literary family . . . which strangely delights in the most afflicting and humiliating of human miseries', Croker describes *Frankenstein* as 'a tissue of horrible and disgusting absurdity'.[8] Croker's review concludes with the quotation of three longer extracts from *Frankenstein* cited to 'agitate the nerves of our readers'[9] and expose what Croker construes in his final two paragraphs as the text's hyperbolic pathos and blasphemous irrationality:

■ It cannot be denied that this is nonsense – but it is nonsense decked out with circumstances and clothed in language highly terrific: it is, indeed

– 'a tale
Told by an idiot, full of sound and fury,
Signifying nothing' –

but still there is something tremendous in the unmeaning hollowness of its sound, and the vague obscurity of its images.

But when we have thus admitted that *Frankenstein* has passages which appal the mind and make the flesh creep, we have given it all the praise (if praise it can be called) which we dare to bestow. Our taste and our judgment alike revolt at this kind of writing, and the greater the ability with which it may be executed the worse it is – it inculcates no lesson of conduct, manners, or morality; it cannot mend, and will not even amuse its readers, unless their tastes have been deplorably vitiated – it fatigues the feelings without interesting the understanding; it gratuitously harasses the heart, and wantonly adds to the store, already too great, of painful sensations. The author has powers, both of conception and language, which employed in a happier direction might, perhaps, (we speak dubiously,) give him [*Editor's note:* Croker's consistent use of the masculine pronoun suggests that he suspects a man – most probably Percy Shelley – to be the anonymous author of *Frankenstein.*] a name among those whose writings amuse or amend their fellow-creatures; but we take the liberty of assuring him, and hope that he may be in a temper to listen to us, that the style which he has adopted in the present publication merely tends to defeat his own purpose, if he really had any other object in view than that of leaving the wearied reader, after a struggle between laughter and loathing, in doubt whether the head or the heart of the author be the most diseased.[10] □

Croker aims to present *Frankenstein* as a nonsensical and deeply immoral work written solely for the perverse gratification of its author and dedicatee. And yet, no matter how determinedly Croker repudiates the novel and disparages its author, he is clearly in awe of the work's powerful suggestiveness. Instead of disdain or contempt, it is panic and dread that motivate Croker's venomous onslaught. As a result, the author of *Frankenstein* emerges from the attack not as a lunatic but a dangerous political adversary whose vision might corrupt society irreparably or, indeed, bring about the end of society as Croker and his kind know and intend to preserve it.

Two more reviews of *Frankenstein* appeared in 1818 (in the *Gentleman's Magazine* and in the *Edinburgh Magazine*), neither of which shares Croker's political paranoia, although both concur with him on the novel's blasphemous attitude and quite regrettable reliance on a string of ungainly and irreverent improbabilities. Unlike Croker's obnoxious outpouring, the writers of these two reviews attempt to be as fair, disinterested and critically balanced as possible in their assessment. Consequently, they are quite capable of condemning the author's choice and treatment of her subject matter without losing sight of the novel's indubitable merits, its compelling attractiveness and display of remarkable artistic talent and skill. Thus, the anonymous reviewer in the *Gentleman's Magazine* refers to *Frankenstein* as 'evidently the production of no ordinary Writer', adding that 'though we are shocked at the idea of the event on which the fiction is founded, many parts of it are strikingly good, and the description of the scenery is excellent'.[11] Similarly, Sir

Walter Scott, who has been identified as the author of the review that appeared in the *Edinburgh Magazine*, feels no need to hide his admiration for *Frankenstein* which he describes as a powerful and intriguing read. 'There never was a wilder story imagined', he exclaims.[12] And yet, Scott's fascination with Shelley's tale never incapacitates his critical faculties that continue to judge the merits of *Frankenstein* against his own high standards of moral propriety as well as the general nineteenth-century predilection for straightforward, no-nonsense narration and plain common sense.

Taken from the very beginning of Scott's review, the first extract reprinted here is characteristic of the ambivalence of Scott's reading of *Frankenstein* expressing both disapproval and genuine enthusiasm. Scott acknowledges Godwin's influence on the novel but seems undecided as to how this influence should ultimately be evaluated. His overall response to the novel's fantastic elements is clearly one of curiosity and intrigue rather than, as in Croker's case, horrified revulsion. Also, whereas he initially appears to make concessions to the literary conventions and ideals of his time, Scott soon embarks on an interrogation of the alleged realism of 'reality'. Citing the spectacular rise and fall of Napoleon Bonaparte (1769–1821) as a historical example, he inquires if 'reality' and 'verisimilitude' ought necessarily always to be regarded as practically synonymous. Not only do actual real-life events display the features and qualities of a story, Scott argues. Occasionally their blatant improbabilities even exceed those that inhere in fiction, presenting us with situations that fundamentally question the terminological usefulness of 'probable' as a critical tool in literary discourse. Scott writes:

■ Here is one of the productions of the modern school in its highest style of caricature and exaggeration. It is formed on the Godwinian manner, and has all the faults, but many likewise of the beauties of that model. In dark and gloomy views of nature and of man, bordering too closely on impiety, – in the most outrageous improbability, – in sacrificing every thing to effect, – it even goes beyond its great prototype; but in return, it possesses a similar power of fascination, something of the same mastery in harsh and savage delineations of passion, relieved in like manner by the gentler feelings. There never was a wilder story imagined, yet, like most of the fictions of this age, it has an air of reality attached to it, by being connected with the favourite projects and passions of the times. The real events of the world have, in our day, too, been of so wondrous and gigantic a kind, – the shiftings of the scenes in our stupendous drama have been so rapid and various, that Shakespeare himself, in his wildest flights, has been completely distanced by the eccentricities of actual existence. Even he would scarcely have dared to have raised, in one act, a private adventurer to the greatest of European thrones, – to have conducted him, in the next, victorious over the necks of emperors and kings, and then, in a third, to have shown him an exile, in a remote speck of an island, some thousands of miles from the scene of his triumphs.[13] □

The final section of Scott's review discusses the conceptual shortcomings and generally controversial nature of *Frankenstein*. Commendably, Scott declines to be categorical in his dismissal of what he evidently regards as the novel's less salubrious aspects; even its potentially blasphemous elements are not automatically dismissed as indicative of the author's moral depravity or 'madness'. However, while the general tone of his reading is one of paternal admonition, Scott remains reluctant to engage in any greater serious detail with the recent developments in nineteenth-century science and philosophy that so conspicuously inform *Frankenstein*. Scott writes:

■ some of our highest and most reverential feelings receive a shock from the conception on which [*Frankenstein*] turns, so as to produce a painful and bewildered state of mind while we peruse it. We are accustomed, happily, to look upon the creation of a living and intelligent being as a work that is fitted only to inspire a religious emotion, and there is an impropriety, to say no worse, in placing it in any other light. It might, indeed, be the author's view to shew that the powers of man have been wisely limited, and that misery would follow their extension, – but still the expression "Creator," applied to a mere human being, gives us the same sort of shock with the phrase, "the Man Almighty," and others of the same kind, in Mr Southey's "Curse of Kehama" [Robert Southey, 1774–1843, English poet]. All these monstrous conceptions are the consequences of the wild and irregular theories of the age: though we do not at all mean to infer that the authors who give in to such freedoms have done so with any bad intentions. This incongruity, however, with our established and most sacred notions, is the chief fault in such fictions, regarding them merely in a critical point of view. . . . We hope yet to have more productions, both from this author and his great model, Mr Godwin [*Editor's note:* Like Croker, Scott clearly considers *Frankenstein* the work of a male author.]; but they would make a great improvement in their writings, if they would rather study the established order of nature as it appears, both in the world of matter and of mind, than continue to revolt our feelings by hazardous innovations in either of these departments.[14] □

Contemporary reviews of *Frankenstein* are dominated by questions of the novel's morality. Hence, early advocates of the novel's merits feel compelled to present it as an instructive allegory that, far from endorsing its protagonist's solitary pursuit of reckless self-fulfilment, seeks to draw attention to the disastrous consequences of an individual's seclusion from society, be it superimposed or self-inflicted. In a little-known review, presumably written in 1817 but first published posthumously in the *Athenaeum* in 1832, Percy Shelley stresses the essential humanity of Frankenstein's monster and suggests the novel is informed by a clear social conscience that presents the reader with a definite moral of universal significance. According to Percy, this moral is:

■ Treat a person ill, and he will become wicked. Requite affection with scorn; – let one being be selected, for whatever cause, as the refuse of his kind – divide him, a social being, from society, and you impose upon him the irresistible obligations – malevolence and selfishness.[15] □

What also significantly contributed to *Frankenstein*'s ever increasing popularity was the theatre's prolific love affair with the novel. In 1823 Richard Brinsley Peake reworked Shelley's controversial material for the stage, rekindling public interest in the novel to such an extent that Shelley's publishers decided to bring out a second edition. Triggered by the immense success of Peake's *Presumption; or, The Fate of Frankenstein*, the next three years saw the production of altogether fourteen dramatic variations on *Frankenstein*, in both English and French.[16] The hitherto heatedly debated issue of *Frankenstein*'s manifold improbabilities and moral ambiguities had practically ceased to signify; what now mattered more than anything was purely the story's captivating appeal. The attitude expressed in a commentary published in the *Knight's Quarterly Magazine* in 1824 seems in many respects symptomatic of the general public's readiness to suspend their disbelief and immerse themselves in the fantastic horrors of *Frankenstein*. 'Grant that it is possible for one man to create another,' the anonymous reviewer writes, 'and the rest is perfectly natural and in course.'[17] Evidently, by the mid-1820s, Mary Shelley's tale had begun to advance from a mere figment of the imagination, or young girl's 'waking dream', to the status of modernity's perhaps most compelling and ominous myth. According to George Levine, *Frankenstein* quickly became 'a vital metaphor, peculiarly appropriate to a culture . . . neurotically obsessed with "getting in touch" with its authentic self and frightened at what it is discovering'. As Levine goes on to suggest, 'latent in the metaphor are some of the fundamental dualisms, the social, moral, political and metaphysical crises of western history since the French Revolution'.[18] However, while the fable of the monster and its maker prospered in the popular imagination, the actual text of the novel, its remarkable conceptual complexity and elaborate intertextual architectonics, fell more and more into oblivion. As Christopher

Small points out, 'to some extent indeed it might be argued that the myth had most hold where the book hasn't been read'.[19]

Subject to manifold popular alterations and remouldings, *Frankenstein* was honed down to its bare essentials. Most significantly perhaps, Frankenstein's creature quickly deteriorated from an eloquent 'noble savage' into an inarticulate and violent brute. Not before the publication of M.A. Goldberg's 'Moral and Myth in Mrs. Shelley's *Frankenstein*' in the *Keats-Shelley Journal* in the late 1950s – of which two extracts are reprinted below – was there any attempt to rehabilitate *Frankenstein* as a literary text worthy of serious scholarly attention. By then, as Goldberg outlines in his introduction, Shelley's novel was in desperate need of a detailed historical recontextualisation that would reveal not only its intricate narrative design but also its solid embedment in a tight network of both mythical and philosophical traditions ranging from the Bible to John Milton's *Paradise Lost* (1667) and Samuel Taylor Coleridge's 'The Rime of the Ancient Mariner' (1798). According to Goldberg, the dramatic monologue of the monster at the core of *Frankenstein*'s narrative concentricity of story-within-story demanded the critic's particular attention since it had clearly suffered most from the novel's widespread reputation as a simple tale of horror and apocalyptic destruction. According to Goldberg, what had to be urgently brought to the attention of Mary Shelley's twentieth-century readers was the early nineteenth century's fascination with the philosopher Edmund Burke's elaborate aesthetics of the sublime. Within the complex framework of Burkean sublimity artistic evocations of 'horror' were never understood to be gratuitous or merely titillating. Rather, they were believed to effect deliberate, often intensely moral repercussions that challenged both the reasoning and emotional faculties of the human psyche. Goldberg explains:

■ [Mary Shelley's] appeal to horror and terror was certainly indicative of no new trend for the early nineteenth century. Almost a hundred years before, [Joseph] Addison [1672–1719, English essayist and poet] had propounded the Great and Uncommon as the most fertile sources for pleasures of the imagination, and by mid-century this had been expanded into a whole esthetic, with Edmund Burke [1729–1797, British statesman and conservative political theorist] contending that the excitation of terror and pain, the true source of sublimity, produces the strongest emotion man is capable of feeling. Yet, unlike modern exponents of horror who revel in the hedonism of violence, the writers who worked within this new esthetic – [Matthew 'Monk'] Lewis [1775–1818] in *The Monk*, Mrs. Radcliffe [1763–1823] in *The Mysteries of Udolpho* – were never devoid of the moral fabric so crucial to eighteenth- and early nineteenth-century England. Though the moralizing was generally crude and obvious, superimposed upon the structure to meet the demands of the public, nevertheless it was consistently present. Even in Burke, where passions have clearly surmounted the newly dethroned reason as the source of art and reality, pleasure in terror bears ethical and social implications. 'The delight we have in such things,' explains the author of *On the Sublime and Beautiful*, 'hinders us from shunning scenes of misery; and the pain we feel, prompts us to relieve ourselves in relieving those who suffer.'[20] Morality in Burke, as with the writers who followed in his wake, is never absent. For Burke, it has simply become instinctive, a branch of the pleasure-pain principle and antecedent to that mainstay of the preceding age, the power of reason.

Unless we allow ourselves to be misled by the intentions revealed in Mrs. Shelley's preface . . . it is in the light of this esthetic that *Frankenstein* must be viewed. To examine the novel for the terror it evokes, without perceiving its relationship to the moral context of early nineteenth-century England, is, in reality, to distort the essence of the tale.[21] □

Goldberg proceeds with an investigation into the moral issues raised by Walton's encounter with Frankenstein in the outer narrative framework of the novel, arguing that the thwarted scientist's tale is intended to serve 'as an *exemplum* aimed at weaning the captain from his obsession'.[22] However, it is the third and final section of the essay, in which Goldberg initiates the beginning of an in-depth exploration of *Frankenstein*'s inter-textual roots and relations, that seems to have triggered, or at least significantly fed into, the revived academic interest that the novel would soon come to instil in a whole new generation of critics. Goldberg writes:

■ Although parallels between the temptations of Frankenstein or Walton and those of Adam or Satan [in *Paradise Lost*] are clearly delineated, it would be a grave distortion to force the analogy without noting pertinent differences. Milton's is a seventeenth-century reinterpretation of the Fall described by the Jehovistic writer of *Genesis*: but Milton's narrative also parallels to no small degree the Hellenic myth of Prometheus who, having usurped the powers of the higher gods, is alienated forever from both men and gods, and chained to the frozen top of the Caucasus. This is an allusion of which Mrs. Shelley was certainly conscious, since she refers to Frankenstein as a 'Modern Prometheus' in her sub-title. Also, Shelley himself was obviously aware of the structural similarity between Milton's narrative and the Greek myth, for in his preface to *Prometheus Unbound* [1819] he remarks that 'the only imaginary being resembling in any degree Prometheus, is Satan.'. . .

. . . Frankenstein's guilt . . . is never completely the crime of *hubris* [(in Greek tragedy) an excess of ambition, pride, etc., ultimately causing the transgressor's ruin] manifested in Aeschylus [c.525–c.456 BC, Greek tragedian] or the failure to recognize derivation which we discern in Milton. Frankenstein's crime, like Walton's, is social. Both sin against society. In syncretizing the Miltonic and Promethean motif Mrs. Shelley has clearly translated her materials into early nineteenth-century terms, just . . . as Shelley transformed the story of Prometheus within his own contemporary framework.

Walton and Frankenstein both sin, not against self or God, but against the moral and social order. Though both begin their pursuit with benevolent intentions, each discovers his error in assuming that knowledge is a higher good than love or sympathy, and that it can be independent of the fellow-feeling afforded by a compassionate society. As a result, what had appeared initially as a benevolent intention becomes in the final analysis misguided pride, a selfish pursuit aimed at self-glory, because it evades the fulfillment of higher duties toward the social community, the brotherhood of man which forms the highest good. Unfortunately, then, Mrs. Shelley's book is paralleled most significantly, not by Aeschylus or Milton, but by her own contemporaries. In Byron's *Manfred* [1817], for example, an analogous 'quest of hidden knowledge' leads the hero increasingly toward a 'solitude . . . peopled with the Furies.' Manfred's avowed flaw ('though I wore the form,/I had no sympathy with breathing flesh') rises from the same ethical assumptions implicit in the guilt-ridden consciousness of Victor Frankenstein. Similarly, Shelley's prefatory remarks on *Alastor or, The Spirit of Solitude* [1816] indicate that 'the Poet's self-centred seclusion was avenged by the furies of an irresistible passion pursuing him to speedy ruin.' Shelley's supposition, that 'the intellectual faculties, the imagination, the functions of sense, have their respective requisitions on the sympathy of corresponding powers in other human beings,' is obviously engendered from the same general principle which has ordered the materials of *Frankenstein*.[23]

Mrs. Shelley offers in her novel – as does [George Gordon] Byron [1788–1824, English poet] in *Manfred* and Shelley in *Alastor* – a theme which is clearly in the tradition of . . . the seventeenth-century Platonists. This is a conception inherited in the eighteenth century by . . . the Scottish Common-Sense School, as represented by Adam Smith [1723–1790, Scottish economist and philosopher]; and finally by William Godwin, who had assumed as basic to his doctrine of political justice that virtue is essentially social. Insistent that reason and free will, as developed in an enlightened society, would naturally result in the subordination of individual pleasures for the good of society as a whole, Godwin set himself in opposition to [François] La

Rochefoucauld [1613–1680, French writer], [Thomas] **Hobbes** [1588–1679, English political philosopher], **and** [Bernard de] **Mandeville** [?1670–1733, English satirist], for whom man was basically selfish and non-social, and to [Jean Jacques] **Rousseau** [1712–1778, French philosopher and writer], who had seen society as a force destructive to natural benevolence. 'No being can be either virtuous, or vicious, who has no opportunity of influencing the happiness of others,' Godwin had contended in his *Enquiry Concerning Political Justice*, insistent that 'the true solitaire cannot be considered as a moral being. . . . His conduct is vicious, because it has a tendency to render him miserable.' Explaining that 'virtue consists in a desire of the happiness of the species. . . . It must begin with a collective idea of the human species,' Godwin argues that true knowledge is also dependent upon the social structure. 'Even knowledge, and the enlargement of intellect, are poor, when unmixed with sentiments of benevolence and sympathy,' he points out; '. . . and science and abstraction will soon become cold, unless they derive new attractions from ideas of society.'[24]

Similarly, Thomas Paine [1737–1809, American political pamphleteer] develops the relationship between happiness and social virtues in *The Rights of Man* [1791–92]. Since nature created man for social life, Paine writes, 'no one man is capable, without the aid of society, of supplying his own wants; and those wants, acting upon every individual, impel the whole of them into society, as naturally as gravitation acts to a centre.' Nature has gone even further than this, Paine continues. 'She has implanted in him a system of social affections, which, though not necessary to his existence, are essential to his happiness. There is no period in life when this love of society ceases to act. It begins and ends with our being.'[25]

This same concept, so crucial to Godwin and Paine, is also central to [Percy] Shelley's thought. 'Love is celebrated every where as the sole law which should govern the moral world,' he announces in his preface to *The Revolt of Islam* [1818], and in an early essay 'On Love' he explains that 'in solitude, or in that deserted state when we are surrounded by human beings, and yet they sympathise not with us, we love the flowers, the grass, and the waters, and the sky. . . . So soon as this want or power is dead, man becomes the living sepulchre of himself, and what yet survives is the mere husk of what once he was.' The closing paragraph of Shelley's preface to *Alastor* unmistakably extends this idea:

> They who . . . keep aloof from sympathies with their kind . . . languish, because none feel with them their common nature. They are morally dead. . . . Among those who attempt to exist without human sympathy, the pure and tender-hearted perish through the

intensity and passion of their search after its communities, when the vacancy of their spirit suddenly makes itself felt. All else, self-ish, blind, and torpid, are those unforeseeing multitudes who constitute, together with their own, the lasting misery and loneliness of the world. Those who love not their fellow-beings, live unfruitful lives, and prepare for their old age a miserable grave.[26]

. . . . . . Through Mrs. Shelley's journal entries we know that during 1816–1817, when *Frankenstein* was conceived, she and Shelley discussed the work many times. We know, too, through [Mary Shelley's journals] that in these years she and Shelley both read Milton's *Paradise Lost*, and that Shelley was immersed at this same time in Godwin's *Political Justice* and Paine's *The Rights of Man*, as well as in the *Prometheus Bound* of Aeschylus. I do not mean to imply that Mary Shelley borrowed her social and moral conceptions from Paine, or from Shelley or Godwin, then deliberately embodied them within her mythological framework. It is perfectly understandable that she shared the social thought of her father and her husband, and that she wove these ideas, which were shared also by many of the enlightened English public during those decades, into an esthetic pattern of her own making.[27] □

Goldberg's acknowledgement of Mary Shelley as an independent writer – no doubt inspired by her husband's ideas, yet ultimately cultivating a creative vision of her own – constituted a crucial first step in the development of late twentieth-century *Frankenstein* studies and must by no means be taken for granted. It is important to remember that, before as well as after the publication of Goldberg's essay, traditionalist critics have persistently found fault with *Frankenstein*, be it thematically or stylistically, and only a few of them have ever hesitated to blame the novel's alleged deficiencies on its author's female sex. For example, in an early biography of Mary Shelley published in 1938, Glynn Grylls deplores 'Frankenstein's fastidiousness and hesitancy' and speculates that the hero's conspicuous effeminacy may find an explanation in Shelley's feeble and inevitably vain attempt to emulate her husband's superior spirit. According to Grylls, 'the heavy Gothic diet, that [Percy] Shelley was strong enough to assimilate and survive, permanently impaired Mary's weaker literary digestion'.[28] Presenting the author of *Frankenstein* as a dilettante and – even though generally quite capable – ultimately rather disappointing epigone, Grylls continues:

■ If [Shelley] had developed in *Frankenstein* and in the later novels the subtler psychology which she touched upon in the monster's *apologia* for his malignity, she would have taken a far higher rank as an artist;

she would have been a novelist and not a 'fictioneer'; but she was content to deal in the stock-in-trade of her generation, and consequently her high gifts of imagination and her command over language, worthy of better things, are lost in a neglect not wholly undeserved. *Frankenstein* remains a 'period piece', of not very good date; historically interesting, but not one of the living novels of the world.[29] □

In a biographical essay from 1970, Sylva Norman follows Grylls's example by likewise comparing Shelley's creative imagination to that of her husband and, as a result, finding it clichéd and unsophisticated. 'She lacked the inner fire', Norman states laconically.[30] In Norman's presentation, *Frankenstein* is reduced to the status of a purely serendipitous achievement that suffers from an acute lack of conceptual coherence and is thus characteristic of Mary Shelley's work as a whole. As far as Norman is concerned, we must eventually ask ourselves 'whether *Frankenstein* is really Mary's masterpiece, or how far it is a masterpiece at all'.[31]

Curiously, the same intellectual and creative immaturity that Norman regards as Shelley's greatest weakness – evident in the alleged omission from her work of 'a unifying motive, whether moral, political, or aesthetic'[32] – is commended as a fortunate asset by Muriel Spark, Shelley's most recent biographer. Spark suggests – quite absurdly it seems – that *Frankenstein*'s success and artistic achievement are due to the author's naivety and total lack of experience at the time the work was composed, implying that Shelley was capable of producing a literary masterpiece only by writing 'automatically', guided not by her own inspired self but by some obscurely unconscious faculty expressing itself, as it were, through her. Accordingly, it would be Shelley's intellectual maturity that is mainly responsible for her later works' relative obscurity and inferior appeal. Spark appears to be arguing that an enduring success like *Frankenstein* could never have been written by a woman in full possession of all her mental faculties, but only by a girl, confused and ventriloquising:

■ 'Methinks,' wrote Byron to John Murray [Byron's publisher], 'it is a wonderful work for a girl of nineteen, – *not* nineteen, indeed, at that time.' But perhaps the wonder of it exists, not despite Mary's youth but because of it. *Frankenstein* is Mary Shelley's best novel because at that age she was not yet well acquainted with her own mind. As her self-insight grew – and she was exceptionally introspective – so did her work suffer from causes the very opposite of her intention; and what often mars her later writing is its extreme explicitness. In *Frankenstein*, however, it is the implicit utterance which gives the theme its power.[33] □

Leaving Goldberg's early attempt aside, the current academic reappraisal of Mary Shelley's literary achievement was effectively set in motion by the publication of *The Endurance of Frankenstein*, a collection of critical essays edited by George Levine and U.C. Knoepflmacher in 1979. As Levine intimates in his own contribution to the volume, the project was intended to re-introduce *Frankenstein* to its readers as 'the most important minor novel in English'.[34] Determined to rehabilitate Shelley's text, Levine and Knoepflmacher assert in their preface that '*Frankenstein* was a novel that could not be put aside with the conventional highbrow dismissals of popular culture',[35] insisting that 'if popular culture has adapted [*Frankenstein*], no part of culture can ignore it' since 'its key images and the central structure of the narrative itself [have entered] both our private and culturally shared store of dreams, fantasy, and myth'.[36] And yet, whilst resolved to emancipate themselves from the traditional values of canonical literary criticism, the editors also seem embarrassed by the sheer audacity of their endeavour. Almost apologetic for their enthusiasm and clearly keen to pre-empt the wrath and ridicule of more serious-minded colleagues, they introduce themselves and their contributors as 'closet aficionados of Mary Shelley's novel'.[37] Then, nervous and highly self-conscious, Levine and Knoepflmacher express their second thoughts about the purpose, feasibility and scholarly worthiness of their project on which, so they claim, they embarked 'half-jokingly':[38]

■ Nonetheless, our eagerness to approach *Frankenstein* with the 'high seriousness' of the Arnoldian literary critic was not without obvious risks. Might not a *Frankenstein* 'perplex' be met with the same mixture of amusement and disbelief always shown by students toward a book assumed to contain nothing more than a story about an awkward and poorly sutured monster? Just as *Frankenstein* lends itself to parodies that belie Mary Shelley's earnest intentions, would not our own collection be received as a self-parody of the solemnity of academic criticism? Our undertaking, we also realized, might raise questions even among those more serious readers who would not have to be convinced that *Frankenstein* is much more than an adolescent flight that has somehow managed to cash in clumsily on popular traditions. Do not the stunning ambivalences of the novel defy analysis? How much of the book's complexity is actually the result of Mary Shelley's self-conscious art and how much is merely the product of the happy circumstances of subject, moment, milieu?[39] □

Over the last twenty years, despite its slightly defeatist editorial preface, *The Endurance of Frankenstein* has become a critical classic, inspiring a wide spectrum of diverse critical works that share a common interest in re-reading whatever generic irregularities and other unruly features

Frankenstein may possess, not as literary flaws, but as the consciously crafted components of a deliberate textual monstrosity. *Frankenstein* has undergone a thorough academic revival. In fact, sometimes it seems as if Mary Shelley's novel has become a bit of an obsession with literary critics and theorists so that Fred Botting may be quite justified in referring to it primarily as 'a product of criticism, not a work of literature'.[40] Rather than wishing to detract from *Frankenstein*'s inherent merits as an inspired artefact of considerable cultural import, Botting's provocative statement aims to contest traditional beliefs in the inalienable, timeless autonomy of literature by highlighting how literary meaning depends invariably on, and changes with, the different historical and cultural contexts into which it is received. Moreover, due to *Frankenstein*'s peculiar subject matter, critical efforts to construe its possible meanings tend to give birth to their own monstrous offspring since they inevitably find themselves at risk of repeating 'Frankenstein's unifying will to dominate and control the text-monster, *Frankenstein*'.[41] As Botting explains in the introduction to *Making Monstrous: Frankenstein, Criticism, Theory*:

■ different critical discourses . . . assemble their own monsters from the partial and dead signifiers that make up the narrative bodies of *Frankenstein*. Critics suture these fragments into their own commentary to produce new and hideous progenies that have lives of their own.[42] □

CHAPTER TWO

Giving Form to Dark, Shapeless Substances: Intertextuality and Ambivalence in *Frankenstein*

F*RANKENSTEIN'S* HISTORY of critical and creative reproduction has added many a terrifying nuance and twist to the significatory potential of Shelley's 'hideous progeny'. However, this must not be allowed to detract from the fact that the great majority of the text's most controversial 'monstrosities' are determined by the particular circumstances of its original composition. It is not just the Monster's highly eclectic reading material that hints at the novel's materialisation from an incidental, even random disparity of sources – including works as diverse as Plutarch's *Lives*, Milton's *Paradise Lost* and Goethe's *The Sorrows of Young Werther*. Equally indicative of *Frankenstein's* essential hybridity is the composite identity of its author, whose full name is Mary Wollstonecraft Godwin Shelley. As the only child of Britain's two most (in)famous political writers of the late eighteenth century, and the wife of English Romanticism's perhaps most ambitious young poet and revolutionary, Shelley was never free from the onerous pressure to fulfil what many of those dear to her regarded as her natural destiny. Almost wearily she notes in her introduction to the novel that 'my husband . . . was from the first, very anxious that I should prove myself worthy of my parentage' (*F* 1831, p. 6). As the present chapter demonstrates, *Frankenstein* was not created entirely from scratch. On the contrary, it is the product of a long and complex literary tradition that incorporates not only the writings of Shelley's most immediate family but also encompasses the literary and philosophical heritage of the Enlightenment, Romanticism, and the French Revolution, as well as Europe's deep-rooted cultural indebtedness to the story lines and imagery of classical mythology and the Bible.

The first two extracts reprinted here are taken from Elisabeth Bronfen's 'Rewriting the Family: Mary Shelley's "Frankenstein" in Its

Biographical/Textual Context', first published in 1994 as part of Stephen Bann's *Frankenstein, Creation, and Monstrosity*.[1] Bronfen reads the novel as a heavily encoded semi-autobiographical text that, thematically and in its multifarious intertextual relations, dramatises the turbulent and often tragic dynamics of Shelley's own family background. In Bronfen's essay, much is made of the pertinent analogy between literary text and monstrous offspring that can be found in the 'Author's Introduction', where Shelley famously bids her 'hideous progeny go forth and prosper' (*F* 1831, p. 10). Inspired by Sigmund Freud's psychoanalytic concept of the 'family romance' in combination with Harold Bloom's highly acclaimed investigation of literary intertextuality, *The Anxiety of Influence* (1973),[2] Bronfen discovers some striking parallels and correspondences between *Frankenstein* on the one hand and Godwin's *St Leon* (1799), Shelley's *Alastor, or the Spirit of Solitude* (1816) and 'The Tale of Jemima' in Mary Wollstonecraft's *The Wrongs of Woman* (1798) on the other. She thus shows how the Shelleys – both husband and wife – were locked in a prolific, yet problematically incestuous intertextual relationship with the Godwins.

According to Bloom's Freudian model of literary influence, there exists an oedipal rivalry between poets from different generations. Young writers tend to feel threatened by the creative prowess of their predecessors, especially those whose work they admire and worship most. A psychic struggle ensues, an imaginary wrestling match, in which the younger poet seeks to clear his work of all traces of a possible indebtedness to tradition. As Bloom demonstrates, this attempt at asserting one's absolute originality must be regarded as a hopelessly impossible endeavour that results in a repression – what Bloom designates as a 'misreading' – of influence, easily diagnosed by the discerning critic who knows that whatever has been repressed must, of course, inevitably return. Curiously, in the particular case of *Frankenstein*, so Bronfen argues, these Bloomian anxieties of literary influence are not repressed but deliberately cultivated. At the same time as Shelley 'reduplicates on a textual level Frankenstein's artificially re-generated body of dead component parts . . . some of the component parts of *her* artificially created being refer back to the writings of other members of her family'.[3] Citing Shelley's artistic principle, that invention does not 'consist in creating out of void, but out of chaos; the materials must, in the first place, be afforded' (*F* 1831, p. 8), Bronfen describes *Frankenstein* as a direct and overt, rather than closeted and desultory, Bloomian 'misreading' of her parents' works.

Bronfen's essay begins with a detailed outline of the conceptual framework within which she intends to read Shelley's novel. She then proceeds to reveal the full dramatic irony of the young Shelleys' oedipally emancipatory struggle with Godwin's and Wollstonecraft's intellectual legacy. Bronfen demonstrates how Mary and Percy faithfully subscribe to the ideals of free love and anarchic self-fulfilment that Mary's mother and father envisaged in their early work, yet ultimately failed to implement in real life. The Shelleys' elopement and unconventional marriage, for example, render them perfect flesh-and-blood realisations of young Godwin's and Wollstonecraft's unruly theoretical attacks on their society's most conservative institutions, standards and norms. According to Bronfen, it seems almost as if the revolutionary spirit of the past had returned to reanimate the parents' discarded theory in the mutinous lives of their children. Bronfen explains:

■ Sigmund Freud suggested that the progress of society depends on the opposition between successive generations. 'The liberation of an individual, as he grows up, from the authority of his parents', he argued, 'is one of the most necessary though one of the most painful results brought about by the course of his development'. Given that this essential liberation is to some extent achieved by every human being by the time the onset of adulthood has been normalized, Freud's concern is for those neurotics whose condition is determined 'by their having failed in this task'.[4] He applies the term 'the neurotic's family romance' to a peculiarly marked imaginative activity engendered by a child's dissatisfaction with the curtailment of parental affection. For in a later stage in the development of her or his estrangement from her or his parents, the neurotic uses the activity of daydreaming as a 'fulfilment of wishes and a correction of actual life' in response to parents she or he feels to be unsatisfactory. In the course of such phantasies the actual insufficient parents are replaced by others 'who, as a rule, are of a higher social standing'.[5] These phantasies exalt the paternal and maternal figure, or, at a later point, denigrate them. As imaginative activities they are an expression of revenge and retaliation, however, that in fact preserves the child's original affection that has been thwarted by the actual events of life. Ultimately these phantasies are an expression of nostalgia and regret, for 'the happy, vanished days when his father seemed to him the noblest and strongest of men and his mother the dearest and loveliest of women'.[6]

Harold Bloom, in turn, resorts to Freud's concept of 'family romance' so as to describe the succession between two generations of poets.[7] In his theory of literary influence, Bloom argues that all poets are intimidated by the strength of their predecessors – and this serves as a source of poetic anxiety that he calls an anxiety of influence. Only by reading their predecessors incorrectly – for which Bloom coins the term creative misreading – can authors carve out for themselves an imaginary space within which they can survive and produce. By virtue of misreading they can repress their true legacy, namely the fact that they owe their creativity to a parent-poet, and this act of repression serves as a second source of anxiety. At the same time, one could add, misreading acknowledges a literary parentage, even as it follows the pattern sketched by Freud. In the act of exalting or denigrating one's literary predecessors, what occurs is a form of re-creation of the parent-poet.

. . . I suggest taking Bloom far more literally than he intended, so as to look at the way that Mary and Percy Shelley's self-conception as authors emerged in a response that significantly merges the spiritual with the actual parents. Though the argument can be made for Percy Shelley as well, I focus on the way Mary Shelley's biography and, especially, her textual creation, *Frankenstein*, can be interpreted as a form of misreading and rewriting the texts by her parents, Mary Wollstonecraft and William Godwin. At the same time I will extend Bloom's term, 'anxiety of influence', so as to emphasize the fact that, as the second generation structures its life, it imitates the writings of the first. What occurs in the process is the recreation of parents in response to a sense of insufficiency that is worked out quite literally by virtue of an imaginary activity. The parents are exalted in a two-fold manner. They are stylized into literary figures, engendering the imaginative or poetic activity of their children, and, as the literary predecessors that they are, idealized. Godwin and Wollstonecraft as texts are thus transformed into figures of the all-sufficient father and mother they never were in life (due to the restrictions exerted by the former and the early death of the latter). One of the crucial questions thus becomes, whether, as a result, the children implement in a consistent way that which their parents only theorized, or whether in this act of self-fashioning they wilfully misunderstood their parents' texts. For what is significant about the Godwin-Shelley family is the fact that here the second generation *does not* repress the importance of their predecessors. Rather, both Mary and Percy seem to have assigned a fetish-like quality to the writings of their parents, as these take on a prototypal function.[8] Furthermore, the repressed ideas of the first generation seem to return and, in the gesture of repetition, become lived reality for the second generation. The children take their bearings precisely from the way they rewrite the lives of their parents, in an act, however, that also refashions these parental biographies.

For the particular family of authors and texts I have chosen, what links the succession of family generations and textual production is an opposition typical for the Romantic period, namely a polarization between solitary artistic activity and natural procreation. At stake is the question of influence and transmission, as well as the mutual interdependence between the question of origins and that of reproduction, between genesis and propagation. Given that my concern is the conflation of two opposites, i.e. the enmeshment of actual and spiritual parentage, my discussion of this interrelation between family and text will itself undertake a heterodox theoretical approach. My reading of *Frankenstein* as Mary Shelley's version of her family romance will collapse a *biographical* approach with the already well-established *thematic* discussion of this gothic tale as an example of the conflict between the ethics of creation and the phenomenon of monstrosity.[9] Within my discussion of the paternity/maternity of Shelley's text, the issue of biography, I will argue, should not be located outside the text but also be sought internal to its structure.

I will begin with a brief sketch of the biographies of my four subjects, always bearing in mind the way the second generation misreads and *mis*produces the writings of the first, in its imaginative effort to recreate its own family romance. The mother in this narrative is Mary Wollstonecraft (1759–97), a courageous, passionate and unconventional feminist, author of *A Vindication of the Rights of Woman* (1792), in which she pleaded for women's rights for self-determination and equality in intellectual, public and private realms. After working as a governess she moved to London, to live there as an independent author. She was the friend of progressive thinkers like Tom Paine and William Blake [1757–1827, Romantic poet, painter, engraver and mystic]. She fell in love with Henry Fuseli [1741–1825, Anglo-Swiss painter] and, given her ideas about free love, wanted to live with him and his wife in a *menage à trois* [household, or sexual relationship, of three]. In 1792 she travelled alone to Paris, where she was at first an ardent supporter of the French Revolution. Two years later she returned to England with her illegitimate daughter, Fanny Imlay [1794–1816], politically and personally disappointed. The infidelities of her American lover, Gilbert Imlay [1754–1828], twice drove her to attempt suicide.

In 1797 she married William Godwin (1756–1836) – the paternal figure in the narrative – a radical political thinker, who had been ordained as a dissenting minister in 1778 but a few years later gave up the clerical profession. Like Wollstonecraft he moved to London to live as an independent writer, and was active in the same intellectual circles. Owing to his polemical *Enquiry Concerning Political Justice* (1793) he was for several years a celebrity, but afterwards fell into obscurity and debt. During his marriage with Mary Wollstonecraft he felt that for the first time in his life he was learning how to combine radical intellect with emotions. Mary died ten days after giving birth to a daughter, also called Mary . . . . . .

The story about the second generation begins some sixteen years after the death of Mary Wollstonecraft, with the appearance in the Godwin household of Percy Bysshe Shelley (1792–1822) – a rebellious, eccentric genius, who was forced to leave Oxford University because of a pamphlet he had written on atheism. He was already married to the sixteen-year-old Harriet Westbrook [1795–1816] when he informed Godwin that he considered Godwin to be his spiritual father and gave him his poem *Queen Mab* [1813] to read, claiming it was a poetic translation of the *Enquiry Concerning Political Justice*. What is interesting about this philosopher/father and poet/son couple, however, is not only the fact that for the older man the young poet seemed to incarnate the lost 'spirit of 1793'. The relationship between the two can, in fact, be seen as a hypertrophic [abnormally intensified] family romance, a superlative elevation of the paternal figure, namely in the translation of written text into life. Godwin had already perceived Shelley's poem *Queen Mab* as a misreading of his theory of political justice. And when the poet eloped with his daughter Mary to Italy, doing so explicitly in the light of Godwin's own treatise against marriage, the father was outraged and wanted to cast off his daughter.[10]

Paralleling Shelley, the daughter Mary (1797–1851) had, in her turn, largely fashioned herself in the image of her dead mother. She constantly read Wollstonecraft's texts and diaries, and did so, further-more, at her mother's grave in St Pancras – which was also the place where Shelley declared his love to her.[11] During their flight through France, accompanied by Mary's half-sister Claire [*Editor's note:* Claire Clairmont (1798–1879), the daughter of Mary Jane Clairmont (1768–1841) who married Godwin in 1801, was Mary Shelley's step-sister, not her half-sister.], Mary and Percy realized the *menage à trois* Wollstonecraft had once imagined for herself, Fuseli and his wife. Paradoxically, against the prohibition and displeasure of the old Godwin, Percy and Mary legitimized their actions by continually re-reading the writings of the young radicals Wollstonecraft and Godwin. Percy's courtship of Mary and their extramarital cohabitation in Switzerland one year later thus marks both the return of the radical French philosophy before 1795 and a concrete, lived realization of Godwin's and Wollstonecraft's political treatises.

Given such behaviour, one could argue that the second generation understood parents as predecessors that encouraged, confirmed and justified their way of living. While the first generation seems to have modified its radical theories when it came to living, the second gener-ation allowed the past to return, but in a far more radical transformation of theory into practice. The relationship between Mary and Percy not only imitates the parents' but transforms into lived reality what they merely *intellectually* conceived as a possibility. In fact, shortly before her suicide in 1816, Harriet Westbrook, who had remained Percy's wife throughout, attributed her husband's infidelity to his *reading* of Godwin's *Enquiry*; 'the very great evil that book has done', she wrote, 'is not to be told.'[12] In the same year, Mary, pregnant for the third time, not only used Harriet's death but also, in turn, her renewed *reading* of Wollstonecraft's *Vindication of the Rights of Woman* to justify to Percy their need to enter into marriage. By this means she hoped to legitimize her children and be recognized again by her father. 1816 is also the year in which she began writing *Frankenstein, or The Modern Prometheus*.[13] □

Throughout the remainder of her intriguing, if often extremely one-dimensional reading of *Frankenstein* as a neurotic encapsulation of Shelley's own life story, Bronfen concentrates on a discussion of the work's allegedly typical Godwinian/Shelleyan characteristics. So persuasive is Bronfen's reading that one almost comes to accept her presentation of what are in actual fact general shifts in the early nineteenth century's socio-political climate as the manifestations of just one single family's intergenerational conflicts, allegiances and tensions. Finally, Bronfen returns to her central theme of the Freudian 'family romance' to explain how the now older, wiser and lonelier Shelley engages in a wishful re-composition of her family as yet another artifice of her 'monstrous' imagination. Towards the end of her argument, Bronfen writes:

■ Through her birth [Mary Shelley] became responsible for the death of her mother, her stepmother disapproved of her and Mary was able to win her affection only after William Godwin's death. Her father disowned her after her clandestine flight with Percy Shelley, and was unwilling even to acknowledge his first grandson [William, 1816–1819], named after him. Due to the unconventionality of her life with Shelley, she was marginalized by English society. She came to feel that her depression caused by her dead children, Shelley's infidelities, and their poverty was a confirmation of her own monstrosity. Thus *Frankenstein* articulates her extremely ambivalent relation to the legacy of her parents. She realizes that to write like her parents is concomitant with a monstrous externalization of her inner phantasies. In an effort to assure herself that she will not be rejected by her reading public, she diffuses this anxiety by appending the author's introduction in the later republication of her novel. What *Frankenstein* also articulates is her realization that the materialization of the liberal political ideas of her parents produced an unbearable social solitude. For in her novel she gives expression to a far more unequivocal argument against solitary artistic practice than one can find in the writings of William Godwin or Percy Shelley. Mary does borrow from her mother the idea of sympathy as the crucial bond among members of a community, but instead of a radical break with conventions she ultimately makes a plea for a radical conformation to social conventions. In other words, in this novel, which at once establishes and deconstructs intertextual family bonds, in the sense that Mary Shelley uses her text to recognize the spiritual legacy of her politically radical parents, she also makes an extraordinarily conservative plea for real family bonds. At the age of nineteen she seems to have had a premonition of the catastrophe of her own life, the loss of her family as a site for 'domestic affection'.[14] Percy Shelley dies four years after the appearance of her novel, only one of her children [Percy Florence, 1819–1889] survives, and for many years Sir Timothy Shelley [her father-in-law, 1753–1844] keeps her from gaining her rightful inheritance. In her own life she was forced to learn that the intellectual legacy of her parents was inextricably interwoven with the monstrosity of being socially outcast.

In a last effort of rewriting her life, Mary Shelley was, however, able to a degree to sublate [resolve] the conflict between family and authorship, which had accompanied her so painfully throughout her relatively long life. If she called her first novel 'my hideous progeny', this designation is equally befitting of her son Percy Florence, who, together with his wife, Lady Jane Shelley, sought to cleanse the public image of his family. In their subsequent refashioning, Shelley's first wife, Harriet, is systematically defamed as a faithless and psychically unstable woman. [*Editor's note:* Harriet's suicide by drowning in December 1816 is most commonly viewed as a desperate response to Shelley's desertion of her and their two children, Ianthe (1813–1876) and Charles (1814–1826). Significantly, however, there are also occasional portrayals of Harriet as an adulteress who committed suicide on finding herself pregnant with another man's child.] Documents that could harm the family reputation were removed from the family archives and burned, for example the correspondence between Wollstonecraft and Fuseli.[15] Percy Shelley himself was raised to the status of a saint, and a room in the house was furnished as a shrine to honour the poet.

Mary Shelley herself collaborated in this exonerating act of refashioning. So as to assure the inheritance of the Shelley estate for her son, she had ceded to Sir Timothy's prohibition against writing a biography of her dead husband. In her memoirs of Godwin, published in 1831, the spiritual bond to Shelley is never mentioned. When in 1838 she received her father-in-law's permission to publish a collected edition of her husband's poetry, she appended her own 'Notes' so as to offer the biographical context from which Shelley's creative genius was shown to have emerged. But these 'Notes', in fact, serve the purpose of transforming her disruptive life into a conventional bourgeois marriage, and in this recuperative gesture Mary effaced all traces of any spiritual debt to Wollstonecraft and Godwin. She recreated, one could say gave birth, to the poet Shelley a second time, now in the image of Victorian expectations – this too an example of 'hideous progeny'. In these seemingly biographical 'Notes', the political urgency of Percy's poetry, as well as any personal weaknesses in the poet's character, are covered up: neither Godwin, nor Harriet, nor Claire Clairmont are mentioned, and their extramarital cohabitation in Switzerland, as well as the many marital crises, are withheld. The revolutionary, the atheist, the renegade is transformed into an alienated, inspired prophet, and his poetry is described as a shield against his disappointment in life. With this fictionalizing biographical rewriting Mary assured her husband an irrevocable position in the pantheon of English poets and integrated him effortlessly into the mainstream of Victorian national culture, namely as the myth . . . of the 'beautiful and ineffectual angel'.

These appended critical and biographical notes are the epitome of Mary Shelley's family romance, the imaginative re-creation of the domestic happiness of family bonds, meant to elevate a husband, by whom she has been disappointed, who had proven insufficient. As Muriel Spark notes, this rewriting of Shelley's life was both a torment – Mary notes in her journal 'I am torn to pieces by memory' – as well as a clever way to circumvent the prohibition of her father-in-law, Sir Timothy, and write a biography of the poet.[16] Yet these 'Notes', creatively misreading her biography as well as the spiritual bonds between her husband and her parents, are also, in Freud's definition of the family romance, nostalgic, for they express her longing for the happy, vanished days when her husband seemed to her both the noblest and the dearest person in the world, when her family bonds offered her a sense of plenitude. Yet the crucial point in my reading of *Frankenstein* . . . resides precisely in the way this novel questions the idea of any original sense of plenitude. These 'Notes', one could say, serve a similar purpose, for they not only function as the imaginative counterpart to Mary Shelley's novel, fashioning an image of domestic happiness where *Frankenstein* traces the slow destruction of the family. They also, in turn, deconstruct their own interest in the conservative image of the family which they (along with the author's introduction of 1831) are meant to afford. For what Mary Shelley obliquely illustrates, even as she makes concessions to comply with the conventions of her time, is that the intact image of the family she offers, like her hideous progeny *Frankenstein* that offers an image of its dissolution, can only be a textual body – always a phantasy, a replacement.[17] ☐

As Bronfen's argument exemplifies, rather than taking *Frankenstein* seriously as a deliberate feat of the author's creative imagination, many critics seem inclined to read it as an obscurely symptomatic document of Shelley's hidden fears and desires. Criticism on the work of Mary Shelley is divided between readings of her fiction as a desultory outpouring of female dreamwork on the one hand and a subtle, consciously crafted expression of authorial intentions, carefully designed and strategically put together, on the other. Due to her sex and remarkably young age at the time of *Frankenstein*'s composition, her independent authorship of the novel has often been contested. Even if most critics do not support the suggestion that large chunks of the novel may in fact have been written by the author's husband,[18] they still seem tempted to regard its main creative impetus as originating in some kind of traumatic sub-conscious stirring. Typically, in Bronfen's account, Shelley's renunciation of her parents' and husband's radicalism, her compliance with her father-in-law's various injunctions, as well as her alleged refashioning of Percy in accordance with a new Victorian ideal of domestic masculinity, fail to be comprehended as a woman's intricate strategies of survival and are instead interpreted as the unfortunate side effects of a 'hysterical', compulsive urge.

In many respects, Bronfen's reading seems inspired by Mary Poovey's earlier essay, 'My Hideous Progeny: Mary Shelley and the Feminization of Romanticism', which was later included as a chapter in Poovey's highly acclaimed study, *The Proper Lady and the Woman Writer: Ideology as Style in the Works of Mary Wollstonecraft, Mary Shelley, and Jane Austen*. Like Bronfen, Poovey presents the author of *Frankenstein* as a woman writing under enormous patriarchal pressure. According to Poovey, the general living conditions of women in the nineteenth century failed to provide them with even the most basic prerequisites for the development of an independent authorial voice. In fact, women were encouraged to curb their desire for self-expression, which was considered unseemly and improper in a lady. Thus entangled in a web of strictly gender-specific behavioural norms, Shelley is introduced by Poovey as an extreme case of what was unfortunately a common dilemma among her female con-temporaries. As Poovey explains, what has often been identified as a basic incongruity or deficiency in Shelley's work must actually be regarded as 'the result of one woman's attempt to conform simultaneously to two conflicting modes of behaviour'. Poovey explains:

■ On the one hand, both as the daughter of William Godwin and Mary Wollstonecraft and as the lover and then wife of Percy Shelley, Mary was encouraged from her youth to fulfill the Romantic model of the artist, to prove herself by means of her pen and her imagination. 'In our family,' Mary's stepsister Claire Clairmont once wryly remarked, 'if you cannot write an epic poem or novel, that by its origin-ality knocks all other novels on the head, you are a despicable creature, not worth acknowledging'. On the other hand, this pressure to be 'original' was contradicted by the more prevalent social expecta-tions that a woman conform to the conventional feminine model of propriety, that she be self-effacing and supportive, devoted to a family rather than to a career.[19] □

While Poovey's reading of Shelley is acutely sympathetic, it is also extremely defeatist. It almost seems as if she expected Shelley's work to be second-rate since, like all women's writing, it must inevitably bear the marks of its author's patriarchal debilitation. According to Poovey, 'Mary Shelley emerges as an important figure, even though she never fully achieved the personal or the aesthetic self-confidence necessary to integrate her imaginative efforts'.[20] Consequently, instead of Shelley's remarkable triumph over the obstacles society thrust in her way, it is quite ironically her alleged failure that assumes prominence in Poovey's attempt to rewrite literary history from a feminist perspective.

Inspired by Poovey's argument yet critical of her conclusions, James Carson rejects all interpretations of *Frankenstein* as an unstructured 'baggy monster' that displays little conceptual stringency or coherence. Rather than regarding Shelley's novel as an obscure emanation from a deep psychological source beyond the author's knowledge or consciousness, Carson reads the unconventional make-up of *Frankenstein* as Shelley's attempt to give voice to a highly self-conscious aesthetics of her own – an aesthetics that transcends acknowledged conflictual tensions as it asserts itself against both traditional patriarchy and male Romanticism, which poses as its anarchic offspring. According to Carson, Shelley neither perpetuates nor succumbs to patriarchal dynamics but, by appropriating three male voices (those of Victor Frankenstein, Robert Walton, and the Monster) within a female-authored frame, skilfully undermines the implicitly gendered positions that inhere in traditional narration. Already Poovey saw in *Frankenstein* a critique of male ambition, and in fact of desire itself, as 'a drive that can and must be regulated – specifically, by the give-and-take of domestic relationships'.[21] However, it is Carson who shows, with reference to Shelley's letters, that her prioritisation of duty over desire is not an expression of her patriarchal conditioning or inveterate conservatism, but a reflection of her belief that only a responsible fulfilment of one's duties is apt to facilitate enduring social change.

As Carson argues, in later life Shelley resolutely dispenses with her husband's noisy acrobatics of revolutionary agitation and embraces a liberalist reformism similar to that of her father. Significantly, once Romantic masculinity has thus been stripped of its exemplary, normative status, the self of the woman writer is able to identify her own aesthetics and determine her own set of values. According to Carson, readers of Shelley's work must discard and learn to emancipate themselves – just as Shelley herself appears to have done – from the critical parameters of traditional, masculinist criticism. It is essential that we stop regarding *Frankenstein* as a random patchwork of half-baked influences that reacts to, but never manages to resolve or reach beyond, the pressure exerted by patriarchal configurations of power. After a careful analysis of the statements on authorship and politics which he finds in Shelley's letters, Carson concludes that 'both her relations with other authors and her refusal of self-assertion suggest that Harold Bloom's model of literary influence may be inapplicable to a woman Romantic writer'.[22] In 'Bringing the Author Forward: *Frankenstein* through Mary Shelley's Letters', first published in an issue of *Criticism* in 1988, Carson posits that the nineteenth-century woman writer deserves to be assessed by her own standards instead of those we expect her to have inevitably internalised. Carson writes:

■ In recent years critics have paid increasing attention to the problem of female authority for Mary Shelley. Ellen Moers, who interprets *Frankenstein* as a birth myth with sources in the author's life, exposes the prejudices on which previous studies of the sources of Shelley's first novel have been based: 'Her extreme youth, as well as her sex, have contributed to the generally held opinion that she was not so much an author in her own right as a transparent medium through which passed the ideas of those around her.'[23] Critics such as Moers have made effective use of biographical evidence, but the recent appearance of an excellent, much expanded collection of Mary Shelley's letters provides new resources for the reader of *Frankenstein*.[24] Mary Shelley's epistolary statements on authorship and gender should prompt us to change the terms of a recent debate in which the author of *Frankenstein* has been viewed as either a failure or a success in a Bloomian struggle to affirm her female self against her male predecessors and contemporaries.[25] By reading Mary Shelley's novel through her letters, I shall show that self-affirmation was not the primary goal at which she aimed. But her refusal to assert her female self would not necessarily make Shelley a less powerful woman writer, for, according to Peggy Kamuf, 'the cult of the individual and the temptation which results to explain to ourselves artistic and intellectual productions as expressions, simple and direct, of individual experience' must be included among 'the fundamental assumptions of patriarchy.'[26] Mary Shelley does not so much compete in a Romantic struggle to assert her creative self as offer an incipient critique of the individualistic notion of originary creativity.

While her unwillingness to bring herself forward is certainly related to specifically female anxieties of authorship, Mary Shelley's self-denial is not a passive gesture but rather both an assertion of ethical value and an indication of the way in which the self is constructed out of unstable social and gender roles. [In 1828] Shelley . . . justified a refusal to become the subject of biography as a legitimate response to a society which confines women to the domestic sphere: 'As to a Memoir, as my sex has precluded all idea of my fulfilling public employments, I do not see what the public have to do with me.'[27] However, the popular success of *Frankenstein*, combined with the growing interest, in the Romantic period, in biographical interpretation, brought Shelley into public notice, a position she exploited in order to emphasize the lack of unity in the female authorial self.

The dangers of slipping into either the vanity of authorship and biographical intrusiveness or the guilt of parental negligence would be especially threatening for a woman writing in her own name the genetic account of a novel published anonymously thirteen years earlier. In the 1831 Introduction to *Frankenstein*, Shelley seeks to overcome the danger of forwardness by insisting on a division between the private and public selves, between what is personal and what pertains to her as an author: 'It is true that I am very averse to bringing myself forward in print; but as my account will only appear as an appendage to a former production, and as it will be confined to such topics as have connection with my authorship alone, I can scarcely accuse myself of a personal intrusion' (*F* 1831, p. 5). It is questionable, however, whether a mere declaration of her aversion to literary forwardness would suffice to exclude Shelley from the egotistical, masculine search for glory exemplified in Walton, Frankenstein, and Clerval. But unlike her creator-hero, the maternal author willingly assumes parental responsibility: 'And now, once again, I bid my hideous progeny go forth and prosper. I have an affection for it, for it was the offspring of happy days, when death and grief were but words, which found no true echo in my heart. . . . But this is for myself; my readers have nothing to do with these associations' (*F* 1831, p. 10). The potential vanity of authorship is cancelled by declaring what is 'my own' to be 'hideous' and, as we shall see, by proposing a theory of invention which denies absolute origination, thereby draining the adjective *my* of most of its possessive force.

Although Mary Shelley did not apparently value female self-assertion, she should not therefore be regarded as simply conventional or as embodying, in advance, a Victorian ideal of self-denying womanhood. The ostentatious self-effacement with which Mary Poovey has recently charged Mary Shelley seems never to have clearly entailed, for Shelley, the belief 'that women's behavior must significantly differ from that of men,' a belief which characterizes the ideology of the 'proper lady'.[28] Mary Shelley advocates duty and self-denial not just as feminine but as human ideals. In a letter she wrote to Robert Dale Owen [1801–1877, eventually an American politician and social reformer], the son of the [Scottish social reformer Robert Owen (1771–1858)] and author of *A New View of Society* (1813), prior to the departure of both father and son for the model American community of Nashoba, Shelley participates in the endeavor, promoted by sentimentalism, to create a new, sympathetic male subject.[29] She commends the self-reliant social reformer Frances Wright [1795–1852, British-American philanthropist, author and social reformer] to Owen's care. She advises him to be very attentive to Wright's situation, for if Wright does not communicate her problems and her need for assistance it will be less on account of secretiveness than of the existing social relations between the sexes:

> we must all be sure of sympathy before we confide at all – & a woman must very highly esteem & love a man before she can tell any of her heart's secrets to him. We have no very excessive opinion of men's sympathetic and self-sacrificing qualities – make yourself an exception.[30]

Mary Shelley clearly recognized not only that woman more fully embodied the qualities of sympathy and self-denial, but that their very success in attaining these ideals would very likely operate to their disadvantage in the current state of society. Hence, in writing to Frances Wright, she tempers her praise with a warning:

> You do honour to our species & and what perhaps is dearer to me, to the feminine part of it. – and that thought, while it makes me doubly interested in you, makes me tremble for you – women are so per[pet]ually the victims of their generosity, – their purer, & more sensitive feelings render them so much less than men capable of battling the selfishness, hardness & ingratitude which is so often the return made, for the noblest efforts to benefit others.[31]

The greater purity of women's than men's efforts to efface the self in doing their duty to humanity and in making those around them happy, as well as the deprivation endured by women because of such self-sacrifice, forms one of the subjects of Mary Shelley's first novel. That Shelley should maintain the human ideal of self-sacrifice, in full awareness of its threat to her sex, suggests that we ought to reassess Gilbert and Gubar's unfavorable comparison of Mary Shelley with Emily Brontë [*Editor's note:* As Carson points out earlier in his essay, Gilbert and Gubar view Shelley 'as an "acquiescent" stage on the road to Emily Brontë's radically corrective "misreading" of Milton'[32]]; for their evaluation is based on the thesis that self-discovery or affirmation of the female self is the telos of nineteenth-century women's writing. Mary Shelley, on the contrary, found it morally reprehensible or merely tiresome to have the self brought forward in writing: 'I have tried to read Mme de Genlis' memoirs, but they are one large capital *I* from beginning to end . . . .'[33] Although Mary Shelley values self-sacrifice over self-affirmation, she does so with a complete awareness of the social implications of her position.[34] □

Carson insists that Shelley is in perfect control of what she thinks and how she writes. Investigating the aesthetic implications of her subtle use of personal pronouns, he explains that critics have found it so exceedingly difficult to acknowledge Shelley's independence, skill and creative maturity because her approach to authorship is fundamentally different, even diametrically opposed, to her famous husband's. Whereas Percy loves to pose as the epitome of inspired originality, Mary quietly withdraws into authorial self-effacement, thereby effectively upstaging the male Romantic ego's masculinist self-fashioning and exposing its obsessive celebration of radical innovation and subjective purity as a pretentious and profoundly asocial act of vanity. As Poovey points out, 'the three-part narrative structure [of *Frankenstein*] enables [Shelley] to establish her role as an artist though a series of relationships rather than through an act of self-assertion'.[35] Shelley clearly prefers a 'chaotic', fragmentary assemblage of others (as facilitated by the traditionally feminine) to a glorification of the self's ultimately impossible integrity and closure (as enacted by the traditionally masculine). In Shelley's aesthetics of authorship, intertextuality is disclosed as a feminine principle that, by rejecting claims of unprecedented originality, incorporates the other and merges with it in a monstrously unruly dialogue that allows for endless re-interpretations. As Carson concludes, 'Mary Shelley's rejection of the "me" and her embrace of non-originary authorship are signs of the anti-elitist, "popular" nature of her work'.[36] Leading up to this final assertion, that presents *Frankenstein* ultimately as a rehabilitation rather than a critical deconstruction of traditional femininity, Carson's argument reads as follows:

■ In *Frankenstein* . . . the pronoun *my* is . . . deprived of much of its possessive force since . . . one should accept responsibility for what is one's own without claiming absolute property in it. A theory of invention that denies origination thus provides an appropriate introduction to Shelley's story of creation:

Every thing must have a beginning, to speak in Sanchean phrase; and that beginning must be linked to something that went before. . . . Invention, it must be humbly admitted, does not consist in creating out of void, but out of chaos; the materials must, in the first place, be afforded: it can give form to dark, shapeless substances, but cannot bring into being the substance itself. (*F* 1831, p. 8)

Within Shelley's genetic account of her novel, she points to the folly of seeking origins. Her account here suggests an infinite regression, while the parody of Genesis in the body of the work implies that new creation is always prompted by and modelled on prior texts. Hence Shelley can only speak of origins 'in Sanchean phrase.' Paradoxically, however, 'to speak in Sanchean phrase' – which refers in Shelley to textual mediation – means in [Miguel de] Cervantes [1547–1616, Spanish writer] to speak proverbially, like the illiterate Sancho Panza [a character in *Don Quixote* (1605)]. Speaking in Sanchean phrase, though the product of literary borrowing, would thus align Mary Shelley with the traditional village culture which is opposed by the enlightened projects of Walton and Frankenstein.

Shelley's humble admission concerning invention becomes even more humble, problematically so, in the course of the Introduction. For, when Shelley comes to discuss her husband's contribution to the work, she limits his influence to matters of *formal* presentation: 'I certainly did not owe the suggestion of one incident, nor scarcely of one train of feeling, to my husband, and yet but for his incitement, it would never have taken the form in which it was presented to the world' (*F* 1831, p. 10). But invention has just been defined as the capacity of 'giv[ing] form to dark, shapeless substances.' The waking dream which Mary Shelley recounts in explaining the genesis of her work would seem to be more on the level of dark substance than of literary form. Does Mary Shelley herself, then, license us to consider Percy Shelley the inventor or author of *Frankenstein*?

Mary Shelley's non-originary and non-assertive authorship would certainly not prompt her to exclude Percy Shelley's writing from the text, but it might lead as well to the recognition that if he is entitled to a share of 'final authority,' then so perhaps are other authors, living and dead, such as Godwin and Milton. Literary influence in *Frankenstein* reinforces the splitting of the narrative *I* and the emptying out of the possessive *my*. The character Frankenstein, on the contrary, engages in Titanic self-assertion. He seeks through his creative project to exceed the human, to take his place among the immortals. Robert Walton shares this ambition to go beyond. He only conceived of a voyage through barren wastes after having aspired to a place in the already crowded poetic mansion: 'I also became a poet, and for one year lived in a Paradise of my own creation; I imagined that I also might obtain a niche in the temple where the names of Homer and Shakespeare are consecrated' (*F* 1831, p. 14). Outside the novel, the humble genre of (women's) terror fiction does not enter into competition with the works of such poetic fathers. Instead, the novelistic activity of exceeding the human through forays into the supernatural can be justified by invoking these consecrated names: *The Iliad, The*

Tempest, Midsummer Night's Dream, and *Paradise Lost* (*F* 1831, p. 11) are all called in to sanction the imaginative procedures of *Frankenstein*. I use the passive in the last sentence, since it is not the 'author' of *Frankenstein* who calls upon Homer, Shakespeare, and Milton. That is to say, it is Percy rather than Mary Shelley who wrote the Preface which contains the defence of supernatural fiction with its attendant appeal to poetic authority.

Yet Mary Shelley is not without ambitions of joining the immortals, however much she may attempt to reconcile these ambitions with the conventional role of the faithful wife, the romantic image of love beyond the grave, and her own ideal of self-denying sympathy:

> But were it not for the steady hope I entertain of joining him what a mockery all this would be. Without that hope I could not study or write, for fame & usefulness (except as far as regards my child) are nullities to me – Yet I shall be happy if any thing I ever produce may exalt & soften sorrow, as the writings of the divinities of our race have mine. But how can I aspire to that?[37]

Shelley aspires to the condition of 'the divinities of our race,' while at the same time denying her own aspirations. She declares that 'fame' is empty for her and that 'usefulness' has value only in the maternal sphere. Just as with Euthanasia in *Valperga* [1823, Shelley's second novel], Mary Shelley uses a conventional feminine role to justify unfeminine ambitions, such as that of mastering classical languages and literature. The study and the exertion of genius that it would take to achieve fame and usefulness are justified by Shelley on the basis of fidelity to her husband, a fidelity which extends to a desire to join him beyond the grave. It is only by not, like Frankenstein and Walton, seeing fame and usefulness as ends in themselves that Mary Shelley may be able to escape from making her own life a 'mockery.' Indeed, for her, divine authors fulfill the feminine function of softening others' sorrows: hence, the God that she made of her father and husband is transformed into a divine being more suitable to her own aspirations, a being who would not wish to supplant her father and wrest away his authority but would hope rather to soften his sorrows in his necessarily dependent human condition. Shelley animates the conventional social roles of daughter, wife, and mother with more than conventional electricity in order both to justify her ambitions and to escape the egotistical endeavors which merely mock divine works.[38] ☐

Frankenstein's departure from literary decorum into alleged incongruity and formal shapelessness is primarily due to Shelley's apparent reluctance to think in the absolutist binaries of originality versus derivation, good versus evil, male versus female, and so forth. *Frankenstein* defies definitive boundaries and continues to blur and confuse distinctions between what has traditionally been regarded as disparate and hence irreconcilable. Apart from embodying Shelley's practice of self-consciously negotiating this disparity of diverse intertextual influences, Frankenstein's monster comes to represent a fitting image of the unpredictable multiplicities of life in general, which it remains impossible to unravel into a neat sequence of clear-cut oppositions. The Monster thus stands as a remarkable feat of both conceptual and textual assimilation: albeit assembled from components of the old order, it is new; seemingly male, its gender assignment must ultimately remain as dubious as that of its father, who is a 'male mother'; and finally, while originally innocent and good, it soon evolves into a merciless killer of women and children. As James O'Rourke finds in '"Nothing More Unnatural": Mary Shelley's Revision of Rousseau', first published in *ELH* in 1989, whenever matters are about to crystallise into clarity, Shelley revokes or deliberately complicates her equations, not whimsically but for good reasons to do with her adamant refusal of partisan representation. Citing from Shelley's journals, O'Rourke quotes her as saying that 'I am not a person of Opinions [because] I feel the counter arguments too strongly'.[39] As *Frankenstein* amply demonstrates, Shelley's personal ambivalence regarding questions of science, art and politics manifests itself in an infinite deferral of textual ambiguities that continues to resist the impossibly neat transparency of any one single 'message'.

In his essay on *Frankenstein*, of which a longer extract is reprinted below, O'Rourke demonstrates how even Shelley's attitude to one of her most fervently admired philosophers, Jean Jacques Rousseau, is torn irresolvably between heartfelt declarations of a deep, familial affinity on the one hand[40] and conflicting sentiments of disapproval and disgust on the other. Rousseau's famous statement that 'man is born free; and everywhere he is in chains', which opens his *Treatise on the Social Compact* (1764) and poignantly expresses his belief that the individual's innate goodness and perfection are invariably corrupted by civilisation, could hardly have failed to appeal to Shelley. However, whereas *Frankenstein* seems in many ways inspired by Rousseau's primitivist anthropology centring on his concept of original, authentic man as a 'noble savage', the novel is probably best understood as a corrective rewrite of Rousseau's hypocritical and intrinsically warped manifesto. Shelley has always been particularly sensitive to the contradictions, inconsistencies and untenable pretence that inform both the politics and poetics of masculine self-representation. Neither her husband nor her father entirely manage to escape her omnipresent, if frequently implicit rather than direct, criticism of man's excessive self-centredness, which is so often prone to drive a wedge between his well-intentioned theoretical ideals and their actual implementation. As far as Rousseau is concerned, a fundamental unevenness between theory and practice was not difficult to detect, and it is this unevenness that, as O'Rourke illustrates in his essay, causes Shelley to digress repeatedly in her encyclopedic essay on Rousseau which she contributed to the Reverend Dionysius Lardner's *Lives of the Most Eminent Literary and Scientific Men of France* (1839). In fact, so O'Rourke argues, Shelley gives us the impression that, rather than a literary rendition of Rousseau's ideas, *Frankenstein* may in fact represent a fierce critique of the philosopher's private life.

As O'Rourke's numerous quotations from Shelley's essay on Rousseau document, the author was incredulous at her idol's cold-hearted abandonment of his five illegitimate children by Thérèse le Vasseur, an illiterate working-class girl. Despite all his apparent concern with a radical reorganisation of society that would safeguard and operate in the individual's best interest, he condemned his own children to a bleak and probably quite short-lived existence in one of eighteenth-century France's most squalid and chronically underfunded orphanages. At times, Shelley's indignation at the philosopher's private life becomes so pronounced that it threatens to disqualify his alleged genius and detract from the enormous influence his ideas exerted on both the insti-gators and supporters of the French Revolution. As so often in Shelley's work, fame and political achievement are considered of little significance as long as they remain unaccompanied by, or are won at the expense of, familial affection. As O'Rourke's re-reading of *Frankenstein* in the light of Rousseau's political anthropology uncovers, Shelley's 'hideous progeny' represents a significant refashioning of Rousseau's Romantic prototype of 'natural man'. Shelley evidently disagrees with Rousseau's dismissal of familial obligations as an integral part of what he condemns as man's burden of societal incarceration. According to Shelley, parental and filial affections are sacred because they are what make us human. To denounce them as particularly sinister constituents of society's (de)for-mative machine of oppression and self-alienation would be, so Shelley insists, deeply barbaric. O'Rourke writes:

■ It is widely understood that *Frankenstein* is to some degree a critique of William Godwin and Percy Shelley. This is grounded in such particulars as the ironic conjunction of the book's impersonal dedication to Godwin and its epigraph from Milton, which . . . suggests a deep ambivalence on Mary Shelley's part towards Godwin, and the use of Percy Shelley's teenage readings in Paracelsus [1493–1541, Swiss physician and alchemist] and Albertus Magnus [1193–1280, German scholastic philosopher], and his juvenile pseudo-nym Victor (which he adopted for a volume of juvenile poetry written in collaboration with his sister Elizabeth) in the creation of Victor Frankenstein.[41] There is, however, a relative scarcity of biographical material that would allow Godwin and Shelley to serve as the prototypes for a father-figure who abandons his creation. . . . Her famous comment that 'my father from age & domestic circumstances & other things could not *me faire valoir*'[42] [*Editor's note:* What Shelley presumably means here is that Godwin simply did not have the means to do her talents justice or show his daughter off to her full advantage.] seems to refer to the time after Shelley's death, and it is, in any event, a very short and qualified criticism. The complicated circumstances that may have led her to blame Shelley, at least in part, for Clara Shelley's death [*Editor's note:* The Shelleys' second daughter died of dysentery in September 1818, aged one.] occurred well after the writing of *Frankenstein*. But there was enough in her experience to allow her to have the monster generalize, in relatively muted tones, on the difference between maternal and paternal behavior:

> I heard of the difference of sexes; of the birth and growth of children; how the father doated on the smiles of the infant, and the lively sallies of the older child; how all the life and cares of the mother were wrapt up in the precious charge. (*F* 1818, p. 97)

The same words, from a more orthodox writer, could be taken simply as a description of a natural difference between the sexes. If it were not for the context of *Frankenstein*, in which a male unilaterally creates and then abandons his creation, this might not even seem a criticism.

For the more extreme instance of paternal neglect, we need to turn from Godwin and Shelley to Rousseau. Rousseau, to Mary Shelley's knowledge, abandoned his five children by Thérèse le Vasseur to the Parisian Foundling Hospital. She wrote about this, with some heat, in an essay on Rousseau for an encyclopedia of French authors. Since this essay is not widely known, and is not easily available outside of a few research libraries, I shall quote liberally from it.

> Even in his *Confessions* [1766–7], where Rousseau discloses his secret errors, he by no means appreciates the real extent of his misconduct on this occasion . . . Theresa was about to become a mother . . . Rousseau did not like to multiply ties between himself and his mistress and her family: he was needy: he had heard young men of rank and fortune allude vauntingly to the recourse they had had on such occasions to the Foundling Hospital. He followed their criminal example . . . Five of his children were thus sent to a receptacle where few survive; and those who do go through life are

brutified by their situation, or depressed by the burden, ever weighing at the heart, that they have not inherited the commonest right of humanity, a parent's care . . . . . .

. . . It is insulting the reader to dwell on the flagrancy of this act. But it is a lesson that ought to teach us humility. That a man as full of genius and aspiration after virtue as Rousseau, should have failed in the plainest dictates of nature and conscience, through the force of example and circumstances, shows us how little we can rely on our own judgment. It shows too, that a father is not to be trusted for natural instincts towards his offspring; for the mother wept, and it needed the control of her own mother, and strong necessity, to induce the weak-minded and misguided girl to consent to part with her offspring.[43]

In the next several pages of her essay, Mary Shelley shows an inability to move away from this subject. Her next paragraph begins, 'We say little of Rousseau's vain excuses as to the probable destiny of his children'; she then lists those excuses. She comments that 'This futile reasoning does not need elaborate refutation,' and then she refutes it. She speculates on what Rousseau's children might have become if they had been kept, 'a help and support in his age,' and even imagines that they might have had the standing to forestall the excesses of the Revolution their father had inspired. She finally seems to wonder at the direction of her own essay (which is, after all, being written for an encyclopedia), saying, 'Such ideas are vain, but will present themselves.' The sentences which follow are well worth quoting in full, both for their resonance for *Frankenstein* and to illustrate the intensity of Mary Shelley's feelings about Rousseau:

Our first duty is to render those to whom we give birth, wise, virtuous, and happy, as far as in us lies. Rousseau failed in this, – can we wonder that his after course was replete with sorrow? The distortion of intellect that blinded him to the first duties of life, we are inclined to believe to be allied to that vein of insanity, that made him an example among men for self-inflicted sufferings. We now dismiss this subject. It was necessary to bring it so far forward as to show the evil effects of so bad a cause; it is too painful to dwell further upon.[44]

But Mary Shelley does not dismiss the subject. She begins to recount how Rousseau's relationship with Thérèse le Vasseur evolved into a common-law marriage, and her commentary begins with an illustration of her own indifference to the legal status of marriage, but it ends on quite a different subject:

This had been praiseworthy as a proceeding founded on tolerant and charitable principles; but when we find that this kindly-seeming society was a Moloch [Semitic deity to whom parents sacrificed their children], whom to pacify, little children were ruthlessly sacrificed, the whole system takes a revolting and criminal aspect from which we turn with loathing.[45]

That is the end of her paragraph; the next paragraph begins, 'However, to go back to narrative,' and it does so.

The essay shifts to an account of Rousseau's first success as an author, with the *First Discourse* [*A Discourse on the Arts and Sciences* (1750)]. Mary Shelley delivers a mixed verdict on Rousseau's speculative anthropology:

The eloquence with which he represented the evils of civilisation, and the blessings of a state of nature, as he called it, fascinated every reader. The freshness and energy of his style charmed; the heart he put into his arguments served instead of reason, and convinced . . . Yet, in point of fact, nothing can be more unnatural than his natural man. The most characteristic part of man's nature is his affections. The protection he affords to woman – the cares required by children; yet Rousseau describes his natural man as satisfying his desires by chance, – leaving the woman on the instant; while she, on her side, goes through childbearing, child-birth, and child-nurture alone. Much may be granted to the strength that human beings enjoy in savage life . . . but, in all, man has ever been found (except in one or two cases, where the human animal descends below brutes), the protector of women, and the source of his children's subsistence; and among all societies, however barbarously constituted, the gentler and nobler individuals among them have loved their wives and their offspring with constant and self-sacrificing passion.[46]

The reader who is familiar with Rousseau's writings will have noticed that Mary Shelley shifts from the *First* to the *Second Discourse* [*A Discourse on the Origin and Causes of Inequality among Men* (1754)] in the material cited from Rousseau. This seems to be a mistake on her part, since she comments briefly on the *Second Discourse* several pages later, calling it simply an extension of the *First*. On the matter of Rousseau's 'natural man,' she is willing to go so far as to characterize the entirety of Rousseau's theory as a rationalization of his own misdeeds:

Poor Rousseau, who had thrust his offspring from parental care to the niggard benevolence of a public charity, found some balm to the remorse that now and then stung him, by rejecting the affections out of his scheme of the state of natural man.[47]

Mary Shelley's challenge to Rousseau's primitivism echoes some of her mother's differences with Rousseau. In *A Vindication of the Rights of Woman*, Mary Wollstonecraft also credited Rousseau's eloquence and disdained his theories when she remarked on 'the brutal state of nature which even his magic pen cannot paint as a state in which a single virtue took root.' Wollstonecraft, like Mary Shelley, found the duties owed to children as a proof against Rousseau, arguing that 'he disputes whether man be a gregarious animal, though the long and helpless state of infancy seems to point him out as particularly impelled to pair, the first step towards herding.'[48] But there are some fundamental differences between Mary Shelley's beliefs and Wollstonecraft's – Wollstonecraft would not have written that 'The most characteristic part of man's nature is his affections' – and these differences make it far more difficult for Mary Shelley to disentangle herself from Rousseau than it had been for Wollstonecraft.

Wollstonecraft grounds her challenge to Rousseau in classic Enlightenment premises, arguing that reason is the distinguishing characteristic of human nature, and that reason is God-given. There is thus a categorical distinction between material being and human capacity in Wollstonecraft's beliefs. But when Mary Shelley suggests that the 'affections' are actually 'the most characteristic part' of human nature, she establishes a continuity between the state of nature and the state of civilization that is characteristic of Rousseauean Romanticism. Mary Shelley's argument with Rousseau is more narrowly an ethical dispute than was Mary Wollstonecraft's. Wollstonecraft maintained a faith in God and reason that provided a metaphysical foundation for believing Rousseau to be ontologically [with respect to the nature of being] wrong in his description of human nature. Mary Shelley had much less faith in such metaphysical sureties, and in the absence of a controlling deity in *Frankenstein*, the ontogeny [individual development] of Victor Frankenstein's creation recapitulates a Rousseauean phylogeny [evolution of humankind as a species].

The two traits that Rousseau attributes to the human animal in a precivilized state are self-preservation and compassion. As he says in the *Second Discourse*, he finds 'two principles prior to reason, one of them interesting us in our own welfare and preservation, and the other exciting a natural repugnance at seeing any other sensible being, and particularly any of our own species, suffer pain or death.'[49] These traits can easily be discovered in Mary Shelley's monster. The monster does not come into existence *tabula rasa* [in a totally uninformed original state; as a 'clean slate'] but begins to show a Rousseauean inner being in his first reaction to light and darkness:

> a stronger light pressed upon my nerves, so that I was obliged to shut my eyes. Darkness then came over me, and troubled me; but hardly had I felt this, when, by opening my eyes, as I now suppose, the light poured in upon me again. (*F* 1818, p. 80)

The first response, to light, is entirely physiological, but this is not so in the reaction to darkness. There is no physical pain associated with darkness; the monster is simply 'troubled.' As this passage echoes Adam's first awakening to consciousness, the monster's distress is Mary Shelley's twist on the belief of Milton's Adam that when 'gentle sleep/First found me,' this might mean that 'I then was passing to my former state/Insensible, and forthwith to dissolve.'[50] The difference between Adam and the monster is precisely that the latter is 'troubled' by this possibility; in this he evinces the Rousseauean instinct for self-preservation that is as automatic as a physiological response. Rousseau argues in the *Second Discourse* that the attainment of a more reflective sense of mortality is a crucial stage in human evolution, 'for no animal can know what it is to die; the knowledge of death and its terrors being one of the first acquisitions made by man in departing from an animal state.'[51] Mary Shelley's monster signals his transition from a state of nature to a more fully human condition in one of his most Rousseauean outbursts that incorporates this growing awareness of mortality:

> Oh, that I had forever remained in my native wood, nor known or felt beyond the sensations of hunger, thirst and heat!
> Of what a strange nature is knowledge! It clings to the mind when it has once seized on it, like a lichen on the rock. I wished sometimes to shake off all thought and feeling; but I learned that there was but one means to overcome the sensation of pain, and that was death – a state which I feared yet did not understand. (*F* 1818, pp. 96–97)

The monster first shows his capacity for compassion when he refuses to take food from the de Laceys' supplies once he realizes that by doing so he causes them hardship. This is the best argument for the original goodness of the monster, for in this case the two primal Rousseauean instincts collide, and the monster chooses to exercise compassion even as it conflicts with his own self-preservation.

The central enigma of *Frankenstein* is the evolution of this benign creature into a child-murderer, and in sketching this development

Mary Shelley uses Rousseauean principles, but she shows an even more fluid transition between the attributes of the natural man and the social being than Rousseau did in his *Discourses*. It could well be the case that rhetorical purpose has to some degree dictated content in both Rousseau's *Discourses* and *Frankenstein*; Rousseau was addressing questions posed by the French Academy that called for a conceptual opposition between nature and civilization, while Mary Shelley was showing the development of a single individual. In any event, it seems clear in *Frankenstein* that the natural instinct to compassion leads directly to the desire for social relations in the monster's dealings with the de Laceys; any such connection is far more difficult to establish in Rousseau.[52] The psychological ground of *Frankenstein* becomes even more complicated when Mary Shelley effaces the distinction made by Rousseau between *amour de soi-meme* and *amour-propre*.

In a footnote to the *Second Discourse*, Rousseau identifies *amour de soi-meme* as a natural instinct and *amour-propre* as an artificial sense of honor born of socialization. *Amour de soi-meme* he calls 'a natural feeling which leads every animal to look to its own preservation,' whereas *amour-propre* is 'a purely relative and factitious feeling, which arises in the state of society, leads each individual to make more of himself than of any other, [and] causes all the mutual damage men inflict one on another.' It follows, in Rousseau's reasoning, that 'in the true state of nature,' there could be 'no feeling arising from comparisons' and the natural being 'could know neither hatred nor the desire of revenge,' since such a being would have no sense of honor to be injured.[53] The congruence between Milton's and Rousseau's accounts of the fall from innocence were clear to Mary Shelley. What Milton called pride, Rousseau called *amour-propre*. Where Milton's Satan could not bear to be placed below the Son of God, Rousseau would identify this indignation with the ability to objectify oneself and make comparisons on points of relative worth. Satan's appeal to Eve was that she might be like a god. This sense of honor rooted in comparison and competition recurs in Mary Shelley's characters. In Frankenstein's initial dreams of glory, he refers to himself in the third person and imagines himself surpassing all of his predecessors: 'So much has been done, exclaimed the soul of Frankenstein, – more, far more, will I achieve' (*F* 1831, p.47). The monster is quite proud of his linguistic prowess, telling Frankenstein, 'I may boast that I improved more rapidly than the Arabian, who understood very little, and conversed in broken accents, whilst I comprehended and could imitate almost every word that was spoken' (*F* 1818, p.95). It should be remembered that the monster is not an otherwise normal being with an unfortunately deformed appearance, and his comparisons of himself to Satan are not entirely laments. When he says that 'Satan had his companions, fellow devils, to admire and encourage him' (F 1818, p. 105), it is noteworthy that he identifies himself with the chief, and 'admired,' rebel and not with any of his 'fellow devils.'

The intensity of the monster's response to his rejection by the de Laceys is rooted precisely in the injury done to his sense of *amour-propre*. He believes that 'to see their sweet looks turned towards me with affection, was the utmost limit of my ambition' (F 1818, p. 107), but his ensuing account of why he believes he will be successful in his quest shows that he has developed the sense of *amour-propre* that marks the transition, in Rousseauean terms, from the natural to the social state: 'The poor that stopped at their door were never driven away. I asked, it is true, for greater treasures than a little food or rest; I required kindness and sympathy; but I did not believe myself utterly unworthy of it' (F 1818, p. 107). Upon the monster's first rejections by human beings, he simply moves away to find new sources of food and shelter. This is the way of Rousseau's 'savage man'; he 'compare[s] the difficulty of conquering his antagonist with the trouble of finding subsistence elsewhere: and as pride does not come in, it all ends in a few blows; the victor eats, and the vanquished seeks provision elsewhere, and all is at peace.'[54] That the monster's response to his rejection by the de Laceys should be a desire for revenge, rather than simple disappointment, is due to his having developed a sense of his own self-worth. This being who cannot trace his existence to a protecting God finds his prospects for happiness controlled by such arbitrary and intractable determinants as his outward appearance, and his sense of justice is outraged. When the monster addresses Frankenstein as 'Cursed, cursed creator' and tells him that 'I declared everlasting war against the species, and, more than all, against him who had formed me' (F 1818, pp. 110–11), he views his entire existence through the prism of his socially acquired sense of justice; he finds his existential condition intolerable, and he focuses his desire for revenge on his creator.

. . . Critics of *Frankenstein* who have seen in the novel an ethical core of condemnation of Victor Frankenstein for his overreaching and his obsessive self-glorification have underestimated the equivocality of Mary Shelley on this subject. It should be kept in mind that the most powerful influence for a strong sense of self-respect in Mary Shelley's life was the life and writings of Mary Wollstonecraft, who argued strongly that the acquisition of a sense of self-respect was the only means by which women and children could escape being degraded by the institution of the patriarchal family. Those who wish to see Victor Frankenstein unequivocally condemned sometimes make Walton a foil to his obsession. This point is made by U. C. Knoepflmacher:

The only surviving male speaker of the novel, Walton, possesses what the Monster lacks and Frankenstein denies, an internalized female complementary principle. Walton begins his account through self-justificatory letters to a female ego-ideal, his sister Margaret Saville. . . . The memory of this civilizing and restraining woman . . . helps him resist Frankenstein's destructive (and self-destructive) course. Frankenstein and the Monster are joint murderers of little William, Justine, Clerval, Alphonse Frankenstein, and Elizabeth; Walton, however, refuses to bring death to his crew.[55]

I do not see, however, that Walton ever makes the decision to return to England. When the crew is deliberating on whether to continue north, Walton says, 'How all this will terminate, I know not; but I had rather die, than return shamefully, – my purpose unfulfilled.' When the crew decides otherwise, Walton writes to Mrs. Saville, 'The die is cast; I have consented to return, if we are not destroyed. Thus are my hopes blasted by cowardice and indecision; I come back ignorant and disappointed. It requires more philosophy than I possess, to bear this injustice with patience' (F 1818, p. 184). Walton, it seems, remains in sympathy with Frankenstein.

Frankenstein himself is quite equivocal as he reflects on his own demise. He first advises Walton to 'Seek happiness in tranquillity, and avoid ambition,' and then immediately reverses himself by saying, 'Yet why do I say this? I have myself been blasted in these hopes, yet another may succeed' (F 1818, p. 186). His disparagement of ambition recalls his earlier advice to Walton: 'how much happier that man is who believes his native town to be the world, than he who aspires to become greater than his nature will allow' (F 1818, p. 35). This advice is cited by George Levine as 'the moral of his story,' but it is a moral that Levine sees 'is argued very ambivalently' by the novel.[56] This ambivalence about the relative value of dreams of glory and domestic happiness can be seen as Mary Shelley's reading of Rousseau, whose native town, as was Victor Frankenstein's, was Geneva. . . .

. . . . . . When Mary Shelley derived from Rousseau the belief that 'the most characteristic part' of human nature is 'his affections,' and showed the operation of those affections in *Frankenstein*, she created characters whose psychologies were inextricable mixtures of altruism and narcissism. Walton identifies the reasons for his journey both as a desire for 'glory' (F 1818, p. 7) and for 'the inestimable benefit which I shall confer on all mankind' (F 1818, p. 6). The monster's first reaction to hearing himself described by the de Laceys as a 'good spirit' is to 'bec[o]me more active' in seeking to discover 'why Felix appeared so miserable, and Agatha so sad' so that 'it might be in my power to restore happiness to these deserving people' (*F* 1818, p.91), but when they injure his own sense of deserving, his entire being comes to be devoted to revenge. Victor Frankenstein, of course, is the most complexly drawn figure in this matter. This is his account of his motivation in the creation of the monster:

> No one can conceive the variety of feelings which bore me onwards, like a hurricane, in the first enthusiasm of success. Life and death appeared to me ideal bounds, which I should first break through, and pour a torrent of light into our dark world. A new species would bless me as its creator and source; many happy and excellent natures would owe their being to me. No father could claim the gratitude of his child so completely as I should deserve their's. Pursuing these reflections, I thought, that if I could bestow animation upon lifeless matter, I might in process of time (although I now found it impossible) renew life where death had apparently devoted the body to corruption. (*F* 1818, p.36)

While criticism of Victor Frankenstein has routinely focused on his desire for the 'gratitude' of this new species, it should not be forgotten, as Ellen Moers has noted, that this passage is also the most direct representation in the novel of the entry in Mary Shelley's journal that describes her dream of reviving her dead child: 'Dream that my little baby came to life again – that it had only been cold & that we rubbed it by the fire & it lived.'[57] The notion that *Frankenstein* can be given an ethical core through the vehicle of a polarized ideology that criticizes Milton, Godwin, Shelley, Rousseau, or others cannot easily accommodate the identification of the overreaching scientist with the most altruistic part of Mary Shelley. The outcome of Mary Shelley's dream – 'I awake & find no baby. I think about the little thing all day – not in good spirits' – subverts the idealisms of both the orthodox and radical traditions. In a Miltonic theology, earthly life serves as a testing ground for a more important hereafter. Wollstonecraft's concerns are less otherworldly than Milton's, but she maintains Milton's metaphysical belief in the essentially spiritual nature of the human being, while Godwin is drawn in his utopian projections to envision, in an appendix to *An Enquiry Concerning Political Justice*, the potential immortality of the human species.[58] Mary Shelley's experiences of having lost her first child and of having been the cause of her own mother's death in childbirth showed her the fallacy of believing death to be a merely 'ideal bound' that could be overcome by force of intellect, but the dream of the recovered baby also showed her the force of the desire behind that illusion.

Mary Shelley never found it easy to engage in the sort of polarized categories that allow for summary ethical judgment. Her unwillingness in the Rousseau essay to approve or disapprove of the trait in Voltaire [1694–1778, pseudonym of François Marie Arouet, French writer] and Rousseau that 'in ordinary men . . . would be named egotism, or vanity' shows the respect that she accords to the question of where the *amour-propre* due to genius becomes excessive. Her conclusion to the Rousseau essay is a marvelously elegant piece of ambiguity. She reiterates, near the beginning of her peroration to the essay, that Rousseau 'neglected the first duty of man by abandoning his children,' and she does not refrain from ethical commentary on the consequences of this neglect:

> He often dilates on simple pleasures – the charms of unsophisticated affections, and the ecstasy to be derived from virtuous sympathy – he, who never felt the noblest and most devoted passion of the human soul – the love of a parent for his child! We cannot help thinking that even while Rousseau defends himself by many baseless sophisms, that this crime, rankling at his heart, engendered much of the misery that he charged upon his fellow creatures.[59]

. . . Mary Shelley then delivers the conclusion to the essay in quite a different key:

> No author knows better than Rousseau how to spread a charm over the internal movements of the mind, over the struggles of passion, over romantic reveries that absorb the soul, abstracting it from real life and our fellow-creatures, and causing it to find its joys in itself. No author is more eloquent in paradox, and no man more sublime in inculcating virtue. While Voltaire taints and degrades all that is sacred and lovely by the grossness of his imagination, Rousseau embellishes even the impure, by painting it in colours that hide its real nature; and imparts to the emotions of sense all the elevation and intensity of delicate and exalted passion.[60]

So soon after a condemnation for having 'neglected the first duty of man by abandoning his children,' is Rousseau really being praised for his skill at 'romantic reveries that absorb the soul, abstracting it from real life and our fellow-creatures'? Can it be said of the same man that he 'neglected the first duty of man' and that 'no man [is] more sublime in inculcating virtue'? Does Mary Shelley approve of Rousseau's talent in 'embellishing the impure'? When this is described as 'painting it in colors that hide its real nature,' it would seem to be pure deception, but there is no mistaking the tone of the final clause, and the valorization of 'the elevation and intensity of delicate passion.'

. . . . . . Faced with the 'hurricane,' to borrow Victor Frankenstein's image, of conflicting affections, what is one's ethical duty? The long journal entry in which Mary Shelley defends herself against criticism for lack of zeal in what she calls 'the "good cause"' comes after fourteen years of relative dormancy of the journal, and is also written in 1838. She does not criticize political activism per se in this entry, saying rather that she has found the 'Radicals' who have pressed her in later life to be more vocal are themselves 'selfish in the extreme . . . rude, envious & insolent,'[61] and, in comparison with Shelley, Wollstonecraft and Godwin, 'mere drivellers'.[62] She goes on to explain what she has and has not done, and why she has not done otherwise:

> If I have never written to vindicate the Rights of women, I have ever befriended women when oppressed – at every risk I have defended & supported victims to the social system – But I do not make a boast . . . for in truth it is simple justice I perform.[63]
>
> If I write the above it is that those who love me may hereafter know that I am not all to blame – nor merit the heavy accusations cast on me for not putting myself forward – I cannot do that – it is against my nature – as well cast me from a precipice & rail at me for not flying.[64]

Besides asserting the inevitability of following one's own nature, this journal entry explicitly addresses the obligation of scrupulous self-examination. In this effort, Mary Shelley takes to heart the precept she derived from her study of Rousseau, 'that a man as full of genius and aspiration after virtue as Rousseau, should have failed in the plainest dictates of nature and conscience . . . shows us how little we can rely on our own judgment.'[65] Rousseau insisted, in closing the *Confessions*, that

> I have told the truth. If anyone knows anything contrary to what I have here recorded, though he prove it a thousand times, his knowledge is a lie and an imposture. . . . I publicly and fearlessly declare that anyone . . . who will examine my nature, my character, my morals, my likings, my pleasures, and my habits with his own eyes and can still believe me a dishonorable man, is a man who deserves to be stifled.[66]

Mary Shelley shows that she has learned from the study of Rousseau to be less certain, and more scrupulous. She says of herself that 'I may distrust my own judgment too much'[67] and, in a Rousseauean summary gesture, she declares: 'Thus have I put down my thoughts – I may have deceived myself – I may be vain – I may be in the wrong. I try to examine myself – & such as I have written appears to me the exact truth.'[68]

This statement of obligation to determine the 'exact truth' about one's life shows the respect Mary Shelley accorded to the Rousseauean project of the *Confessions*, which she described as 'an invaluable book, [that] discloses the secret of many hearts to those who have the courage to penetrate into the recesses of their own.'[69] As she showed in her essay, however, she did not think that Rousseau exercised sufficient judgment either in his life or in his self-examination. The impulse to justify is not easy to avoid; Frankenstein tells Walton on his deathbed, 'During these last days I have been occupied in examining my past conduct; nor do I find it blameable' (*F* 1818, p. 185). As Frankenstein fills the roles both of Milton's God, the unilateral male creator, and Rousseau, the father who abandoned his children, he is put into the position of trying, and failing, to justify the ways of God or man.[70] □

Reaching beyond all the various intertextual correlations introduced and discussed above, and perhaps most immediately indicative of *Frankenstein*'s radically composite nature as a merger of tradition and the individual talent, is the novel's full title: *Frankenstein, or The Modern Prometheus*. While the juxtaposition of Frankenstein and Prometheus establishes a connection between the mythic past and Shelley's own creative initiative in the present, the term 'modern' encapsulates and projects the work's ominous implications for the future.[71] *Frankenstein* can be read as an allegory of the modern age in which, due to its scientific progress and increasing knowledge in all areas of life, humanity has outgrown the medieval order of a God-given universe and begun to think itself the maker of its own world. In this respect, the rise of modernity represents simultaneously both a triumph and a fall, signalling humankind's enfranchisement and liberation from intellectual servitude as well as its irretrievable loss of innocence and existential security. Consequently, Shelley's novel leaves us wondering if, as a typical representative of modern man, Victor commits an unforgivable sin by attempting to emulate God's creative power or if, alternatively, he could possibly be seen as a heroic rebel against divine tyranny, whose science constitutes an awesome tool of human emancipation.

As Theodore Ziolkowski explains in 'Science, Frankenstein, and Myth', an essay first published in the *Sewanee Review* in 1981, this fundamental promethean ambivalence of Victor's heroic status is a direct result of Shelley's precarious conflation of the classical pagan myth with the biblical narrative of Genesis. Shelley's chief protagonist displays an affinity with both guilt-ridden Adam expelled from Eden and defiant Prometheus widely admired for his intransigence and superhuman audacity. According to Ziolkowski, modern man is a scientist, never too sure if his experiments are legitimate or constitute a crime, or if he will ever be able to strike a sustainable balance between his progress, ethics and desire. Significantly, Ziolkowski himself is not writing out of a political vacuum. His essay, of which a brief extract is reprinted below, dates from the early 1980s when the Cold War between East and West was about to culminate in a paranoid frenzy of nuclear armament and people feared the world might be annihilated through the accidental misfortune of a single technical error. Allegorically speaking, Frankenstein was evidently at it again, yet still it was not clear if his actions ought ultimately to be endorsed or reprehended. Stressing the enduring cultural topicality of *Frankenstein*, Ziolkowski elaborates on the problematic ambivalence of the novel's title as follows:

■ after the title page . . . it remains for the reader to deduce in what respects Victor Frankenstein can be said to be a modern Prometheus. The frequent references in the novel to electricity and lightning remind us that Prometheus incurred the wrath of the gods by stealing fire for mankind. A further analogy can be detected in the legend according to which Prometheus created the human race by fashioning men of clay. But that is as far as the analogy can be pursued. For his theft of fire Prometheus was punished by being chained to a mountain in the Caucasus, where each day an eagle appeared to eat away his liver, which renewed itself for the eagle's delectation every day for thirty thousand years. Unlike Frankenstein, however, Prometheus never succumbs to his punishment. He was beloved by the Romantics precisely because of his titanic spirit of rebelliousness. Far from being beset by doubts, the romantic Prometheus is, in [Percy] Shelley's words, 'the type of the highest perfection of moral and intellectual nature, impelled by the purest and the truest motives to the best and noblest ends.' What distinguishes him from such rebels as Satan and makes him more poetical, Shelley continues in the preface to *Prometheus Unbound*, is the fact that 'in addition to courage, and majesty, and firm and patient opposition to omnipotent force, he is susceptible of being described as exempt from the taints of ambition, envy, revenge, and a desire for personal aggrandisement.' These words could hardly be applied to Victor Frankenstein, who apart from his obsession with fire is a Prometheus *manqué* [unfulfilled or would-be]: he creates a man, to be sure, but it is a flawed man. Instead of serving society, Frankenstein becomes its nemesis [agency of retribution and vengeance], having created a monster that threatens its destruction. Indeed his name itself has become anathema [a curse], the very definition of the evil scientist. The ambivalence of Mary Shelley's modern Prometheus is produced, I would argue, through its contamination by a parallel legend from a totally different source: the biblical Adam.

Here the text does help us, for although it lacks specific references to the myth of Prometheus, it is replete with images borrowed from the first few chapters of Genesis. Most frequently, to be sure, it is the monster himself, fresh from his study of *Paradise Lost*, who sees himself as a new Adam, rambling in the fields of Paradise but soon abandoned by his creator. In this analogy, of course, Frankenstein is equivalent to God the Creator. But in several other passages Frankenstein uses biblical imagery to characterize his own situation. At one point, after the monster has warned him that he will seek him out on his wedding night, Frankenstein thinks of his beloved Elizabeth. 'Some softened feelings stole into my heart and dared to whisper paradisaical dreams of love and joy; but the apple was already eaten, and the angel's arm bared to drive me from all hope' (*F* 1818, p. 159) – a clear allusion to the sin of knowledge, which Frankenstein took upon himself by his search for forbidden knowledge.

This cluster of images alerts us to another dimension of the novel. Adam, like Prometheus, is both functionally and by etymological designation a scientist. He performs the typically scientific functions of naming and classifying nature. And, as the serpent tells Eve, if she and Adam will eat of the fruit of the Tree of Knowledge, they will become as gods, knowing (*scientes*) good and evil. There is an essential difference, however. Whereas Prometheus was venerated for his scientific achievements, Adam was lamented. From the sixth century B.C. the quest for scientific knowledge provided one of the most powerful motivations for Greek culture. The Hebrews had an entirely different conception. 'In much wisdom is much grief; and he that increaseth knowledge [the Vulgate [fourth-century version of the Bible] uses the term *scientia*] increaseth sorrow' (Ecclesiastes 1:18). The ambivalence regarding science that we encounter in *Frankenstein* results from a conflation of these two opposing views. In both cultures we encounter the paradigm of the scientist who seeks to increase knowledge by probing hitherto forbidden secrets; in both cases new consciousness is brought to the human race as a result of the scientific discovery; and both scientists receive typically political punishment for their transgressions: Prometheus is imprisoned and Adam is sent into exile. But the difference between their respective reactions to their fates produces the ambivalence toward science in our modern society, which arises from the dual traditions of Judeo-Christian and Greco-Roman culture: Adam skulks out of Eden, ashamed of his knowledge and deplored for all eternity for his fall, while Prometheus remains defiant in his attitude, cheered by the gratitude of the human race, until he is ultimately liberated by a tyrannical Zeus [supreme god of the ancient Greeks].

The analogy between the two myths has been recognized by theologians and poets since the Renaissance ... In the nineteenth century the interest [began to focus specifically on] the analogy between

Adam and Prometheus, who were seen to exemplify the differences between Nazarene [Christian] and Hellene [Greek] that had been made popular by Heinrich Heine [1797–1856, German poet and essayist] and Matthew Arnold [1822–1888, English poet, essayist and literary critic], among others. This tradition culminates in [Friedrich] Nietzsche [1844–1900, German philosopher, poet and critic], who argues in *The Birth of Tragedy* [1872] that the myth of Prometheus has the same characteristic significance for 'Aryan' man as does the myth of the Fall for Semitic man. In both cases, Nietzsche suggests, mankind achieves its highest goal, cognition, through an act of sacrilege. In the Greek myth the sacrilege is perpetrated consciously in the interest of human achievement and dignity; in the Hebrew myth, in contrast, it is prompted by idle curiosity and the reaction is shame.

We can now see that Mary Shelley's novel represents a surprisingly early conflation of the two representative myths. It is well known that during the composition of the novel Mary Shelley and her husband studied *Paradise Lost* and *Prometheus Bound* – that the Bible and Aeschylus' drama were therefore very much in her mind as she worked. But it has not been sufficiently stressed that her inability to reconcile the conflict inherent in her two sources – between pride and shame in cognition – produced for the first time that ambivalence toward scientific knowledge that we have come to regard as characteristically modern.[72] □

As the wide-ranging and often conspicuously incompatible interpretations by Bronfen, Carson, O'Rourke and Ziolkowski indicate, Shelley's novel constitutes a highly ambivalent text that is not only inspired but crucially informed by a variety of different sources or 'intertexts'. What also becomes evident is that each critical reading of *Frankenstein* has to be critically evaluated within the framework of its own conceptual parameters. Of special interest in this context would be the assumptions readers are invariably prone to cultivate with respect to the role of the critic and his or her relationship to the text and its author. This general interpretive dilemma is examined in greater detail in the next chapter which pays particular attention to the methods and principles of psychoanalytic criticism.

CHAPTER THREE

A Dream That Haunts Literature: Consciousness, Authority and Signification in *Frankenstein*

ABDICATING ALL conscious responsibility for the fantastic horror that informs her tale, Shelley claims in her 'Author's Introduction' that the original inspiration for *Frankenstein* came to her from 'far beyond the usual bounds of reverie' (*F* 1831, p.9) out of the deep recesses of her half-suspended, daydreaming mind. Her 'hideous progeny', she appears to be saying, is made of the stuff that nightmares are made of, its textual being issuing from a chaotic welter of psychic impulses whose exact source and motivation her consciousness cannot grasp. Accordingly, some critics have suggested that, in order to make 'proper' sense, the work's dream narrative needs to be subjected to a psychoanalytic probing that would unveil the encoded meanings that allegedly inhabit its allegorical utterances. Due to *Frankenstein*'s universal appeal – that is, its proven capacity to horrify all of us without exception – readers have been quick to believe that the novel draws on a common set of deep-rooted, archetypal patterns and configurations that reflect not only the author's own mental disposition, but also the psychocultural foundations of society as a whole and the workings of the human mind in general.

This chapter intends to provide no representative survey of different psychoanalytic readings (Freudian, Jungian, Lacanian, and so forth), all of which draw on an exegetical model of their own and therefore often come to mutually exclusive and incompatible conclusions.[1] Instead, it introduces two *meta*psychoanalytic perspectives whose particular readings of *Frankenstein* address the strife for predominance between literary and critical modes of representation and interrogate the claims of legitimacy and 'truth' that are invariably at stake in psychoanalytic renditions of literary meaning. The first extract is taken from Paul Sherwin's '*Frankenstein*: Creation as Catastrophe', first published in the *PMLA* in

1981 and reprinted in Harold Bloom's *Mary Shelley's Frankenstein* six years later. As Fred Botting illustrates, Sherwin seeks 'to outplay the repetitions and extravagances of psychoanalytic readings' in order to reaffirm literature's creative authority and unleash once again its indomitably subversive potential.[2] Combining a sympathetic investigation of the methods and objectives of Freudian literary criticism with a parody of its impossibly dense, often impenetrable style, Sherwin's challenging reading falls into altogether three sections, of which the first one is reprinted below. While emphasising the thoroughly helpful, illuminating effect of many a deep-psychological reading of literature, Sherwin deplores the widespread tendency of psychoanalytic critics to forget about the experimental origin and intrinsic playfulness of the Freudian model of interpretation. As a result, instead of opening up the text's ambivalent being-in-flux, these critics are inclined to constrain it, even close it for good. Sherwin argues that not Freud himself but the dogmatic zeal of some of his followers is responsible for bringing psychoanalytic criticism into disrepute. It is the latter who choose to ignore that the representational potential of a work like *Frankenstein* will endlessly continue to oscillate between the literal and the literary, the conscious and the unconscious. Texts like *Frankenstein* have to be understood as restive, agitated constructions of the imagination that are caught up in a never-ending, and ultimately vain, search for unequivocal symbolic signification. Any worthwhile reading of Shelley's novel must therefore remain indeterminate, concentrating not on the birth of one definitive textual meaning but engaging in a continuous delivery of interpretive meaning-making.

Sherwin concludes the first part of his argument suggesting that we re-invoke Freud's 'spirit of creativity'. Although his effort to demonstrate what exactly he means by this in the concluding two parts of his essay remains very vague, this cannot detract from his dazzling performance in Part I, which has established itself as a classic interrogation of the critical reception of *Frankenstein*. Sherwin writes:

■ Mary Shelley might well have titled her novel *One Catastrophe after Another*. For Frankenstein, who is dubiously in love with his own polymorphously disastrous history, the fateful event to which every other catastrophe is prelude or postscript is the creation. According to the archaic model implicit in his narrative, transcendence is equivalent to transgression, and his presumptuous deed is invested with the aura of a primal sin against nature that somehow justifies the ensuing retributive bother. Condemned by nature's gods to limitless suffering, the aspiring hero learns his properly limited human place. *Frankenstein*, however, knows differently. A reading alert to the anti-Gothic novel Mary Shelley inscribes within her Gothic tale will discover that nothing is simple or single. The critical event is impossible to localize, terms such as 'justice' and 'injustice' do not so much mean as undergo vicissitudes of meaning, and all the narrators are dispossessed of their authority over the text. As the central misreader, Frankenstein is the chief victim of the text's irony, the humor becoming particularly cruel whenever he thinks he is addressing the supernatural powers that oversee his destiny, for his invocatory ravings never fail to conjure up his own Creature. Indeed, the evacuation of spiritual presence from the world of the novel suggests that *Frankenstein* is more a house in ruins than the house divided that its best recent critics have shown it to be. The specter of deconstruction rises: doubtless future interpreters will describe a text that compulsively subverts its own performance and that substitutes for its missing center the senseless power play of a catastrophic Gothic machine. Yet the Gothic is always already demystified, the ruin of an anterior world of large spiritual forces and transcendent desires that the most relentless of demystifiers cannot will away. *Frankenstein*, although arguably a Gothic fiction, remains a living novel because it is a haunted house, ensouled by the anxious spirit that perturbs all belated romances.

While the unconsummated spirit raised by *Frankenstein* cannot be put to rest, one might suppose that *das Unheimliche* [the uncanny] can be contained within the spacious edifice of Freudian psychoanalysis. Freud's antithetical system provides an interpretive context for many of the anomalies disclosed by an ironic reading: the dissonance of overt and implicit meanings, the obscure sense of having trespassed on sacred ground, the appalling secret that craves expression yet must be protected as though it were a holy thing. In addition, the novel's catastrophic model functions in a way strikingly similar to the Freudian psychic apparatus. Instead of hubris, there is the drive's excess; instead of a downcast hero assaulted by phantasmagoria [a shifting medley of real or imagined figures, as in a dream], there is the boundless anxiety occasioned by the proliferation of repressed desire; and instead of the restrictive gods, there is the exalted secondary process, intended to keep the apparatus stable by binding or incarcerating mobile energy. More telling, the catastrophic model is an almost exact duplicate of the oedipal scenario, the most privileged psychoanalytic thematic and the dynamic source of Freud's mature topography [mapping] of the psyche. The way is opened for a recentering of the novel's unresolved intellectual and emotional turmoil.

Of course, the Freudian way has increasingly become, and always was, a wildly extravagant detour or series of detours, and staking out a position in the psychoanalytic field can be as agonizing as 'choosing' a neurosis. Still, when one reads that Walton is about to enact the favorite dream of his youth, seeking a passage through the ice to the warm Pole, where he may 'discover the wondrous power which attracts the needle' (*F* 1831, pp. 13–14), or that Frankenstein struggles 'with a child's blindness' to break through 'the fortifications and impediments that seemed to keep human beings from entering the citadel of nature' (*F* 1831, p. 39), it is hard not to translate such statements into the formulations of a recognizably classical psychoanalysis. I should acknowledge here that I am averse to reducing the questing drive in *Frankenstein* to a desire for primordial union with, or active possession of, the maternal body and that I think it is a dangerous critical error to conceive the novel as a tale told by an idiot, signifying. . . . Psychoanalysis, it may be said, is properly attuned to an important element in the life of the mind; its problem is that it fancies that part the whole.

A reading of the oedipal drama the novel re-enacts can begin with a notice of the first overt catastrophe recorded in Frankenstein's narrative: his witnessing, at fifteen, the terrible power of a lightning bolt during a thunderstorm. When the adult Frankenstein describes the event, which occurred at a time when his enthusiasm for alchemy had redoubled the urgency of his endeavors to penetrate nature's secrets, his excited rhetoric betrays the insistent presence of a forgotten childhood scene. 'I remained, while the storm lasted, watching its progress with curiosity and delight. As I stood at the door, on a sudden I beheld a stream of fire issue from an old and beautiful oak . . . and so soon as the dazzling light vanished the oak had disappeared, and nothing remained but a blasted stump' (*F* 1831, p. 40). In the original version of the text it is the father who discourses on the nature of lightning and who controls the symbolically castrating bolt that cripples desire: 'he constructed a small electrical machine, and exhibited a few experiments . . . which drew down that fluid from the clouds' (*F* 1818, p. 24). The son is, as it were, shocked into the latency stage [(in psychoanalysis) a period, from the age of about five to puberty, when sexual interest is diminished]; a sudden influx of self-revulsion impels him to denounce 'natural history and all its progeny as a deformed and abortive creation . . . which could never even step within the threshold of real knowledge . . . an unusual tranquility and gladness of soul . . . followed the relinquishing of my ancient and latterly tormenting studies' (*F* 1831, p. 41).

The next critical event in Frankenstein's history is his mother's death, and a period of mourning delays his departure for the University. Once there, he abruptly resumes his former studies, reconverted by Professor Waldman's panegyric [eulogy] on modern chemists: 'these philosophers . . . penetrate into the recesses of nature . . . They ascend into the heavens . . . they can command the thunders of heaven' (*F* 1831, pp. 46–47). The difficult work of mourning – the guilt-ridden withdrawal of attachment to the mother, a process allied to the transferral of Frankenstein's love to Elizabeth and his decision to leave home – is undone. Waldman's vision of the master who can refind the lost object and command limitless power has the character- istically unsettling impact of a pubescent irruption of libido [psychic/sexual energy emanating from the id], and the idea of the mother, set free by death for fantasy elaboration, becomes the focus of the regressive descent into phantasmagoria that constitutes Frankenstein's reanimation project. Within the secretive darkness of vaults and charnels, he dabbles in filth, his heart sickening at the work of his hands as he disturbs, 'with profane fingers, the tremen- dous secrets of the human frame' (F 1831, p. 53). The imagery has an unmistakably anal and masturbatory cast. At once feces and phallus, the filth is also the maternal presence he is assembling from phantas- mal body parts and buried wishes. In sum, Frankenstein's descent is a grotesque act of lovemaking, the son stealing into the womb that bore him in order to implant his seed. Having fully re-membered the form of his desire, the mother restored by a far more radical rescue than the one by which the father claimed her, he is ready to draw rebellious Promethean fire down from the heavens and realize his grandiose con- ception, the creation proper.

Or so Frankenstein dreams: the time never can be right for this obsessional neurotic:

> With an anxiety that almost amounted to agony, I collected the instruments of life around me, that I might infuse a spark of being into the lifeless thing that lay at my feet. . . . my candle was nearly burnt out, when . . . I saw the dull yellow eye of the creature open, and a convulsive motion agitated its limbs. How can I describe my emotions at this catastrophe . . . ? (F 1831, p. 56)

What is most strange here is that the Creature is a sleeping beauty until its orgasmic stirring rouses Frankenstein to recognize the mon- strosity before him. We confront the antithetical aspects not only of the fantasy mother but of the son's desire. The Creature is thus a befouled version of the son who would usurp the father's prerogatives, the would-be transcendent father of himself who now beholds the squalor of his actual origins and wishes. But such an interpretation is still oversimplified. The scene scatters the self into every possible familial position; the Creature, on the contrary, is a massively overdetermined representation of the entire scene as well as of the related Oedipus complex. We can infer that the Creature also embodies the fantasy father because it is as much a ubiquitous gaze under which Frankenstein cowers as a nightmare image that bewilders his sight.

The convulsive agitation of the aroused Creature suggests ejaculation; yet although this 'filthy mass' (F 1831, p. 142) represents a monstrously oversized phallus, its dread-provoking *corps morcelé* [fragmented body] bears the stigma of castration, calling to mind the Lacanian castrated phallus. This difficulty can be resolved if the Creature is viewed as Frankenstein's renounced phallic self, the self he yields to the father, perhaps detached in the very achievement of orgasm, at once the moment of the organ's autonomy and a repetition of the father's act of begetting. Whatever the interpretation, when Frankenstein mimics the Creature's convulsions after his flight and subsequent nightmare, the appropriate description, given his regressed condition, is anal evacuation, which Freud claims is the child's typical response to the primal scene. Here we may note that Mary Shelley writes in the Introduction of 'the working of some powerful engine' (F 1831, p. 9), but Frankenstein has a spark, not a bolt, and as he begins to infuse life, his candle has dwindled. Already defeated by his own scene of origins, Frankenstein is barred from the compensatory replay he intends. Instead the creation precipitously repeats the occasion of his mental trouble, the traumatic fixation he is fated to suffer again and again.

It is not until several chapters later and some two years after the creation that the novel, approaching another dangerous crossing, is disturbed into strength. By now the abandoned or liberated Creature has embarked on its career of murderous inroads into Frankenstein's family romance, and the creator, increasingly abandoned to morbid anxiety, gravitates to the Alps, whose 'savage and enduring scenes' (F 1831, p. 91) become the stage for an attempted reworking of his defining scene. Alternately plunging and mounting for three days, he is at last urged to penetrate the mists rising like incense from the ravine of Arve toward the surrounding heights, coming to a halt in a spectacular setting where 'a power mighty as Omnipotence' (F 1831, p. 91) manifests itself. As in the lightning scene of his youth, he stands apart, gazing ecstatically. From the recess of a rock, he looks across the troubled surface of *La Mer de Glace*, the glacier poured down from the summits in an eternally solemn procession, and in the distance the stupendous bright dome of Mont Blanc rises 'in awful majesty' (F 1831, p. 95) before him. Power, throughout this section of the novel, is envisioned as the power to wound: 'the . . . silence of this glorious presence-chamber of imperial Nature was broken . . . by . . . the cracking . . . of the accumulated ice, which, through the silent working of immutable laws, was ever and anon rent and torn, as if it had been but a plaything' (F 1831, p. 93). To be where Power is would mean to be above the turmoil of desire, the desire of and for the mother (*la mère*),[3] whom the father controls and possesses by right. Restaging his primal-scene fantasy under the gaze of the terrific god of the Alps,

Frankenstein has a dual aim. While he would seem to be propitiating the father, submitting to the law that freezes or castrates desire, he may also be seeking a way out of his oedipal impasse by identifying with a transcendent paternal principle that enables the son, in his turn, to put on the power of the father.

The scene dissipates when Frankenstein's call to the 'wandering spirits' (F 1831, p. 95) of his mountain god summons the Creature, his own errant spirit. Rising up to demand a mate from *his* father, the Creature forces Frankenstein into the unamiable role of a jealously restrictive frustrate father, a lame parody of his dread paternal imago [idealised image]. A possible explanation for this failed oedipal normalization is that the excessive harshness of the agency whose function is to suppress the complex actually reinforces Frankenstein's most primitive longings. But such an overweening superego [that part of the unconscious that acts as a conscience for the ego] is too deeply contaminated by unregenerate desire to be construed as autonomous. Rather, it is a phantasmic derivative of the complex, a shadowy type of that relentless internal danger which the Creature consummately represents. At least the Creature is almost a representation. Though actualized in the world of the fiction, out of narrative necessity, the Creature is so uncannily fearful that it cannot in fact be seen. Yet how is one to comprehend a representation that transcends representation, that is apparently the thing itself? Frankenstein's astonishing psychic achievement, in Freudian terms, is the construction of a primal repression, whose constitutive role in psychic development is to structure the unconscious as an articulate erotogenic zone. His sorrow is that this catastrophically global repression, or rerepression, is so radically alienated from the ego that it disqualifies any attempt at integration, insistently transmitting its full affective charge and thus preventing the institution of a firm psychic apparatus.

The developing plot of the novel elaborates the grim psychic consequences of Frankenstein's deepening subjugation to his dark double. The Creature is cast as the active partner in what amounts to a bizarre conspiracy, rehearsing in another register the scandalous history of the creator's desire, with Frankenstein bound to what Melanie Klein [1882–1960, Austrian psychoanalyst] calls the 'depressive position.' As a recognizable human world recedes and the Creature becomes a progressively more enthralling superpower, Frankenstein joins in the frenetic dance of death that impels these mutually fascinated antagonists across the waste places of the earth. By now wholly the Creature's creature, he must be considered a florid psychotic, pursuing the naked form of his desire in a fantastic nowhere that is his own. Of course, the consummating thrust of the sword eludes Frankenstein, who is drained by his interminable quest, but the Creature, that monstrous embodiment of his unremitting parental nightmare, can say 'I am satisfied' (F 1831, p. 196).

I am not, nor in fact is the Creature, though admittedly the coherence and audacity of this psychoanalytic reading give it considerable authority. While it is true that by the end of Frankenstein's narrative creator and Creature form a kind of symbiotic [interdependent] unit whose significance various orthodox analytic schools are well suited to explain, such pathological relatedness can be as cogently elucidated by [Georg] Hegel's [1770–1831, German philosopher] master-slave dialectic or by its derivatives in [Jacques] Lacan [1901–1981, French psychoanalyst] and [René] Girard. This fearful symmetry, moreover, stems largely from a perverse misreading that Frankenstein sets in motion and that the traditional psychoanalytic critic refines on.

Consider a privileged psychoanalytic moment in the text, Frankenstein's nightmare after the creation and his subsequent response:

> I thought I saw Elizabeth, in the bloom of health, walking in the streets. . . . Delighted and surprised, I embraced her; but as I imprinted the first kiss on her lips, they became livid with the hue of death; her features appeared to change, and I thought that I held the corpse of my dead mother in my arms; a shroud enveloped her form, and I saw the graveworms crawling in the folds of the flannel. I started from my sleep with horror . . . every limb became convulsed: when, by the dim and yellow light of the moon . . . I beheld . . . the miserable monster whom I had created. He held up the curtain of the bed; and his eyes, if eyes they may be called, were fixed on me. His jaws opened, and he muttered some inarticulate sounds, while a grin wrinkled his cheeks. He might have spoken, but I did not hear, one hand was stretched out, seemingly to detain me, but I escaped . . . I took refuge in the courtyard . . . fearing each sound as if it were to announce the approach of the demoniacal corpse . . . A mummy again endued with animation could not be so hideous . . . (F 1831, p. 57)

Restricting the interpretive game to a psychoanalytic strategy and overlooking those automatic signals (Elizabeth as streetwalker, the mummy-mommy pun) with which a prevalent mode of subcriticism clutters the mind, what can we deduce from the passage? Most simply, there is a treacherous wishing-dreading circuit that links Elizabeth and the Creature to the mother, the central term of the triad. As symbolic counter, Elizabeth is the mother's corpse, and in embracing this cousin-sister-bride Frankenstein reaches through her to take hold of the maternal body he intends to possess.[4] The hungry phallic worms

only faintly disguise his wish, and when it comes too close to fulfillment he wakens excitedly on the bed of his desire, where he is
confronted by the Creature as demoniacal corpse, its negativity a token
of the repression that distorts the wish even in the dream. Once this
basic fantasy material is unearthed, numerous variations on the dream
scenario are possible: Elizabeth is killed off because she tempts
Frankenstein to a sublimated version of his true desire; Frankenstein's
lust is overwhelmed by his fear of being sucked into the cloaca of the
vampirish mother; and the Creature is alternatively or simultaneously
the accusatory phallic father, the rephallicized mother, and (in view of
the multiplication of genital symbols in the dream) the castrated self.

At issue is where and how closely such a commentary touches the
passage. Clearly a psychoanalytic reading is attuned to Frankenstein's
anxious, conflict-ridden experience, but the bewilderment of his
desire and his relationships is at most tangentially allied to sexuality
and not at all to incest, which is a poor trope [figure of speech] for the
disturbing center of the dream. To reopen the text we must reverse the
process by which the analyst translates the teasingly idiomatic world
of the dream into a too familiar context of anticipated meanings. At the
outset we need to recall that Frankenstein has devoted two years to his
animation project; that, aside from a few detours into the abyss, he has
been soaring in a rarefied atmosphere where it is impossible to
breathe; and that now he is responding to the dissolution of his hopes
as well as to the embarrassing fact of the Creature, a singular enormity
for which there is no place in his experiential horizon. His response is
revealing: first literal flight, then flight into sleep, and finally flight
from both the dream and the Creature. The dream itself, the way it is
lived, beautifully testifies to the disorienting shock of Frankenstein's
reentry into reality. The dreamer does not know what is happening to
him. He exists discontinuously, overwhelmed by sudden, appalling
contrasts and baffled by the uncertain boundaries between the real
and the phantasmal. When the imagery of the dream's core, derived
from the creator's descent into the house of the dead, is brought
together with the family world he bracketed during the creation, the
most canny (*heimlich*) of worlds, the effect is peculiarly poignant.
Elizabeth is present because she is a fit emblem of the dream of loveliness that has slipped away from him, and the mother is there mainly
because she is the only dead person who matters to him. Waking,
within the dream, into emptiness and worse, Frankenstein beholds
the idealized form of his mother, preserved intact by his memory as by
the shroud in the dream, falling prey to anonymous malforming
powers. He has nothing to hold onto except the body of death, and as
he wakens he spills out of one nightmare into another, finding himself
face to face with the abomination he has created.

For Frankenstein there is an inescapable connection between the intruding 'graveworms' of the dream and the monster that invades his curtained bed. Only after the Creature's narrative cuts into his and compels us to reread the passage do we appreciate how mistaken Frankenstein is. He will not hear and cannot see. Reading a sinister intention into this newborn's clumsy gestures, he is terrified by a shadow of his own casting, a bad interpretation that climaxes all the traumatic events and that irrevocably determines the creation as The Bad Event. The process of misreading is most clearly exemplified when he next encounters the Creature, during a nocturnal storm in the Alps. The figure is suddenly illuminated by a bolt of lightning. A series of staccato flashes enables Frankenstein to make out the Creature's dizzying course as it leaps from crag to crag, and in the intervals of darkness, while his eye is recovering from each blinding glance, he reflects. None but this 'devil' could have strangled his little brother or framed the saintly Justine for the murder. 'No sooner did that idea cross my imagination, than I became convinced of its truth' (F 1831, p.73). Unlike those who convict Justine on the basis of mere appearance, Frankenstein has the facts right, but his imputation of diabolical designs to the Creature is a gross distortion, as is his sum- mary judgment, which marks him as the prototypical psychoanalytic reader of his own text: 'I conceived the being . . . in the light of my own vampire, my own spirit let loose from the grave, and forced to destroy all that was dear to me' (F 1831, p.74). The proper analytic rejoinder is that Frankenstein is an overreacting, moralizing mis- reader, rather like the self-blinded ego [the conscious mind] that travesties the id [the mass of primitive instincts and energies in the unconscious mind that underlies all psychic activity]. The analogy is admissible, however, only if it is restricted to an illustrative function. Reading it literally, the critic perpetuates Frankenstein's interpretive error, violating the Creature's spiritual integrity and evading the aesthetic problem this figure poses.

The overriding ironies are that it is the psychoanalytic reader, not the Creature, who reenacts the history of Frankenstein's desire in another register and that what enables the analyst to articulate this desire so persuasively is what discredits the interpretation. Both protagonist and critic are family-obsessed (or, rather, preoccupied with that aspect of the familial which is an adjunct to the personal), backward-looking, fatalistic, fixated on a terrible secret. They exist within the same dis- turbed conceptual horizon, conceiving experience and the experiential universe in solipsistic [self-centred] terms. Once again the alchemist is reborn in the scientist: the projector would look or crash through the phenomenal to an occult, transcendent reality. An apparent difference is that while Frankenstein, who is by turns indifferent to and sickened by appearances, views reality as the elixir that will grant him power over things, the analyst sees appearances, no matter how superficially hideous, as a deceptively appealing screen and reality as a squalor. Yet that squalor is the critic's secret of secrets, the means of pouring the light of meaning into the dark world of desire and so of overpowering the text . . . The image – world or text – shatters, and one is left holding onto a corpse. That form of alienation, for the orthodox psychoanalytic critic, is the literal, dead letter of the Freudian corpus, the petrified formulations of an introjected mystery religion that are interposed as a barrier between reader and text. But such 'repression' of the text results in a solution that merely replays an element in the text, its most conventional, superficial, or manifest dimension: that of Gothic melodrama. In this intense, simplistically dualistic world of obsessional neurosis, the analyst discovers truth.

One thinks of the novel's melodramatic climax, the Creature's ravishment of the bride on Frankenstein's wedding night: if any literary work can be opened up by a psychoanalytic approach, this incident suggests that *Frankenstein* must be the text. Reflecting 'how fearful the combat which I momentarily expected would be to my wife' (*F* 1831, p. 188), Frankenstein bids Elizabeth retire to the bridal chamber while he paces restlessly through the house in anticipation of the Creature's advent. Roused by a scream, he rushes in to find her limp body thrown across the bed, when, through the open casement, he beholds his monstrous rival: 'he seemed to jeer as with his fiendish finger he pointed towards the corpse . . . I rushed towards the window and, drawing a pistol from my bosom, fired; but he eluded me . . . and, running with the swiftness of lightning, plunged into the lake' (*F* 1831, p. 190). However polymorphously perverse an analytic rendering of the incident, I would not seriously dispute its applicability to Frankenstein, whose evocation the reading is based on, though it could be claimed that an exposition of his sexual trouble merely brings one to the horizon of a larger spiritual problem. But how apposite [apt] is such a commentary to Elizabeth? Where the analyst would place sexuality, for her there is a void. As for the Creature, he is not, at this point, sexless, his desire having become eroticized because his hideousness limits him to spying on the women of the De Lacey household and to gazing on the loveliness of Frankenstein's mother and Justine in the aesthetically distanced form of a portrait or a sleep-. ing body. Unless Elizabeth somehow means these images, it is hard to understand why she should matter to the Creature. Frankenstein does matter to him, however – certainly not because of some repressed homosexual attachment and not because Frankenstein is the Lacanian or Girardian 'other' who confers value on the object of (the other's) desire. What, then, does the Creature want from Frankenstein? He seeks reparation for his sorrows, and to this end he attempts to engage Frankenstein in dialogue, again not because Frankenstein is the Lacanian 'Other' whose recognition is all he really wants[5] [*Editor's note:* The Lacanian 'Other' allows for more than one single reading and must be clearly distinguished from the concept of 'other' (with a small 'o') which means the specular other, the mirror image of the self. The 'Other' is defined not in complementation but in opposition to the self and designates whatever occupies the position of the 'not-me', for example, the maternal body or the opposite sex.[6]] but because Frankenstein alone can provide a suitable mate with whom to share his enforced solitude. After Frankenstein breaks his word, mangling the half-finished monsteress in full view of the Creature, the Creature keeps his. The killing of Elizabeth is at once a way of establishing a relationship with the only human being to whom he can claim kinship and a desperately antierotic act designed to teach his creator what he suffers. The Creature's murderous career, an ingenious counterplot, compels Frankenstein to read what amounts to a Freudian text in reality.

The foregoing may seem not only naively overliteral but sentimental. Am I not . . . excusing the Creature because he is an 'exception,' and how can I justly argue that his truth is intersubjectivity when his only contacts are hypothetical? In dealing with the Creature one needs to exercise the hesitancy such questions induce; that is, the critic should, insofar as possible, respect the text. When J. M. Hill, a psychoanalytic adept, claims that the Creature 'cannot fathom the depths of passion which urge vengeance'[7] and when a generally skeptical George Levine remarks that the Creature 'doesn't fully understand the power of irrational energies which he himself enacts',[8] they are presumably thinking about the unconscious of the unconscious, whatever that means, but I am fairly sure these are not critical statements. Despite appearances, the Creature remains a scandal for analytic readers because he does not fit Freud's specifications: his unpresentable outside (only apparently idlike) balks (but not purposefully, as in Freudian repression) his unambiguously presentable inside. Of course, given the sophisticated rhetorical techniques of the psychoanalytic arsenal, there is nothing to prevent critics from remaking the Creature in whatever image they wish, from transforming any presence into an absence or any absence into a presence, as they see fit. Critics can thereby preserve the coherence of a reading, but in so doing they sacrifice too much. For the Creature's story is something finer than just another version of, or a sentimental recoil from, Frankenstein's, and the Creature himself is *Frankenstein*'s great, original turn on tradition, a disturbingly uncanny literal figuration that ought to rouse the critical faculties to act.

An editor of a recent collection of essays on *Frankenstein* observes,

'So pervasive has been the recognition that the Monster and Frankenstein are two aspects of the same being that the writers in this volume assume rather than argue it.'[9] Among the powerful forces responsible for collapsing the two into one is the inertial drift of both reading and textuality, fostered here by the mystifying allure of those grand figures of thought, doubling and monsterism. Within us there is also a need, perhaps a compulsion, to return things to an originative, determining source, especially when the human producer of an object or act is involved. This exigency is manifest in forms ranging from the ghoulish rage of [Percy] Shelley's Count Cenci [a character from the play *The Cenci* (1820)], who would reappropriate a 'particle of my divided being' by raping his daughter, to the comparatively mild critical reduction of the Creature to the dark complement of Frankenstein's light or of creator and created to epiphenomena [secondary or additional components] of some larger whole, be it Blake's inconceivable unfallen Albion, Mary Shelley's psyche, or the Freudian psychic apparatus.[10] At this stage of *Frankenstein* criticism, the motif of the double can be useful only if it sharpens awareness of the irreducibly complex otherness intrinsic to the self or of the Creature as an autonomous 'other self' duplicitously representing the traditional alter ego. Even supposing that the Creature owes his engenderment to Frankenstein's oedipal scene, he is no more reducible to it than any of us is to what our parents happened to be thinking when they conceived us. How different from Frankenstein's is the Creature's recurrent catastrophic scene of rejection and exclusion. The Creature's utmost desire is that another reciprocate his need for sympathetic relationship, and even after he becomes searingly conscious of his exclusion from the human community and begins to objectify the negativity he arouses in others, we recognize that his aggression is a by-product of disintegration, not an innate drive that has been cathartically unbound.[11] If, with a reader's ideal blindness, we can hear the bereavement of the Creature's whole self, we recognize too that he looks back at us with 'speculative eyes' (*F* 1831, p. 9). Freed, by the end, from his creator's self-consuming rage, he makes his destiny his choice, emblazoning himself as a giant form of Solitude, an existence made absolute by its confinement to the hell of being itself.

Still, the Creature's fate is to be misread, and any thematic capture necessarily restricts, however much it restitutes. In a moment of remarkable self-awareness he reflects that if he had been introduced to humanity not by the patriarchal De Laceys but 'by a young soldier, burning for glory and slaughter,' he would 'have been imbued with different sensations' (*F* 1831, p. 126). His history, then, is only a possible actualization of his essence, which is to say that the Creature's principal virtue is virtuality. A kind of wandering signifier, the

Creature proceeds through the text triggering various signifying effects. As the reader increasingly acknowledges the larger cultural and biographical context that constitutes the penumbra [obscure or blurred fringe] of the fiction, critical representations of what the Creature represents multiply endlessly. If, for the orthodox Freudian, he is a type of the unconscious, for the Jungian he is the shadow, for the Lacanian an *objet a* [any cause of desire sustaining the illusion of meaning], for one Romanticist a Blakean 'spectre,' for another a Blakean 'emanation'; he also has been or can be read as Rousseau's natural man, a Wordsworthian child of nature, the isolated Romantic rebel, the misunderstood revolutionary impulse, Mary Shelley's abandoned baby self, her abandoned babe, an aberrant signifier, *différance* [*Editor's note:* In the French philosopher Jacques Derrida's theory of deconstruction, *différance* designates 'a structure and a movement that cannot be conceived on the basis of the opposition presence/absence [or any other hierarchical opposition]. *Différance* is the systematic play of differences, of traces of differences, of the spacing by which elements relate to one another. This spacing is the production . . . of intervals without which the "full" terms could not signify.'[12]], or as a hypostasis [the person of Christ as one part of the Holy Trinity] of godless presumption, the monstrosity of a godless nature, analytical reasoning, or alienating labor. Like the Creature's own mythic version of himself, a freakish hybrid of Milton's Adam and Satan, all these allegorizations are exploded by the text. The alert reader, at a given moment of interpretive breakdown, will resort to another signifying chain, and thence to another, and will be left wondering whether to receive this overload of signification as a mutually enriching profusion of possibilities or as an unmeaning chaos.

While the most sensible response may be a benign ecumenical [universally unifying] acceptance of difference, certain problems remain: for instance, how can the same text sustain divergent critical representations and what authorizes or disqualifies any representation at a particular moment? Moreover, such negative capability [a phrase coined by the Romantic poet John Keats (1795–1821) describing a willingness to accept mystery, ambiguity and doubt, and an ability to live in existential uncertainty] is likely to mask mere incapacity or a failure of will and is rarely conducive to interesting readings. Exemplary of a potentially stronger critical position are the psychoanalytic readers who would compound with the world of the text's imaginings by penetrating to its center of mystery. Entering the circle of the text and operating Freud's ingenious meaning-making machine, they will discover that an oedipal focus limits only the range of interpretive options, and if they are open to the possibility that the oedipal material they uncover may defend against other types of psychic conflict, their critical anxieties will mount. To salvage their integrity they must found a reading by arbitrarily limiting it, restricting at the same time their own cognitive, erotic, and imaginative capabilities. To construct a plausible narrative they will resort to such tactics of secondary revision as lacunae [gaps or spaces, especially in a book or manuscript], decontextualization, distortion, and rationalized contradiction, and to persuade us that their story is not simply another revocable text they will enlist the aid of some extratextual model to underwrite both the fiction and the critical discourse. Ultimately, however, the authorizing model relies on an interpretation of how things are (or, for the growing number of the novel's psychobiographers, how things were), and whether or not the representation is privileged depends on the particular analyst's rhetorical skill and our willingness to be lied to.

A possible way out of or around this hermeneutic [interpretive] circle is to stop viewing the Creature as a thing apart. We might consider 'meaning' as a constantly shifting relational event, asking what the Creature means, at a certain point in the novel, to himself, Frankenstein, Elizabeth, or such and such a reader. The danger here is hazy relativism, an openness akin to the indifferent free trafficking that deconstructionists tend to elevate to a principle of principles. Even misreading has its map. Why one interpretive pathway should be preferred to another may be impossible to determine, but we must not forget that all must pass through the Creature, that something is there to solicit us. That something demands careful scrutiny because of its unsettling effect on our habitual ideas about what signs may be up to. Luckily barred from the overwhelming presence of the Creature, in the face of which interpretation becomes mute, we must dream our dreams of the Creature not only as a signifier in search of its proper signification but as a literal being that means only itself. The literal Creature, in other words, is as much a figuration as the figurative Creature, and in reflecting on what the letter of the text allows us to surmise about the Creature, whose 'reality' we know is but a textual effect, we are always in an indeterminate borderline situation. Frankenstein never speaks more truly than when he calls the Creature his 'daemon.' A marginal or boundary being, the daemon is a powerful representation of our uncertain lot, suspended as we are between knowledge and power, nature and supernature, objectivity and subjectivity.[13] Conceiving the Creature as a genius of liminality [a state of transition or blurred identification], a type of art's duplicitous interplay of revelation and concealment, restores his virtuality, which is betrayed as soon as he comes to signify something determinate. An emphasis on meaning as process also encourages the interpreter to participate in the work of the work, a dreamwork more efficacious than that of the mind abandoned to sleep. The literalizing power of Frankenstein is, of course, only a dream that haunts literature. But 'labour is blossoming' [a phrase taken from 'Among School Children' by the Irish poet William Butler Yeats (1865–1939)] within this marginal ontological zone, where letter and spirit forge a meaning that can never be anything more than a dreaming to signify, to become significant, to touch reality. We are touched by the passion of the signifier, a perpetually renewed *dreaming to* that no dream of satisfaction can satisfy.

Who, in our century, understood or exemplified the insistence of the dream of signification better than Freud? Psychoanalysis, for him, was always a stopgap until the real thing (biochemistry) would come along, but his inventive genius transformed the analytic field into an ample domain of spirit, an autonomous power that his system goes on calling by false names. Decentered or detraumatized, the Freudian corpus becomes an indispensable guide to the intentional play of forces that keeps meaning wandering restlessly through the mind. From Freud we can gather many enabling fictions, forms of the spirit's cunning and resourcefulness, and he can instruct us in the virtues of hovering attention, the need to look at something again and again until it begins to declare itself, and of alertness to the heterogeneous [intrinsically diverse].[14] □

Doubtlessly more sceptical than Sherwin of the methods and objectives of psychoanalysis, Fred Botting reads *Frankenstein* as an allegory of the manifold conflictual tensions that haunt the relationship between texts and their critics. Botting argues that the dialectic of mastery and slavery that underlies Shelley's novel is 'a dialectic which is repeated in the relationship between literature and psychoanalysis',[15] a relationship that turns both the text and the (female) author into patients who are obliged to surrender their secret existence to the critic-analyst's inquisitive gaze. The mystery of literature is made to unravel and explain itself in accordance with the critic's interpretive apparatus of preconceived diagnostic schemes and devices. The literary work is dissected into symptoms that are 'known' to characterise a certain pathological complex, condition, or instance of traumatic repression. Almost inevitably lost in this monstrous process of critical translation are the text's individual singularity, its ambivalence and idiosyncratic unruliness, or what Botting designates as the text's inherent 'differences'. In 'Allure, Authority and Psychoanalysis: the "Case" of *Frankenstein*', a chapter from *Making Monstrous: Frankenstein, Criticism, Theory* (1991), Botting begins his investigation of textual authority by identifying the main problems inherent in literature's fraught relationship with criticism and psychoanalytic criticism in particular. Botting writes:

■ There are moments in the psychoanalytic criticism of *Frankenstein* when a certain unease appears, hesitant reflections which cast suspicion upon the limits and dangers of the Freudian framework and urge a cautionary approach to any application of its terms. Nonetheless, the allure of the text remains powerful. As a text that surrounds its benevolent fathers, heavenly mothers and 'more than sisters' with monstrous figures of death and desire and depicts, too, a dream in which Frankenstein embraces his adopted sister as she transmutes into the corpse of his mother (recalling also the Introduction's statement of the novel's oneiric origins [the novel's origins in a 'waking dream']), as well as having a double as its central relationship, *Frankenstein* appears a most appropriate subject for analysis to revel in and reveal the effects of profound unconscious wishes and traumas, conflicts of ego and id and, of course, oedipal anxieties and fantasies. Despite initial hesitancy on the part of the critic, the demand for analysis, the seductive promise of the presentation of meaning, is too strong an attraction to resist: 'however reluctant one might be to apply psychoanalytic dream theory to literature, Frankenstein's necrophobial fantasy with its Oedipal implications might tempt even the most circumspect of readers into such a line of criticism'.[16] The conjunction of *Frankenstein* and psychoanalysis seems too potent a mixture for critics to escape its intoxicating effects, though the preliminary reluctance suggests that submitting to temptation entails an offence against critical sobriety.

> How conscious she was of the meaning of her dream transcript and its elaboration in the novel is beside the point. Frankenstein's dream world is her world; his terrifying journey of self-discovery also leads deep into the mind of Mary Shelley . . . It would be presumptuous to go too far in psychoanalyzing the author through her novel. But the temptation is strong.[17]

That the temptation to employ psychoanalysis ought to be resisted is indicated not only by the reluctance on the part of the literary critic but by the concern that giving in to such temptations is 'presumptuous' and excessive. Involving a dangerous presumption that incites the reader to 'go too far', the temptation of psychoanalysis for the literary critic implies a conflict over whether or not certain prohibitions should be ignored, whether decorous limits should be transgressed or specific rules broken. It constitutes a dilemma which, though overcome, displays the anxieties of the one enticed to transgress. This dilemma, moreover, raises the question of the legitimacy of applying psychoanalysis to literature since the codes that govern the latter are broken in the process.

While psychoanalysis promises the discovery of the Meaning of the text 'deep in the mind of Mary Shelley', thereby fulfilling the desire for critical authority, it does so only by displacing the author. No longer a creator in control of the text's meaning, the author, a figure crucial to ideas of literature, is supplanted by the forces of 'her own' unconscious. Indeed, the emergence of the unconscious as the site and producer of meaning renders the author obsolete and, undermining a fundamental literary principle, relegates traditional approaches that identify a creative consciousness and artistic intention to the status of a misguided pursuit: the conscious intentions of the writer are now 'beside the point'.

There remains an unease in the face of temptation even as criticism excludes the author and retrieves its authority over meaning by a move elsewhere, a move within the discourse of psychoanalysis. The reluctance, produced in the conflict between assumptions about literature and those of psychoanalysis, destabilises the position of criticism, unsure whether to describe itself as 'literary' or 'psychoanalytic'. And as it submits to the allure of psychoanalysis, criticism experiences, perhaps, a moment of guilt and doubt: guilt because the abandonment of the author constitutes a betrayal of previous literary values, and doubt since, in the insecurities exposed by the transition, there lingers, shadowed by literary figures, a suspicion about the truth of psychoanalytic authority.[18] □

After briefly sketching out the advantages and drawbacks of a number of different psychobiographical readings of *Frankenstein*, Botting proceeds to reflect on literature's inexhaustibly multi-faceted relationship with the psychoanalytic critic, a relationship that seems just as prone to result in exploitative misreadings as it is likely to propagate the formation of mutually beneficial, quasi-symbiotic allegiances. Invariably, however, what remains problematic is the issue of textual authority and independence. Should literature be made to comply with the critic's desire and yield its 'truth', or should it be allowed to sustain its puzzling ambivalence as an awesome, ultimately unfathomable 'monstrosity'? What these tensions between literature and psychoanalysis help to uncover are the essentially Frankensteinian attributes of the critic. Whereas some accuse critics of recklessly experimenting on the vulnerable body of literature and thereby delivering a disastrous brood of interpretive monsters, others applaud their 'heroic' endeavour to enhance, resuscitate, perhaps even to immortalise, the cultural significance and value of important literary works. In a second extract from *Making Monstrous* Botting continues to read *Frankenstein* in the light of this fundamental ambivalence of all psychoanalytic attempts at a meaningful interpretation of literary 'truth':

■ [T]here is the temptation to take the discourse of psychoanalysis seriously and reduce all texts to allegories dramatising Freud's truth, a truth of and in the unconscious.[19] The effect this has on the author is frequently resisted. Instead of becoming merely a passive transcriber of unconscious dictates, literature's central figure begins a reassertion of authorial identity within positions which assert the primacy of the unconscious: 'to an astonishing extent, Mary Shelley half knows what her fiction is about.'[20] Indeed, as the conscious mind of the artist is reaffirmed, the unconscious becomes the text's meaning, a meaning that resolves the conflict between unconscious wishes and the values of community: 'Mary answers by dramatising obsessive regression in Frankenstein's life. She reveals the cost of failure to curb the wishes of the unconscious. Implicitly, we must live a comparative moderation of our desires if we want sanity.'[21] The unconscious is effaced as the discovery of meaning in the unconscious makes it conscious. The meaning, also, like the means by which meaning is produced, is the same: the author returns to announce the need to consciously control the disturbing effects of the unconscious.

Reaffirming author, meaning and critical authority, the return or persistence of literature or literary values occupies and assimilates the terms of Freud and also serves to reconstruct the literary creator as a psychoanalyst *avant la lettre*: 'Freud has given us a model and a vocabulary by which to understand how things come to be, but he was the first to confess how well artists have always known intuitively the substance of his discoveries.'[22] Furthermore, the acknowledgement of Freud's opinion that 'writers have always known about the unconscious' attempts to balance the relationship between literature and psychoanalysis so that literature becomes the unconscious of psychoanalysis.[23]

Thus both literature and psychoanalysis retain their authority, an authority established by their shared revelation of human nature and elevating them to the status of truth. That authors can prefigure and intuitively know the substance of Freud's discoveries effaces temporal change and, transcending historical differences, defines such truths as universal: 'the creature is artificial, non-human; and within the "inhuman" breast there could be dramatized the sexual and violent passions which Freud would find widespread in the fantasies of most civilized men'.[24] The shared knowledge of the enduring human condition and its humanisation of history seemingly confirms the critic-analyst's authoritative position. Yet what is human cannot be defined in itself, but only by what it is not, by its difference from others: as the figure of the monster is introduced to affirm the primacy of humanity, it succeeds only in reiterating differences in their monstrous form. The revelation of truth turns out to be a repetition of differences that returns to separate human from inhuman and disarms the desired authority by foregrounding, yet again, the differences between literature, criticism and psychoanalysis.

As the tension between the terms is repeated, the temptations of psychoanalysis are rendered suspect and disrupt the relation between literature and criticism. The threat thus posed by psychoanalysis – that it may tempt one to go too far and upset the differences on which critical authority is based – seems to require some means of making it safe, of instituting some mechanism of defence against its disturbing effects. Defusing the serious implications of psychoanalysis demands that it be rendered trivial. In a section entitled 'Amateur Psychoanalysis' Robert Wexelblatt tries to negotiate between the dangers and pleasures of psychoanalytical reading: 'well, let us suppose that young Mary Wollstonecraft Shelley had not written a novel but instead sought an appointment with a psychoanalyst to deal with an elaborate recurrent nightmare'.[25] In a similar manner, Martin Tropp begins his analysis of Frankenstein's dream: 'in order to interpret this nightmare, we must play psychiatrist and investigate Frankenstein's childhood'.[26] Psychoanalysis is reduced to a game of make-believe, a playing of roles that restricts the play of differences and permits the critical explorer to wander, safely inoculated, in potentially contaminating zones.

But it remains a serious game and a dangerous play in which the status of the analytic relationship becomes rather unclear: though Mary Shelley occupies the role of patient, does the novel function as a symptom of her neurosis, as an unconscious wish produces a dream, or is it a form of therapy, a result of therapeutic practices, equivalent to the analytic treatment that 'deals with' the dream?[27] That analysis may be a substitute for writing a novel implies yet another problematic displacement. Irreconcilably split between the symptom of an illness and the cathartic treatment, the text thus destabilises the position of the critic-analyst.

What are the implications of the alignment of analyst and text which emerges almost despite the games of truth that are played by the critic? In what way does text as treatment attempt a therapeutic resolution of psychic conflicts, and what further displacements are suffered by the critic as (make-believe) analyst? As the setting where the analyst encounters the author-as-patient the text seems to occupy the transferential space of the scene of treatment, and yet the possibility couched in the quotation from Wexelblatt is that analysis may be a substitute for writing a novel: instead of writing the author attends analysis to 'deal with an elaborate recurrent nightmare'. Curiously, analysis and the authorial process are equated, so that analysis replaces writing. But this act of replacement constitutes yet more writing, as is shown by the critical insertion of 'recurrent' to describe the nightmare. Rewriting the novel's Introduction, which retrospectively accounts for *Frankenstein*'s origin in a moment of imaginative possession, 'gifting the successive images that arose in my mind with a vividness far beyond the usual bounds of reverie' (*F* 1831, p. 9), the addition of 'recurrent' constitutes a telling 'slip': the critic-analyst, whose rewriting also causes the nightmare to recur, assumes the mantle of author by his inscriptive or creative addition.

Analytic criticism thus becomes more than simply reading or seeing the truth in a text, for it involves the use of a technique, a way of seeing that enables the possessor to reveal the truth that is concealed in the depths of the unconscious: 'Indeed, the terrible figures of dream are subject to aesthetic controls, elaboration, palliating disguise and finally purgation. In the process, *if we know how to look*, much of what those figures signify is revealed. Their story is spoken, as with dream, in the oddities of expression cast in relief against conscious awareness.'[28] Psychoanalysis which also knows *where* to look is marked out as a mode of interpretation that prescribes what need be known in order that looking can be successful. The gaze of the critic is not only preceded and made possible by the structuring knowledge of psychoanalysis, but must restructure or reorganise the text as a reflection of the truth it already knows, so that the truth can merely be recognised. Looking involves the recognition of a true and prescribed reflection, the reflection of the truth of psychoanalysis. Thus the conjunction of text and analyst 'deals with' the problem of authority through a mutual reflection of shared truth. As id replaces ego and unconscious is made conscious the text is constructed as a site both of and for the inscription of truth, a place of writing on which critical reading (in the form of writing) takes place. Displacements and resistances are overcome at the instant of transference that conjoins analyst, patient, writer and reader in an overjoyed identification of and with the text as their own.

The imagined completeness installed by an identification of and with the text as truth, however, is sustained only by a blind forgetfulness which excludes the differences of the text, a repression perhaps symptomatic of authorial anxiety. Indeed, critical desires for authority seem to be anticipated in the figure of Frankenstein, practically an analyst himself, whose project displays the figures that provide a frame for the mirror in which criticism will see itself.

Frankenstein's research aims towards the discovery of final truths by which to confirm his authority. Dissatisfied with superficialities and not content to appreciate the appearances of things, in contrast to Elizabeth, Victor 'delighted in investigating their causes', seeking profound insights of universal scope: the 'hidden laws of nature' (*F* 1831, p. 36). Frankenstein's attempts to unfold these secrets are phrased in quasi-sexual terms: like a lover courting his beloved he 'pursued nature to her hiding places' (*F* 1831, p.53). But, 'insensible to the charms of nature' (*F* 1831, p.53), he desires only one thing, 'embued with a fervent longing to penetrate the secrets of nature' (*F* 1831, p.39). It seems, indeed, that female nature is to be ravished by the masculine desires for sexual conquest.

Unveiling the truth of the novel's nature involves penetrating the unconscious depths of the female author's mind to steal the secret of the text's life. It constitutes another, critical, violation of textual difference and authorial distance, an attempt to possess a knowledge presumed to lie within the scope of criticism's penetratingly recuperative gaze. This repetition of Frankensteinian desires, however, implicates the critic in the anxieties associated with repetition. Victor Frankenstein fails to realise his project of mastery and complete unification and instead becomes embroiled in conflicts. Struggling with nature and then the product of natural/unnatural creation, the scientist is entangled in a battle in which the prize of unity can never be won, though it remains tantalisingly on offer. Participating in the undisclosed sexuality of psychoanalysis by assuming masculine priority and privilege, and by aspiring to the control and possession of meaning, criticism constructs and subordinates the text as woman, as other. In the process, the locus of authority slides. Withdrawn from the mind of the female author, authority is invested in the name of the father, Freud, guarantor of meaning, of truth.

At this point, the allure of authority becomes a lure, for, in dispossessing the author and subordinating her and 'her' text to analysis's own authoritative meaning, criticism severs itself from the literary values it privileges and attempts to preserve, blurring the boundaries on which its identity depends. Is it literary criticism or psychoanalysis? Criticism is thus lured into conflicts that question its values, function and identity and prevent the fulfilment of its authorial aspirations. Torn between celebrating or suppressing literature's differences, the conflict leaves criticism unsure of itself, uncertain whether to proclaim the genius of the author or to steal her fire and supplant it with the flame of critical authority.[29] □

With respect to *Frankenstein*, the question of authorial control is of course crucial. Is the text a product of creative labour and deliberate craftsmanship, or does it merely record – without much purpose, aim or principle – the instance of a spontaneous unconscious stirring, whose meaningful comprehension relies entirely on the analytic skills of the critic? As Devon Hodges shows in '*Frankenstein* and the Feminine Subversion of the Novel', first published in 1983 in an issue of *Tulsa Studies in Women's Literature*, this question becomes particularly urgent in the context of a feminist reading of Shelley's novel. Hodges reads *Frankenstein* as a female-authored work of strategic subversion, a textual embodiment of feminine defiance wholly impervious to conventional strategies of inter-pretation. As such, it poses a deliberate challenge to psychoanalytic criticism which has traditionally aligned itself with, and thus strength-ened and reinscribed, the fixed symbolic structures of patriarchy and, most notably perhaps, its hierarchical oppositioning between masculinity as the superior self and femininity as its inferior other.[30] Due to their sys-tematic oppression under patriarchy, so Hodges speculates, women find themselves in the position of culture's repressed and are therefore likely to identify with the marginality of dreams or, within the realm of litera-ture, the generic turbulence and intransigence of the fantastic. Thus, in its original capacity as a nightmare, *Frankenstein* represents a radically deconstructive project, intent on promoting the emancipation of feminine difference and toppling the traditional hierarchies that are so solidly embedded in (literary) language. As Hodges explains, the unusual narra-tive form and disturbing imagery of *Frankenstein* must be seen as illustrations of the woman writer's dream to explode the patriarchal order from within by experimenting with hitherto unemployed, new techniques and devices of female self-representation:

■ What dislocates the narrative might simply be the irrational logic of the dream, of the unconscious. Yet dream logic may be in the service of a woman writer's critique of prevailing structures. . . . Dreams allow something to speak that is not normally present in the patriarchal course of things. Through the agency of dream, this order confronts something it cannot fully account for, something it has excluded or repressed. Such a bringing to the surface of troubling otherness, some-times explicitly connected to the unconscious, has been described as an effect of women's writing. . . . It is disturbing because it exposes the inadequacy of the symbolic order, the limits of its knowledge.[31] □

The woman writer is no longer prepared to consign her voice to silence and oblivion but begins 'to deform, to transgress literary structure from within – demonstrating the inadequacy of the paternal narrative by opening it up to what it excludes'.[32] Hence, simply to dismiss Frankenstein's monster as some kind of oneiric accident would be totally to ignore its role as a powerfully disruptive vehicle in Shelley's attempt to release a woman's perspective from patriarchal literature's crippling cata-logue of strictly gender-specific conventions. As Hodges indicates, the most significant drawback of traditional psychoanalytic criticism is its tendency to read as pathological symptoms of repression what are in fact counterdiscursive strategies of female resistance. Instead of betraying the woman writer's alleged authorial incompetence, Shelley's monster epitomises the failure of male-authored science to realise its warped aesthetic ideals of size, power and integrity. 'Mak[ing] Frankenstein undergo his own experience of incoherence and exile', so Hodges argues, the Monster operates as a deliberately devised 'figure of feminine text-uality'[33] that destroys its oppressor's single-minded masculinist world in an act of perfectly justifiable retaliation.

As its political commitment and strongly rehabilitative impetus indi-cate, Hodges's reading of *Frankenstein* is clearly inspired by the tenets and practices of feminist literary criticism whose enormous impact on the late twentieth-century reappraisal of Shelley's novel is recorded in greater detail in the next chapter.

CHAPTER FOUR

Whose Body Does the Text Display?: Representations of Gender in *Frankenstein*

U P UNTIL the late 1970s when *Frankenstein* first began its belated career as an extremely popular course text in further and higher education, Mary Shelley's importance for literary history had widely been considered a passive and indirect one, 'aris[ing] not from her own writings but from the fact that she was the second wife of poet Percy Bysshe Shelley and the daughter of political philosopher William Godwin and pioneering feminist Mary Wollstonecraft'.[1] This biased and deeply condescending view of the author of *Frankenstein* began to change dramatically with the publication of *Literary Women*, Ellen Moers's highly acclaimed study of women's writing, in 1977. In 'Female Gothic', which became the study's most famous chapter and was reprinted in Levine and Knoepflmacher's *The Endurance of Frankenstein* only two years after its original publication, Moers reads Shelley's novel as a woman's intimately personal, autobiographical fiction. 'No other Gothic work by a woman, perhaps no literary work of any kind by a woman, better repays examination in the light of the sex of its author', Moers asserts. 'For *Frankenstein* is a birth myth, and one that was lodged in the novelist's imagination . . . by the fact that she was herself a mother.'[2] Between the ages of 16 and 21 Shelley had been almost constantly pregnant, suffering several miscarriages and giving birth to four children, three of whom died in infancy or early childhood. This traumatic experience, so Moers argues, combined with the fact that Mary's relationship with Percy was illegitimate until she married him after his first wife's suicide in December 1816, must have had a major impact on the novel Shelley was writing at the time. Moers's strictly woman-centred perspective quickly won the status of an influential classic, inducing many future critics 'to see Victor Frankenstein's disgust at the sight of his creation as a study of postpartum depression, as a representation of maternal rejection of a new-born infant, and to relate the entire novel to Mary Shelley's mixed feelings about motherhood'.[3] Years passed before it was found necessary to revisit Moers's interpretation. Mary Jacobus was among the first to realise that, no matter how productive it had been in the 1970s, Moers's unequivocal biologising of women's writing ultimately helped only to perpetuate patriarchy's hierarchical oppositioning of the sexes. The popular understanding of Frankenstein as a 'birth-myth', so Jacobus explains, 'may tell us about women's lives, but it reduces the text itself to a monstrous symptom'.[4]

The second most important early feminist reading of *Frankenstein* is 'Horror's Twin: Mary Shelley's Monstrous Eve', a chapter in Sandra Gilbert and Susan Gubar's best-selling study, *The Madwoman in the Attic: The Woman Writer and the Nineteenth-Century Literary Imagination*, published in 1979. Gilbert and Gubar read *Frankenstein* as a 'daughterly' – that is, at once obedient and mutinous – rewrite of John Milton's *Paradise Lost*. Resolutely ignoring the explicit maleness of *Frankenstein*'s chief protagonists, Gilbert and Gubar decode Victor and his monster's quandary as an allegorical configuration of female anxiety, discontent, and defiant resistance to a hoary male-authored tradition of patriarchal oppression. Gilbert and Gubar are convinced that 'femaleness . . . is at the heart of this apparently masculine book'. They acknowledge the novel's many biblical parallels, yet in doing so protest that, 'though Victor Frankenstein enacts the roles of Adam and Satan like a child trying on costumes, his single most self-defining act transforms him definitively into Eve'.[5] It is not only Victor's predicament that reminds Gilbert and Gubar of our biblical foremother's fall and punishment; they also suggest that 'Victor Frankenstein's monster may really be a female in disguise'.[6] The Monster's ordeal as an ostracised autodidact with little hope of public recognition resembles the fate of nineteenth-century women intellectuals who found themselves categorically excluded from political debates and condemned as 'unnatural' should they – like Mary Shelley's mother – be bold enough to take the initiative and openly speak their mind. Accordingly, while to Robert Walton Victor and his monster may look 'like God and Adam, Satanically conceived', in Gilbert and Gubar's feminist view Shelley's male protagonists have been 'Eve and Eve all along'.[7]

A third classic feminist commentary on *Frankenstein*, that takes the readings of Moers and Gilbert and Gubar an important step further, is Barbara Johnson's review article 'My Monster/My Self', first published in *Diacritics* in 1982 and later reprinted in Harold Bloom's *Mary Shelley's Frankenstein*. Providing a general overview of the then newly burgeoning field of nineteenth-century women's studies, Johnson's essay is an attempt to account for the many evident textual inconsistencies that call Shelley's feminist commitment seriously into question. How, for example, can

Frankenstein sincerely intend to teach us anything about the issue of femininity, or the difficult problem of female authorship, when it not only categorically silences women's voices but actually clears the text of all main women characters by killing them off one by one? Helpfully, Johnson suggests that instead of necessarily signalling a complicitous, androcentric bias on Shelley's part, *Frankenstein*'s focusing on the lives of men rather than women may represent a poignant critique of the mutually injurious oppositioning of the sexes under patriarchy. Johnson speculates that Shelley may quite possibly have been rebelling against the all-male peer pressure exerted on her by her husband and Lord Byron's creative authority. As a result, she may have 'fictively transposed her own frustrated female pen envy into a tale of catastrophic male womb envy' – a tale which suggests 'that a woman's desire to write and a man's desire to give birth would both be capable only of producing monsters'.[8]

According to Johnson, the full significance of *Frankenstein* can only be grasped against the background of the dilemma of the nineteenth-century woman writer. As representatives of an allegedly weaker, inferior sex, women were not only denied, but believed incapable of, expressions of any intellectual or emotional complexity. Commonly considered to be of a simple, kind, and congenitally unassuming disposition, women were not thought complicated enough to understand, let alone experience, the challenges and mental torments endemic to the allegedly more sophisticated and susceptible male. Hence, what Shelley confronted in her composition of *Frankenstein*, so Johnson explains, was patriarchal literature's inability to accommodate, or ignorant refusal to allow for, adequate representations of female experience unless, that is, they manifested themselves vicariously or were couched in an oblique allegorical imagery denoting absence, mutilation and death:

■ It is . . . perhaps the very hiddenness of the question of femininity in *Frankenstein* that somehow proclaims the painful message not of female monstrousness but of female contradictions. For it is the fact of self-contradiction that is so vigorously repressed in women. While the story of a man who is haunted by his own contradictions is representable as an allegory of monstrous doubles, how indeed would it have been possible for Mary to represent feminine contradictions *from the point of view of its repression* otherwise than precisely in the *gap* between angels of domesticity and an uncompleted monsteress, between the murdered Elizabeth and the dismembered Eve?[9] □

Rather than providing any longer extracts from these three seminal, if now slightly outdated works, the present chapter focuses on a number of more recent readings which give a good indication of the wide variety of different approaches to the representation of gender in *Frankenstein* that have developed over the last two decades. Reprinted here with no major cuts, the first example is Anne Mellor's 'Possessing Nature: The Female in *Frankenstein*', first published in 1988 as part of *Romanticism and Feminism*, a collection of critical essays edited by Mellor herself. Mellor presents us with a popular, but in many respects rather old-fashioned feminist reading that views Shelley's novel as a variation on the ancient theme of 'the battle of the sexes'. Motivated by womb envy and driven by a typically masculine desire for heroic self-aggrandisement, Victor Frankenstein is a male scientist who experiments on and thus violates the sacred body of Mother Nature. Threatened with emasculation by the female's pro-creative resourcefulness, the male makes it his chief objective to usurp nature's position of absolute power in order to assert and indelibly inscribe his own status of an allegedly God-given cultural superiority. Traditionally feminine values, such as familial affection and domestic peacefulness, are superseded by the seemingly self-perpetuating dynam-ics of an inveterate male egotism fuelled and compounded by misogynous paranoia. Ominously redolent of Walton's confession to his sister that 'there is something at work in my soul, which I do not under-stand' (*F* 1831, p. 19), the male pursuit of adventure, power and progress seems at once warped and irresistibly compelling. Quite evidently, Mellor's reading is part of a critical trend that relies on the current popu-larity of *Frankenstein* as a metaphor for the general late twentieth-century distrust of science and male-authored science in particular. For example, in *Fathering the Unthinkable*, his book on masculinity, scientists and the nuclear arms race, Brian Easlea effectively employs Shelley's tale as some kind of leitmotif or conceptual structuring principle that accentuates his profeminist and anti-militaristic line of argumentation. 'Masculine science . . ., as Mary Shelley conceived it', so Easlea writes, 'is an obsessive quest not only for power over nature, described in metaphors of sexual pene-tration and phallic creativity, but also for public acclaim and glory'.[10]

What ultimately disqualifies Mellor's reading is its tendency to deteriorate into a neat moral fable in which masculine science features as the villain while feminine nature is both the damsel in distress and her (own) saviour. Displaying little regard for *Frankenstein*'s enduring ambivalence, Mellor reads the novel as if it were working towards a definitive final showdown in which 'Divine Nature' descends on Victor and retaliates by destroying him. Mellor's feminist perspective seems almost reactionary in that it opts not for genuine change but for a simple reversion of the existing power relations between the male and female, replacing patriarchal structures of hegemony and subordination with equally one-dimensional and oppressive matriarchal ones. Clearly, Mellor's reading of Frankenstein's tragedy would have greatly benefited from heeding certain less sexist, more subtle and egalitarian developments in modern feminism like those one finds pithily expressed in the work of Angela Carter who writes, for example, that ultimately 'mother goddesses are just as silly a notion as father gods'.[11] While good at pointing out the oppositional contrasts between masculinity and femininity that inform the novel, Mellor remains largely insensitive to Shelley's latently subversive introduction of a complicated blurring and merging of traditional gender formations. Most problematic in this context is surely Mellor's penchant for a moral assessment of gender roles, equating maleness with immoral, antisocial dissipation and femaleness with goodness, innocence and fortitude. Also, although Mellor clearly understands femininity not as a biological given but as an oppressive construction of patriarchal discourse, she fails to recognise that men, too, may experience their gender assignment not as a privilege but, on the contrary, as a coercive and debilitating behavioural straitjacket of deleterious imperative ideals. Mellor writes:

■ When Victor Frankenstein identifies Nature as female – 'I pursued nature to *her* hiding places' (*F* 1818, p. 36) – he participates in a gendered construction of the universe whose ramifications are everywhere apparent in *Frankenstein*. His scientific penetration and technological exploitation of female nature . . . is only one dimension of a more general cultural encoding of the female as passive and possessable, the willing receptacle of male desire. The destruction of the female implicit in Frankenstein's usurpation of the natural mode of human reproduction symbolically erupts in his nightmare following the animation of his creature, in which his bride-to-be is transformed in his arms into the corpse of his dead mother – 'a shroud enveloped her form, and I saw the graveworms crawling in the folds of the flannel' (*F* 1818, p. 39). By stealing the female's control over reproduction, Frankenstein has eliminated the female's primary biological function and source of cultural power. Indeed, for the simple purpose of human survival, Frankenstein has eliminated the necessity to have females at all. One of the deepest horrors of this novel is Frankenstein's implicit goal of creating a society for men only: his creature male; he refuses to create a female; there is no reason that the race of mortal beings he hoped to propagate should not be exclusively male.[12]

On the cultural level, Frankenstein's scientific project – to become the sole creator of a human being – supports a patriarchal denial of the value of women and of female sexuality. Mary Shelley, doubtless inspired by her mother's *A Vindication of the Rights of Woman*, specifically portrays the consequences of a social construction of gender that values the male above the female. Victor Frankenstein's nineteenth-century Genevan society is founded on a rigid division of sex roles: the male inhabits the public sphere, the female is relegated to the private or domestic sphere.[13] The men in Frankenstein's world all work outside the home, as public servants (Alphonse Frankenstein), as scientists (Victor), as merchants (Clerval and his father), or as explorers (Walton). The women are confined to the home; Elizabeth, for instance, is not permitted to travel with Victor and 'regretted that she had not the same opportunities of enlarging her experience and cultivating her under-standing' (*F* 1818, p. 127). Inside the home, women are either kept as a kind of pet (Victor 'loved to tend' on Elizabeth 'as I should on a favorite animal' [*F* 1818, p. 21]); or they work as housewives, childcare providers, and nurses (Caroline Beaufort Frankenstein, Elizabeth Lavenza, Margaret Saville) or as servants (Justine Moritz).

As a consequence of this sexual division of labor, masculine work is kept outside of the domestic realm; hence intellectual activity is segregated from emotional activity. Victor Frankenstein cannot do scientific research and think lovingly of Elizabeth and his family at the same time. His obsession with his experiment has caused him 'to forget those friends who were so many miles absent, and whom I had not seen for so long a time' (*F* 1818, p. 37). This separation of mascu-line work from the domestic affections leads directly to Frankenstein's downfall. Because Frankenstein cannot work and love at the same time, he fails to feel empathy for the creature he is constructing and callously makes him eight feet tall simply because 'the minuteness of the parts formed a great hindrance to my speed' (*F* 1818, p. 35). He then fails to love or feel any parental responsibility for the freak he has created. And he remains so fixated on himself that he cannot imagine his monster might threaten someone else when he swears to be with Victor 'on his wedding-night.'

This separation of the sphere of public (masculine) power from the sphere of private (feminine) affection also causes the destruction of many of the women in the novel. Caroline Beaufort dies unnecessarily because she feels obligated to nurse her favorite Elizabeth during a smallpox epidemic; she thus incarnates a patriarchal ideal of female self-sacrifice (this suggestion is strengthened in the 1831 revisions where she eagerly risks her life to save Elizabeth). She is a woman who is devoted to her father in wealth and in poverty, who nurses him until his death, and then marries her father's best friend to whom she is equally devoted.

The division of public man from private woman also means that women cannot function effectively in the public realm. Despite her innocence of the crime for which she is accused, Justine Moritz is executed for the murder of William Frankenstein (and is even half-persuaded by her male confessor that she is responsible for William's death). And Elizabeth, fully convinced of Justine's innocence, is unable to save her: the impassioned defense she gives of Justine arouses public approbation of Elizabeth's generosity but does nothing to help Justine, 'on whom the public inclination was turned with renewed violence, charging her with the blackest ingratitude' (*F* 1818, p. 64). Nor can Elizabeth save herself on her wedding night. Both these deaths are of course directly attributable to Victor Frankenstein's self-devoted concern for his own suffering (the creature will attack only him) and his own reputation (people would think him mad if he told them his own monster had killed his brother).

Mary Shelley underlines the mutual deprivation inherent in a family and social structure based on rigid and hierarchical gender divisions by portraying an alternative social organization in the novel: the De Lacey family. The political situation of the De Lacey family, exiled from their native France by the manipulations of an ungrateful Turkish merchant and a draconian legal system, points up the injustice that prevails in a nation where masculine values of competition and chauvinism reign. Mary Shelley's political critique of a society founded on the unequal distribution of power and possessions is conveyed not only through the manifest injustice of Justine's execution and of France's treatment first of the alien Turkish merchant and then of the De Lacey family, but also through the readings in political history that she assigns to the creature. From Plutarch's *Parallel Lives of the Greek and Romans* and from Volney's *Ruins, or Meditations on the Revolutions of Empires*, the creature learns both of masculine virtue and of masculine cruelty and injustice. 'I heard of the division of property, of immense wealth and squalid poverty; . . . I learned that the possessions most esteemed . . . were high and unsullied descent united with riches' (*F* 1818, p. 96). 'Was man, indeed, at once so powerful, so virtuous, and magnificent, yet so vicious and base?' the creature asks incredulously. Implicit in Mary Shelley's attack on the social injustice of established political systems is the suggestion that the separation from the public realm of feminine affections and compassion has caused much of this social evil. Had Elizabeth Lavenza's plea for mercy for Justine, based on her intuitively correct knowledge of Justine's character, been heeded, Justine would not have been wrongly murdered by the courts. As Elizabeth exclaims,

> how I hate [the] shews and mockeries [of this world]! when one creature is murdered, another is immediately deprived of life in a slow torturing manner; then the executioners, their hands yet reeking with the blood of innocence, believe that they have done a great deed. They call this *retribution*. Hateful name! when the word is pronounced, I know greater and more horrid punishments are going to be inflicted than the gloomiest tyrant has ever invented to satiate his utmost revenge. (*F* 1818, p. 67)

In contrast to this pattern of political inequality and injustice, the De Lacey family represents an alternative ideology: a vision of a social group based on justice, equality, and mutual affection. Felix willingly sacrificed his own welfare to ensure that justice was done to the Turkish merchant. More important, the structure of the De Lacey family constitutes Mary Shelley's ideal, an ideal derived from her mother's *A Vindication of the Rights of Woman*. In the impoverished De Lacey household, all work is shared equally in an atmosphere of rational companionship, mutual concern, and love. [*Editor's note:* Mellor ignores that this apparent idyll is facilitated by the blindness of the De Lacey patriarch. She also fails to acknowledge that in the 1831 edition of *Frankenstein*, Shelley distances herself from her earlier, idealised representation to return to traditional gender stereotyping: 'The young man [Felix] was constantly employed out of doors, and the girl [Agatha] in various laborious occupations within' (*F* 1831, p.107).] As their symbolic names suggest, Felix embodies happiness, Agatha goodness. They are then joined by Safie (*sophia* or wisdom). Safie, the daughter of the Turkish merchant, is appalled both by her father's betrayal of Felix and by the Islamic oppression of women he endorses; she has therefore fled from Turkey to Switzerland, seeking Felix. Having reached the De Lacey household, she promptly becomes Felix's beloved companion and is taught to read and write French. Safie, whose Christian mother instructed her 'to aspire to higher powers of intellect, and an independence of spirit, forbidden to the female followers of Mahomet' (*F* 1818, p.99), is the incarnation of Mary Wollstonecraft in the novel. Wollstonecraft too traveled alone through Europe and Scandinavia; more important, she advocated in *A Vindication* that women be educated to be the 'companions' of men and be permitted to participate in the public realm by voting, working outside the home, and holding political office. [*Editor's note:* Shelley's representation of Safie is by no means as definitive and wholly unequivocal as Mellor makes out but bears some rather sinister implications. Safie's impression that the West is markedly less misogynous than the East is a delusion revealing the insidious eurocentrism of western patriarchy. Although in early nineteenth-century Europe women were not treated as slaves, their inferior status as second-class citizens was never seriously called into question.]

But this alternative female role-model of an independent, well-educated, self-supporting, and loving companion, and this alternative nuclear family structure based on sexual equality and mutual affection, is lost in the novel, perhaps because the De Lacey family lacks the mother who might have been able to welcome the pleading, pitiable creature. When Safie flees with the De Lacey family, we as readers are deprived of the novel's only alternative to a rigidly patriarchal construction of gender and sex roles, just as Mary Shelley herself was deprived of a feminist role-model when her mother died and was subsequently denounced in the popular British press as a harlot, atheist, and anarchist. Safie's disappearance from the novel reflects Mary Shelley's own predicament. Like Frankenstein's creature, she has no positive prototype she can imitate, no place in history. That unique phenomenon envisioned by Mary Wollstonecraft, the wife as the lifelong intellectual equal and companion of her husband, does not exist in the world of nineteenth-century Europe experienced by Mary Shelley.

The doctrine of the separate spheres that Victor Frankenstein endorses encodes a particular attitude to female sexuality that Mary Shelley subtly exposes in her novel. This attitude is manifested most vividly in Victor's response to the creature's request for a female companion, an Eve to comfort and embrace him. After hearing his creature's autobiographical account of his sufferings and aspirations, Frankenstein is moved by an awakened conscience to do justice toward his Adam and promises to create a female creature, on condition that both leave forever the neighborhood of mankind. After numerous delays, Frankenstein finally gathers the necessary instruments and materials together into an isolated cottage on one of the Orkney Islands off Scotland and proceeds to create a female being. Once again he becomes ill: 'my heart often sickened at the work of my hands . . . my spirits became unequal; I grew restless and nervous' (*F* 1818, p. 137).

Disgusted by his enterprise, Frankenstein finally determines to stop his work, rationalizing his decision to deprive his creature of a female companion in terms that repay careful examination. Here is Frankenstein's meditation:

> I was now about to form another being, of whose dispositions I was alike ignorant; she might become ten thousand times more malignant than her mate, and delight, for its own sake, in murder and wretchedness. He had sworn to quit the neighborhood of man, and hide himself in deserts; but she had not; and she, who in all probability was to become a thinking and reasoning animal, might refuse to comply with a compact made before her creation. They might even hate each other; the creature who already lived loathed his own deformity, and might he not conceive a greater abhorrence for it when it came before his eyes in the female form? She also might turn with disgust from him to the superior beauty of man; she might quit him, and he be again alone, exasperated by the fresh provocation of being deserted by one of his own species.
>
> Even if they were to leave Europe, and inhabit the deserts of the

new world, yet one of the first results of those sympathies for which the daemon thirsted would be children, and a race of devils would be propagated upon the earth, who might make the very existence of the species of man a condition precarious and full of terror. Had I a right, for my own benefit, to inflict this curse upon everlasting generations? . . . I shuddered to think that future ages might curse me as their pest, whose selfishness had not hesitated to buy its own peace at the price perhaps of the existence of the whole human race. (*F* 1818, p. 138)

What does Victor Frankenstein truly fear, which causes him to end his creation of a female? First, he is afraid of an independent female will, afraid that his female creature will have desires and opinions that cannot be controlled by his male creature. Like Rousseau's natural man, she might refuse to comply with a social contract made before her birth by another person; she might assert her own integrity and the revolutionary right to determine her own existence. Moreover, those uninhibited female desires might be sadistic: Frankenstein imagines a female 'ten thousand times' more evil than her mate, who would 'delight' in murder for its own sake. Third, he fears that his female creature will be more ugly than his male creature, so much so that even the male will turn from her in disgust. Fourth, he fears that she will prefer to mate with ordinary males; implicit here is Frankenstein's horror that, given the gigantic strength of this female, she would have the power to seize and even rape the male she might choose. And finally, he is afraid of her reproductive powers, her capacity to generate an entire race of similar creatures. What Victor Frankenstein truly fears is female sexuality as such. A woman who is sexually liberated, free to choose her own life, her own sexual partner (by force, if necessary), and to propagate at will can appear only monstrously ugly to Victor Frankenstein, for she defies that sexist aesthetic that insists that women be small, delicate, modest, passive, and sexually pleasing – but available only to their lawful husbands.

Horrified by this image of uninhibited female sexuality, Victor Frankenstein violently reasserts a male control over the female body, penetrating and mutilating the female creature at his feet in an image that suggests a violent rape: 'trembling with passion, [I] tore to pieces the thing on which I was engaged' (*F* 1818, p. 139). The morning after, when he returns to the scene, 'The remains of the half-finished creature, whom I had destroyed, lay scattered on the floor, and I almost felt as if I had mangled the living flesh of a human being' (*F* 1818, p. 142). However he has rationalized his decision to murder the female creature, Frankenstein's 'passion' is here revealed as a fusion of fear, lust, and hostility, a desire to control and even destroy female sexuality.

Frankenstein's fear of female sexuality is endemic to a patriarchal construction of gender. Uninhibited female sexual experience threatens the very foundation of patriarchal power: the establishment of patri-lineal kinship networks together with the transmission of both status and property by inheritance entailed upon a male line. Significantly, in the patriarchal world of Geneva in the novel, female sexuality is strikingly repressed. All the women are presented as sexless: Caroline Beaufort is a devoted daughter and chaste wife while Elizabeth Lavenza's relationship with Victor is that of a sister.

In this context, the murder of Elizabeth Lavenza on her wedding night becomes doubly significant. The scene of her death is based on a painting Mary Shelley knew well, Henry Fuseli's famous 'The Nightmare.' The corpse of Elizabeth lies in the very attitude in which Fuseli placed his succubus-ridden woman: 'She was there, lifeless and inanimate, thrown across the bed, her head hanging down, and her pale and distorted features half covered by her hair' (F 1818, p. 165). Fuseli's woman is an image of female erotic desire, both lusting for and frightened of the incubus (or male demon) that rides upon her, brought to her bed-chamber by the stallion that leers at her from the foot of her bed; both the presence of this incubus and the woman's posture of open sexual acceptance leave Fuseli's intentions in no doubt.[14] Evoking this image, Mary Shelley alerted us to what Victor fears most: his bride's sexuality.[15] Significantly, Elizabeth would not have been killed had Victor not sent her into their wedding bedroom *alone*. Returning to the body of the murdered Elizabeth, Victor 'embraced her with ardour; but the deathly languor and coldness of the limbs told me, that what I now held in my arms had ceased to be the Elizabeth whom I had loved and cherished' (F 1818, p. 166). Victor most ardently desires his bride when he knows she is dead; the con-flation with his earlier dream, when he thought to embrace the living Elizabeth but instead held in his arms the corpse of his mother, signals Victor's most profound erotic desire, a necrophiliac and incestuous desire to possess the dead female, the lost mother.

To put this point another way, we might observe that Victor Frankenstein's most passionate relationships are with men rather than with women. He sees Clerval as 'the image of my former self' (F 1818, p. 131), as his 'friend and dearest companion' (F 1818, p. 155), as his true soul mate. His description of Clerval's haunting eyes – 'languish-ing in death, the dark orbs covered by the lids, and the long black lashes that fringed them' (F 1818, p. 154) – verges on the erotic. Similarly, Walton responds to Frankenstein with an ardor that borders on the homoerotic. Having desired 'the company of a man who could sympathize with me; whose eyes would reply to mine' (F 1818, p. 8), Walton eagerly embraces Frankenstein as 'a celestial spirit' (F 1818,

p. 16) whose death leaves him inarticulate with grief: 'what can I say,' Walton writes to his sister, 'that will enable you to understand the depth of my sorrow?' (*F* 1818, p. 186). Finally, Frankenstein dedicates himself to his scientific experiment with a passion that can be described only as erotic: as Mary Shelley originally described Frankenstein's obsession, 'I wished, as it were, to procrastinate my feelings of affection, until the great object of my affection was compleated.' Frankenstein's homoerotic fixation upon his creature, whose features he had selected as 'beautiful' (*F* 1818, p. 39) . . . , was underlined by Mary Shelley in a revision she made in the Thomas copy of *Frankenstein*. Describing his anxious enslavement to his task, Frankenstein confesses: 'my voice became broken, my trembling hands almost refused to accomplish their task; I became as timid as a lovesick girl, and alternate tremor and passionate ardour took the place of wholesome sensation and regulated ambition.' [*Editor's note:* The Thomas copy of the 1823 edition, from which the above quotation is taken, is named after an acquaintance of Mary Shelley's during her time in Albaro, Italy. Shelley gave Mrs Thomas an autographed copy of her novel containing handwritten suggestions for a revised edition, some of which eventually found their way into the edition of 1831. Wisely, Mrs Thomas noted on the title page of her copy that 'I preserve this Booke and (Mary Shelley's) Autograph Notes to me – as at some future day they will be literary Curiosities'.[16]] In place of a normal heterosexual attachment to Elizabeth, Victor Frankenstein has substituted a homosexual obsession with his creature,[17] an obsession that in his case is energized by a profound desire to reunite with his dead mother, by becoming himself a mother. [*Editor's note:* On closer inspection, Mellor's argument proves highly problematic. By identifying the misogynous overreacher as a latent homosexual, Mellor implicitly sanctions the behaviour of 'normal', heterosexual men – despite the fact that it is primarily the latter who perpetrate, or are complicit with, the systemic oppression and violation of the female. According to Mellor, Frankenstein wreaks havoc on his family and society at large not because he is 'typically' male but because he may turn out to be 'queer'. If only he had been 'normal'!]

To sum up, at every level Victor Frankenstein is engaged upon a rape of nature, a violent penetration and usurpation of the female's 'hiding places,' of the womb. Terrified of female sexuality and the power of human reproduction it enables, both he and the patriarchal society he represents use the technologies of science and the laws of the polis [state] to manipulate, control, and repress women. Thinking back on Elizabeth Lavenza strangled on her bridal bier and on Fuseli's image of female erotic desire that she replicates, we can now see that at this level Victor's creature, his monster, realizes his own most potent lust. The monster, like Fuseli's incubus, leers over Elizabeth, enacting Victor's own repressed desire to rape, possess, and destroy the female. Victor's creature here becomes just that, his 'creature,' the instrument of his most potent desire: to destroy female reproductive power so that only men may rule.

However, in Mary Shelley's feminist novel, Victor Frankenstein's desire is portrayed not only as horrible and finally unattainable but also as self-destructive. For Nature is not the passive, inert, or 'dead' matter that Frankenstein imagines.[18] Frankenstein assumes that he can violate Nature and pursue her to her hiding places with impunity. But Nature both resists and revenges herself upon his attempts. During his research, Nature denies to Victor Frankenstein both mental and physical health: 'my enthusiasm was checked by my anxiety, and I appeared rather like one doomed by slavery to toil in the mines, or any other unwholesome trade, than an artist occupied by his favourite employment. Every night I was oppressed by a slow fever, and I became nervous to a most painful degree' (F 1818, p. 38). When his experiment is completed, Victor has a fit that renders him 'lifeless' for 'a long, long time' and that marks the onset of a 'nervous fever' that confines him for many months (F 1818, p. 43). Victor continues to be tormented by anxiety attacks, bouts of delirium, periods of distraction and madness. As soon as he determines to blaspheme against Nature a second time, by creating a female human being, Nature punishes him: 'the eternal twinkling of the stars weighed upon me, and . . . I listened to every blast of wind, as if it were a dull ugly siroc [hot southerly wind] on its way to consume me' (F 1818, p. 123). His mental illness returns: 'Every thought that was devoted to it was an extreme anguish, and every word that I spoke in allusion to it caused my lips to quiver and my heart to palpitate' (F 1818, p. 132); 'my spirits became unequal; I grew restless and nervous' (F 1818, p. 137). Finally, Frankenstein's obsession with destroying his creature exposes him to such mental and physical fatigue that he dies at the age of twenty-five.

Appropriately, Nature prevents Frankenstein from constructing a normal human being: an unnatural method of reproduction produces an unnatural being, in this case a freak of gigantic stature, watery eyes, a shriveled complexion, and straight black lips. This physiognomy causes Frankenstein's instinctive withdrawal from his child, and sets in motion the series of events that produces the monster who destroys Frankenstein's family, friends, and self.

Moreover, Nature pursues Victor Frankenstein with the very electricity he has stolen: lightning, thunder, and rain rage around him. The November night on which he steals the 'spark of being' from Nature is dreary, dismal, and wet: 'the rain . . . poured from a black and comfortless sky' (F 1818, p. 40). He next glimpses his creature during a flash of lightning as a violent storm plays over his head at Plainpalais; significantly, the almighty Alps, and in particular Mont Blanc, are represented in this novel as female, as an image of omnipotent fertility[19] – on his wedding day, Victor admires 'the beautiful Mont Blanc, and the assemblage of snowy mountains that in vain endeavour to emulate *her*' (*F* 1818, p.163; my italics). Before Frankenstein's first encounter with his creature among the Alps, 'the rain poured down in torrents, and thick mists hid the summits of the mountains' (*F* 1818, p.74). Setting sail from the Orkney island where he has destroyed his female creature, planning to throw her mangled remains into the sea, Frankenstein wakes to find his skiff [light rowing boat] threatened by a fierce wind and high waves that portend his own death: 'I might be driven into the wide Atlantic, and feel all the tortures of starvation, or be swallowed up in the immeasurable waters that roared and buffetted around me. I . . . felt the torment of a burning thirst; . . . I looked upon the sea, it was to be my grave' (*F* 1818, p.144). Frankenstein ends his life and his pursuit of the monster he has made in the arctic regions, surrounded by the aurora borealis, the electromagnetic field of the North Pole. The atmospheric effects of the novel, which most readers have dismissed as little more than the traditional trappings of Gothic fiction, in fact manifest the power of Nature to punish those who transgress her boundaries. The elemental forces that Victor has released pursue him to his hiding places, raging round him like avenging Furies.

Finally, Nature punishes Victor Frankenstein the life-stealer most justly by denying him the capacity for natural procreation. His bride is killed on their wedding night, cutting off his chance to engender his own children. His creature – that 'great object, which swallowed up every habit of my nature' (*F* 1818, p.37) – turns against him, destroying not only his brother William, his soul mate Clerval, his loyal servant Justine, his grief-stricken father, and his wife, but finally pursuing Victor himself to his death, leaving Frankenstein entirely without progeny. Nature's revenge is absolute: he who violates her sacred hiding places is destroyed.

Mary Shelley's novel thus portrays the penalties of raping Nature. But it also celebrates an all-creating Nature loved and revered by human beings. Those characters capable of deeply feeling the beauties of Nature are rewarded with physical and mental health. Even Frankenstein in his moments of tranquillity or youthful innocence can respond powerfully to the glory of Nature. As Walton notes, 'the starry sky, the sea, and every sight afforded by these wonderful regions, seems still to have the power of elevating his soul from earth' (*F* 1818, p.16). In Clerval's company Victor becomes again the same happy creature who, a few years ago, loving and beloved by all, had no sorrow or care. When happy, inanimate nature had the power of bestowing on me the most delightful sensations. A serene sky and verdant fields filled me with ecstacy. (*F* 1818, p.51)

Clerval's relationship to Nature represents one moral touchstone of the novel: since he 'loved with ardour . . . the scenery of external nature' (*F* 1818, p.130), Nature endows him with a generous sympathy, a vivid imagination, a sensitive intelligence and an unbounded capacity for devoted friendship. His death annihilates the possibility that Victor Frankenstein might regain a positive relationship with Nature.

Mary Shelley envisions Nature as a sacred life-force in which human beings ought to participate in conscious harmony. Elizabeth Lavenza gives voice to this ideal in her choice of profession for Ernest Frankenstein:

I proposed that he should be a farmer . . . A farmer's is a very healthy happy life; and the least hurtful, or rather the most beneficial profession of any. My uncle [wanted him] educated as an advocate . . . but . . . it is certainly more creditable to cultivate the earth for the sustenance of man, than to be the confidant, and sometimes the accomplice, of his vices. (*F* 1818, p.45)

Nature nurtures those who cultivate her; perhaps this is why, of all the members of Frankenstein's family, only Ernest survives. [*Editor's note:* Mellor fails to acknowledge Shelley's substantial revision of this passage in the 1831 edition where, rather than learning to nurture and take care of nature, Ernest is allowed to enter into – potentially (self-)destructive – patriarchal service and fulfil his manly dream of becoming a soldier, 'a true Swiss' (*F* 1831, p.62).] Mary Shelley shares Wordsworth's concept of a beneficial bond between the natural and the human world, which is broken only at man's peril. Had Victor Frankenstein's eyes not become 'insensible to the charms of nature' (*F* 1818, p.37) and the affections of family and friends, he would not have defied Mary Shelley's moral credo:

A human being in perfection ought always to preserve a calm and peaceful mind, and never to allow passion or a transitory desire to disturb his tranquillity. I do not think that the pursuit of knowledge is an exception to this rule. If the study to which you apply yourself has a tendency to weaken your affections, and to destroy your taste for those simple pleasures in which no alloy can possibly mix, then that study is certainly unlawful, that is to say, not befitting the human mind. (*F* 1818, p.37)

As an ecological system of interdependent organisms, Nature requires the submission of the individual ego to the welfare of the family and the larger community. Like George Eliot [1819–1880, pseudonym of Mary Ann Evans, English novelist] after her, Mary Shelley is profoundly committed to an ethic of cooperation, mutual dependence, and self-sacrifice. The Russian sea-master willingly sacrifices his own desires that his beloved and her lover may marry; Clerval immediately gives up his desire to attend university in order to nurse his dear friend Victor back to health; Elizabeth offers to release her beloved Victor from his engagement should he now love another. Mary Shelley's moral vision thus falls into that category of ethical thinking which Carol Gilligan has recently identified as more typically female than male. Where men have tended to identify moral laws as abstract principles that clearly differentiate right from wrong, women have tended to see moral choice as imbedded in an ongoing shared life. As Gilligan contrasts them, a male 'ethic of justice proceeds from the premise of equality – that everyone should be treated the same' while a female 'ethic of care rests on the premise of nonviolence – that no one should be hurt.'[20] This traditional female morality can probably be traced to what Nancy Chodorow and Dorothy Dinnerstein have shown to be the daughter's greater identification with the mother.[21] Whereas the son has learned to assert his separateness from the mother (and the process of mothering), the daughter has learned to represent that gendered role and thus has felt more tightly (and ambivalently) bound to the mother. Less certain of her ego boundaries, the daughter has been more likely to engage in moral thinking which gives priority to the good of the family and the community rather than to the rights of the individual.

Insofar as the family is the basic social unit, it has historically represented the system of morality practiced by the culture at large. The hierarchical structure of the Frankenstein family embodies a masculine ethic of justice in which the rights of the individual are privileged: Frankenstein pursues his own interests in alchemy and chemistry, cheerfully ignoring his family obligations as he engages 'heart and soul' in his research, and is moreover encouraged to leave his family and fiancée for two years . . . In contrast, the egalitarian and interdependent structure of the De Lacey family ideologically encodes a female ethic of care in which the bonding of the family unit is primary. Felix blames himself most because his self-sacrificing action on behalf of the Turkish merchant involved his family in his suffering. Agatha and Felix perform toward their father 'every little office of affection and duty with gentleness; and he rewarded them by his benevolent smiles'; they willingly starve themselves that their father may eat (F 1818, p. 87). [Editor's note: All these instances could of course equally well be interpreted as evidence of the children's total internalisation of ultimately self-annihilative patriarchal structures.] Safie's arrival particularly delighted Felix but also 'diffused gladness through the cottage, dispelling their sorrow as the sun dissipates the morning mists' (F 1818, p. 93). In portraying the De Laceys as an archetype of the egalitarian, benevolent, and mutually loving nuclear family, Mary Shelley clearly displayed her own moral purpose, which Percy Shelley rightly if somewhat vaguely described in his Preface as 'the exhibition of the amiableness of domestic affection, and the excellence of universal virtue' (F 1818, pp. 3–4).

Mary Shelley's grounding of moral virtue in the preservation of familiar bonds (against which Frankenstein, in his failure to parent his own child, entirely transgresses) entails an aesthetic credo as well. While such romantic descendants as Walter Pater [1839–1894, English essayist and critic] and Oscar Wilde [1854–1900, Irish writer and wit] would later argue that aesthetics and morality, art and life, are distinct, Mary Shelley endorsed a traditional mimetic aesthetic that exhorted literature to imitate ideal Nature and defined the role of the writer as a moral educator. Her novel purposefully identifies moral virtue, based on self-sacrifice, moderation, and domestic affection, with aesthetic beauty. Even in poverty, the image of the blind old man listening to the sweetly singing Agatha is 'a lovely sight, even to me, poor wretch! who had never beheld aught beautiful before' (F 1818, p. 85). In contrast, Frankenstein's and Walton's dream of breaking boundaries is explicitly identified as both evil and ugly. As Walton acknowledges, 'my day dreams are . . . extended and magnificent; but they want (as the painters call it) *keeping*' (F 1818, p. 9). 'Keeping,' in painting, means 'the maintenance of the proper relation between the representations of nearer and more distant objects in a picture'; hence, in a more general sense, 'the proper subserviency of tone and colour in every part of a picture, so that the general effect is harmonious to the eye' (*OED*). Walton thus introduces Mary Shelley's ethical norm as an aesthetic norm; both in life and in art, her ideal is a balance or golden mean between conflicting demands, specifically here between large and small objects. In ethical terms, this means that Walton must balance his dreams of geographical discovery and fame against the reality of an already existing set of obligations (to his family, his crew, and the sacredness of Nature). Similarly, Frankenstein should have better balanced the obligations of great and small, of parent and child, of creator and creature. Frankenstein's failure to maintain *keeping*, to preserve 'a calm and peaceful mind' (F 1818, p. 50), is thus in Mary Shelley's eyes both a moral and an aesthetic failure, resulting directly in the creation of a hideous monster.[22] □

While Mellor's reading no doubt opens up an important new set of perspectives on the representation of gender in *Frankenstein*, it remains
oblivious of the complex ambiguities that inform Shelley's text. Mellor's
reading thus appears to lack the subtlety, sophistication and analytical
detail that characterise Burton Hatlen's discussion in 'Milton, Mary
Shelley, and Patriarchy', first published in the *Bucknell Review* in 1983.
Hatlen's piece, of which three extracts are reprinted here, takes us back
to the issue of intertextuality and, in particular, Gilbert and Gubar's reading of *Frankenstein* as 'a female fantasy of sex and reading . . . a gothic
psychodrama reflecting Mary Shelley's own sense of what we might call
bibliogenesis, that *Frankenstein* is a version of the misogynistic story
implicit in *Paradise Lost*'.[23] While traditional criticism has paid little attention to the subversive potential of either *Paradise Lost* or *Frankenstein*,
feminist critics have often categorically prioritised Shelley's achievement
over that of her famous male predecessor. By thus mistaking *Paradise Lost*
for a mere paraphrase – orthodox and dogmatic – of the biblical book of
Genesis, Gilbert and Gubar fail to acknowledge the strongly revolutionary disposition of Milton's work. At the same time, Shelley's rewrite of
Milton's epic is grossly misrepresented as an index of her 'apparently
docile submission to male myths . . . [which] may conceal fantasies of
equality that occasionally erupt in monstrous images of rage'.[24] As
Hatlen aims to show, *Frankenstein* has to be regarded as a self-conscious,
skilfully designed effort to dismantle 'the patriarchal mythos of creation',
an endeavour brought to fruition rather than hampered by Shelley's
detailed knowledge of *Paradise Lost*:

■ Both John Milton and Mary Shelley were revolutionary writers:
Milton in his advocacy of individual liberty in an epoch of aristocratic
and theocratic tyranny, and Mary Shelley in her exploration of the
corrosive effects that inequalities of power and status exercise on personal relations. But bourgeois literary criticism has attempted in
various ways to obscure the revolutionary implications of the works of
both these writers. . . . To recover the revolutionary content of the
works of Milton and Mary Shelley, it is useful, I believe, to read
Frankenstein and *Paradise Lost* in conjunction. For *Frankenstein* is at least
in part a commentary on and amplification of *Paradise Lost*, designed to
uncover certain egalitarian and libertarian motifs that are at work in
Milton's poem, but which are there partly suppressed by an overlay of
religious orthodoxy. That there is a direct connection between
Frankenstein and *Paradise Lost* has not gone unnoticed by the critics, but
the principal discussions of the relationship between these texts have
been distorted by the . . . conservative bias of most recent criticism. For
example, Leslie Tannenbaum, seeing *Paradise Lost* as purely and simply
a defense of divine authority, argues that Mary Shelley's allusions to

Milton primarily serve to establish a contrast between the legitimate power and authority of God and Victor Frankenstein's illegitimate claims to a similar power and authority.[25] No less than the conservative Tannenbaum, the cultural feminists Sandra Gilbert and Susan Gubar also obscure the revolutionary content of both the texts here under discussion. Gilbert and Gubar see Milton as the archetypal misogynist. *Paradise Lost*, they argue, sets out to show that women are responsible for all the ills of humankind. And the 'divagations' of Mary Shelley's parody, they contend, 'merely return to and reinforce the fearful reality of the original. For by parodying *Paradise Lost* in what may have begun as a secret, barely conscious attempt to subvert Milton, Shelley ended up telling, too, the central story of *Paradise Lost*, the tale of "what misery the inabstinence of Eve/Shall bring on men!"'[26] Unlike both Tannenbaum on the one side and Gilbert and Gubar on the other, I believe (and, perhaps more to the point, the Romantics also believed) that *Paradise Lost* conceals some unexpectedly revolutionary implications. And I further believe that the purpose of Mary Shelley's parody of *Paradise Lost* is, not to reveal the inadequacy of would-be human imitators of God, nor to reassert Milton's presumed view of woman as the source of all evil, nor even to 'subvert Milton' – but rather to explode what I shall here call the patriarchal mythos of creation. According to the patriarchal mythos, the act of creation is the exclusive prerogative of the male of the species, and it entails rights of ownership both over the 'means' of creation (that is, the female) and over the end result of this act. This patriarchal mythos is central to *Paradise Lost*; therefore Mary Shelley develops her critique of patriarchy primarily through a series of allusions to Milton's poem. But like most of the Romantics Mary Shelley seems to assume that Milton was secretly on the side of the rebel against patriarchy. Therefore her goal is less to 'destroy Milton' than to liberate the 'true' Milton from this false mythos. Her secondary aim, I propose, is to point toward an alternative mythos of cooperation and equality, in the belief that only such a mythos can resolve the sterile struggle between creator and creature. It is the struggle between these two mythoi, the mythos of patriarchy and the mythos of equality, as that struggle unfolds within the dialogue between Mary Shelley and John Milton, that I shall attempt to trace out . . . ,[27] with the ultimate goal of recovering the revolutionary energies that Mary Shelley in her time discovered in *Paradise Lost*, and the revolutionary hopes to which she herself gave expression in *Frankenstein*.[28] □

Hatlen argues that Shelley's novel is strongly influenced by the radical egalitarianism of the French Revolution reflected in her parents' work as well as that of her fellow Romantics. Notably, the Romantics sympathise and indeed identify with Milton's Satan whose insurrection they see as indicative of the general significance of *Paradise Lost* as a powerful poetic counterdiscourse against theocratic oppression. However, whereas the male Romantics are inclined to focus on a reading of Adam's plight, or Satan's struggle against God, as an allegory of the historical class dialectic of master and slave, Shelley's rewrite considerably compounds these tensions between self and other by encapsulating all of patriarchy's schismatic hierarchies within the ambiguous imagery of a single psychic dualism – that of Victor and his monster. Moreover, by introducing Eve into the equation, Shelley supplies the Romantic reappraisal of Milton with a hitherto unprecedented feminist perspective. Victor and his monster are shown to bear not only many significant correspondences with the union of a mother and her child but also with the 'marriage' of Adam and Eve. In fact, so Hatlen argues, rather than representing a feeble or failed Bloomian 'misreading' of *Paradise Lost*, *Frankenstein* aims to fulfil the dormant feminist potential of Milton's epic by modelling Victor's monster deliberately on the biblical blueprint of Eve. Thus, Shelley's novel presents us with the figure of the categorically disempowered and demonised female as a kind of ancestral prototype whose dilemma illustrates the emancipatory struggle of all patriarchal 'creations'. Hatlen explains:

■ The writings of Godwin and Wollstonecraft and the daily conversation of Byron, Percy Shelley, and other radicals established the intellectual environment within which Mary Shelley wrote *Frankenstein*. Mary Shelley's diary indicates that during the time she was writing *Frankenstein* she read and reread the works of both her parents, and that Percy Shelley read aloud to her all of Milton's works – a reading presumably interspersed with discussions of the implications of these poems. And when the book was finished, she dedicated it to her notorious father. Clearly, then, if we wish to understand the metamorphosis that Milton's treatment of the patriarchal mythos undergoes in the crucible of Mary Shelley's imagination, we cannot ignore the effects upon her of the libertarian and egalitarian ideals that pervaded her environment.

If we wish to understand Mary Shelley's response to Milton, we must also recognize that for the thinkers who most influenced her the importance of Milton's work lay not in his apparent defense of traditional conceptions of hierarchy and obedience but rather in what the Romantics saw as his half-suppressed but still powerful inclination to subject to a ruthless critique all forms of inequality and arbitrary power. To the Romantics, Milton was a great hero in the ongoing human struggle for liberty and equality. The Romantics, Joseph Wittreich notes, saw Milton as 'a "revolutionary artist," which means

that he works with, not within, poetical traditions and that he criticizes the very systems – political and theological – that he postulates in
his poetry and prose.'[29] Blake's summation of this Romantic conception of Milton was seminal: 'The reason Milton wrote in fetters when
he wrote of Angels and God, and at liberty when of Devils and Hell, is
that he was a true poet and of the Devil's party without knowing it.'[30]
The emphasis here on the disparity between Milton's conscious intent
and the actual effects of his verse, between his apparent celebration of
authority (God's over Satan and man, Adam's over Eve) and his latent
sympathy for the rebel who rejects all claims to authority, is typical of
Romantic commentary on Milton. In the *Enquiry* Godwin echoes
Blake's description of Satan as the archetype of the rebel against arbitrary authority: 'Why did [Satan] rebel against his maker? It was, as he
himself informs us, because he saw no sufficient reason for that
extreme inequality of rank and power which the creator assumed.'[31]
Even Mary Wollstonecraft, while noting that many passages in *Paradise
Lost* imply a derogatory view of women, saw a conflict within Milton
between an overt belief in male superiority and a latent desire for
male/female equality: 'It would be difficult,' she says, 'to render two
passages which I now mean to contrast, consistent.' And she then juxta-
poses Eve's statement to Adam ('God is thy law, thou mine') with
Adam's own request that God create for him a mate who will be his
equal ('Among unequals what society/can sort, what harmony or true
delight?').[32] Finally, and perhaps most significantly, Percy Shelley
consistently saw *Paradise Lost* as a profoundly subversive critique of
arbitrary authority:

> Milton's Devil as a moral being is as far superior to his God, as One
> who perseveres in some purpose which he has conceived to be
> excellent in spite of adversity and torture, is to One who in the cold
> security of undoubted triumph inflicts the most horrible revenge
> upon his enemy, but with the alleged design of exasperating him to
> deserve new torments.[33]

And in *Prometheus Unbound*, Shelley set out, it would seem, to rewrite
Paradise Lost:

> The only imaginary being resembling in any degree Prometheus, is
> Satan, and Prometheus is, in my judgment, a more poetical charac-
> ter than Satan, because, in addition to courage, and majesty, and
> firm and patient opposition to omnipotent force, he is susceptible
> of being described as exempt from the taints of ambition, envy,
> revenge, and a desire for personal aggrandisement, which, in the
> Hero of *Paradise Lost*, interfere with the interest.[34]

This statement by Shelley invites us to see *Prometheus Unbound* as a 'purified' *Paradise Lost* in which the false crust of 'orthodoxy' that overlays Milton's poem is stripped away to liberate the revolutionary myth hidden within, and in this effort to uncover the presumed latent but 'true' content of Milton's poem, Percy Shelley's poetic drama establishes itself as part of one of the major projects of Romanticism – the ongoing effort to rescue Milton from Christian orthodoxy.

William Godwin, Mary Wollstonecraft, and Percy Shelley all influenced the developing intellect and imagination of Mary Shelley, and *Frankenstein* represents . . . both a powerful synthesis of the responses to Milton summarized above and an important step forward in the dialogue (a dialogue centered upon the themes of authority and equality) between the Romantics and Milton. Mary Shelley shared with her husband an empathy with the rebel against arbitrary authority. But for her, as U. C. Knoepflmacher has shown, authority embodied itself with particular intensity in the figure of her own father, William Godwin.[35] Mary Shelley found herself in the role of the Other standing over against the Father, legitimate authority, in two ways: first as child, and second as female. For Mary, then, the relationship between the master who claims authority and the rebel who denies that claim became intertwined with the relationships between creator and creature and between man and woman. In *Paradise Lost* Mary Shelley found all of these linked analogies at work. *Paradise Lost*, before it is a poem about sin and the Fall, is a poem about creation, and thus inevitably a poem about the mutual rights and responsibilities of the creator and the creature. *Paradise Lost* is also, inevitably but in some ways surprisingly, about the relationship of male and female – a relationship that assumes an archetypal form in the story of Adam and Eve. Milton inherited certain ideas and images on all of these matters from the Bible specifically (which gave him, for example, the story that Eve was created out of Adam's rib) and more broadly from the Judeo-Christian heritage (his image of Satan, for example, derives more from folklore and the Church Fathers than from the Bible). In pulling together this complex of material *Paradise Lost* offered Mary Shelley, as it offered many other English writers, an invaluable summation of the Judeo-Christian mythos of creation – or as I have here described it, the mythos of patriarchy. But Milton also, as his prose writings on politics and on marriage demonstrate, had some novel, occasionally revolutionary, ideas of his own on the relationship of rulers to ruled and of men to women. In *Frankenstein* Mary Shelley responds to all these dimensions of *Paradise Lost*: the 'traditional' and the 'revolutionary,' the cosmological and the psychological, the political and the personal. Like Percy Shelley in *Prometheus Unbound*, Mary Shelley has set out to rewrite *Paradise Lost* – not as tragedy but rather as nightmare, perhaps even as farce. Because *Frankenstein* draws together all the principal motifs of Milton's poem, it seems to me a more subtle response to *Paradise Lost* than is *Prometheus Unbound*. Mary Shelley recognizes the degree to which inequalities of power distort not only our cosmogonic myths and our political institutions but also (and Percy was blind to this point) our family structures and sexual relations. Thus Mary pushes beyond Percy's critique of arbitrary power to develop a critique of the total cultural and psychological system that in our society sustains relations of inequality both in and outside the family. And as the patriarchal mythos dissolves in the corrosives of Mary Shelley's parody, the possibility of an alternative mythos also moves into the foreground. In this respect *Frankenstein* not only 'liberates' the 'hidden' content of *Paradise Lost* but also, I here want to argue, moves beyond not only Milton's poem but also any text by Mary Shelley's own contemporaries in the attempt to discover a genuine alternative to patriarchy.

. . . . . . From my (and also, I think, from Mary Shelley's) point of view, the significance of Milton's description of the process of creation arises from his unusually detailed exposition of . . . the patriarchal mythos of creation, and from his own apparent uneasiness about this mythos. Milton did not invent this mythos. Rather, he inherited it from his sources (both the Bible and Greek philosophy), and he absorbed it from his environment. To the seventeenth century, the patriarchal conception of creation was, quite simply, true, and Milton seems to have accepted it as such. I call this conception of creation 'patriarchal' because it assumes that the generative power is exclusively male. The female is at best a 'vessel' that temporarily contains and nurtures the new life generated by the male. This conception of the process of creation derives directly from the Bible: the famous list of 'begats' in the first chapter of Matthew suggests that each male in the line of David generated his own son, with at best incidental assistance from an occasional woman. On the theological level, the doctrine that a (male) God single-handedly generated the universe reflects and re-inforces the belief that the generative power is uniquely male. And at least in the rigidly masculinist gospel of John, God also seems to generate his own son in (apparently) a single act of the will, and in turn the son with his own hands shapes Adam out of the dust. In demonic parody of these processes, Satan generates Sin out of his own head and on earth Adam himself gives birth to Eve, by an operation not unlike Caesarian section. Until the last books of the poem, then, the power to give birth is a power almost exclusively exercised by males. (The one exception is Sin, who engages in incestuous intercourse with her father and as a consequence gives birth to Death.) It should also be noted that in all these instances of male birth, the creature is in some degree 'lesser' than his creator. The son 'is' God, but he is also contained within his father, who is thus 'larger' than he. The Son creates Adam, a clearly inferior being, and Adam, after giving birth to Eve, learns from Raphael [the Archangel] that he should treat her as an inferior . . .

There seems to be a general principle here: the 'male mother' in some fashion 'owns' the creature to which he gives birth. Nor can the 'Son' ever grow up, to become the 'Father' in his own right. The Son is, eternally, the Son. So too Eve is presumably intended by God to remain forever an obedient appendage of Adam. Again Sin, the mother of Death, is the exception that seems to prove the rule. Born of woman, Death is not an obedient extension of his mother. Rather, he sullenly threatens both his mother and his father, who control him only by promising that someday he will be permitted to satiate freely his appetites. At this point the pattern seems clear. The creator, if he is male and if he gives birth without the intercession of woman, 'owns' the creature. It is an extension of him, and, theoretically at least, it finds its fulfillment in obeying him. The patriarchal cosmos, it seems, is a perfectly hierarchical world, descending by stages from God, the 'author' of all creation. And each creature in this hierarchy, recognizing that it owes its existence to a creator who occupies a higher level in the hierarchy, responds (or in theory should respond) with gratitude and obedience.

Insofar as *Paradise Lost* postulates as the original order of things a perfectly hierarchical world, the poem may seem to lend credence to the currently widespread theory that Milton was a proponent of order, tradition, authority and masculine superiority. However, it is difficult to reconcile this image of Milton with his political career as a defender of the Puritan rebellion against royal authority . . . .

Mary Shelley's desire to disentangle Milton's 'counter-poem' is first demonstrated by the passage she chooses for her epigraph:

Did I request thee, Maker, from my clay
To mold me man, did I solicit thee
From darkness to promote me?[36]

Adam's anguished question to his maker remains, in *Paradise Lost*, unanswered. Brought into being without his request or consent, Adam has been commanded to love and obey his creator. Summoned to play a game governed by rules (all of them set by God) he does not understand, Adam is now to be punished for breaking these rules. Is not there something a little cruel about a God who creates in human beings the capacity to sin, and who foreknows that they will sin, but who nevertheless insists on punishing them when they do sin? This is the question that Adam's plaint raises. But in *Paradise Lost* this moment of brutal understanding quickly passes. Adam himself reasons his way from accusation of God to self-accusation, and beyond self-accusation to (with the help of Eve) repentance. Yet by abstracting this moment out of context, and by elaborating Adam's accusatory question into an entire novel, Mary Shelley forces us to confront the possibility that the creator (i.e., the patriarchal creator as envisioned in the Judeo-Christian mythos, and as poetically portrayed in Milton's poem) is at best incompetent, and at worst a cruel sadist. The possibility that the real object of Mary Shelley's bitterness is God himself seems to make many commentators on *Frankenstein* acutely nervous. Tannenbaum, for example, denies any significant similarity between Frankenstein and Milton's God: 'Frankenstein approaches Milton's God only in terms of the characteristic that the Satanist view of *Paradise Lost* most frequently attributes to him, his vindictive nature.'[37] Yet the monster's response to *Paradise Lost* suggests a far broader similarity between God and Frankenstein:

> But *Paradise Lost* excited different and far deeper emotions. I read it as I had read the other volumes which had fallen into my hands, as a true history. It moved every feeling of wonder and awe that the picture of an omnipotent God warring with his creatures was capable of exciting. I often referred the several situations, as their similarity struck me, to my own. Like Adam, I was apparently united by no link, to any other being in existence; but his state was far different from mine in every other respect. He had come forth from the hands of God a perfect creature, happy and prosperous, guarded by the especial care of his Creator; he was allowed to converse with and acquire knowledge from beings of a superior nature, but I was wretched, helpless, and alone. Many times I considered Satan as the fitter emblem of my condition, for often, like him, when I viewed the bliss of my protectors, the bitter gall of envy rose within. (*F* 1831, p. 126)

What Satan and Adam have principally in common is their status as secondary, created beings – creatures who at least in theory owe gratitude and obedience to their creator. In absorbing into himself the qualities of both Adam and Satan, the Monster becomes the universal embodiment of the creature. Standing over against him, as creator, is Frankenstein, just as Milton's God stands over against the entire created universe. Can the ways of the creator toward the creature be justified? This is the question Milton poses in *Paradise Lost*. His 'official,' public answer is yes. But, as we have seen, the Romantics detected in *Paradise Lost* a half-suppressed countervoice which, rather than putting man on trial before the bar of God's justice, instead hungered to put God on trial before man's idea of justice. In *Frankenstein* Mary Shelley does what Milton, in the eyes of the Romantics, wanted but did not dare to do: she puts the patriarchal creator on trial, and she finds him guilty. That is, she works through the possibility that the creator's ways toward the creature are not and cannot possibly be just – that whatever justice may exist in the universe is created not by God but by humankind as we assume collective responsibility for our own destiny.

The most significant similarity between God and Victor Frankenstein is their common status as 'male mothers.' Victor Frankenstein gives birth to his creature without any sort of assistance from a woman. As we have already seen, a similar pattern of 'male motherhood' is at work within *Paradise Lost*: God, Satan, and Adam all 'give birth' in the course of Milton's poem. Simply because Milton's myths are all more or less 'orthodox,' we may well read *Paradise Lost* without sensing anything perverse in the poem's insistence that the ability to create new life is a power possessed exclusively by males. But if we read *Paradise Lost* 'through' *Frankenstein*, then the central position that 'male motherhood' occupies in Milton's poem (and, of course, also in the Judeo-Christian myths upon which he draws) becomes apparent. . . . Moreover, if we read *Paradise Lost* with Mary Shelley's parodic description of 'male motherhood' fresh in our minds, we begin to sense that there is something intrinsically monstrous in this idea. That male motherhood is inherently monstrous is apparent, first, in the inability of the patriarchal creator, whether God or Frankenstein, to create the kind of being he sets out to create. The monstrous physiognomy [bodily features] of Victor Frankenstein's creature serves as an objective correlative of the monstrous act that brought him into existence. Here we encounter an apparent contradiction between *Paradise Lost* and *Frankenstein*. For as the Monster himself notes, God's creative labors issue in a beautiful creature, while Victor horribly botched the job:

> Accursed Creator! Why did you form a monster so hideous that even you turned from me in disgust? God, in pity, made man beautiful and alluring, after his own image; but my form is a filthy type of yours, more horrid even from the very resemblance. (*F* 1831, p. 126)

Yet the contrast here may be more apparent than real, for Adam's beautiful exterior conceals a fatal flaw: a propensity toward sin that brings upon humankind untold misery. Why did God, knowing full well that sooner or later human beings would sin, create in them the capacity to sin? The events in *Paradise Lost* force us to ask this question, but neither God nor Milton will stay for an answer. Mary Shelley, less sanguine than Milton, demands an answer. And if we let ourselves read *Paradise Lost* through her eyes, we cannot help but wonder whether the male mother who gives birth to Adam is any more competent than the male mother of Mary Shelley's nameless Monster. Furthermore, Mary Shelley suggests a specific reason why male motherhood is 'monstrous': it issues exclusively from the will rather than the heart.[38] Victor Frankenstein creates the Monster not out of love for the developing creature but purely out of a need to demonstrate his mastery over the process of nature. The Monster, we might say, leaps full-grown (indeed, overgrown) from the mind (not the loins) of his creator like Athena [Greek goddess] from the head of Zeus, like Sin from the mind of Satan, like the Son from the mind of God, like Eve from the side of Adam. The last of these acts of birth is perhaps less monstrous than the others, because Eve at least emerges from a place in reasonable proximity to Adam's sexual organ, and because she is created out of Adam's need for a companion. But God has no 'need' of the Son or of Adam, nor does Satan 'need' Sin. No possibility of reciprocity exists in these cases, and thus the act of creation itself seems motivated solely by the creator's desire to possess an inferior being over whom he can exercise power. By this means Mary Shelley forces us to recognize that all these male births, insofar as they issue from motives other than love, are in varying degrees unnatural – that the true 'monster' here is not the creature but his creator.

If the motives that impel God and Frankenstein to bring their creatures into existence are similar, so too are the ways in which they behave toward their creatures. To both creators the act of creation entails a descent from the spiritual toward the material: Milton's God is pure light, while Adam and Eve are creatures of flesh and blood. Why is God willing to let his 'image' be degraded by this entrance into matter? Even Milton has difficulty answering this question: at one point Raphael speculates neo-platonically that perhaps God will someday allow the human soul to ascend from the material prison in which it is entrapped, and this notion seems to imply that the very creation of the material world was in some sense a 'fall.' In any case, between a purely spiritual God and his material creature a great gulf is fixed. The creature is by his very nature an 'other,' eternally standing over against a creator whose nature is fundamentally different from (and immeasurably superior to) the nature of the creature. Between Frankenstein and his creature there is a similar gulf. Victor 'dreams' his creature. But when this dream stands over against him in inescapably physical form, he is appalled by the incommensurability between his spirit and this gross body:

> I had worked hard for nearly two years, for the sole purpose of infusing life into an inanimate body. For this I had deprived myself of rest and health. I had desired it with an ardour that far exceeded

moderation; but now that I had finished, the beauty of the dream vanished, and breathless horror and disgust filled my heart. (*F* 1831, p. 56)

Both God and Frankenstein also 'abandon' their creatures. Victor's refusal to take responsibility for his 'child' is obvious: he takes one look at what he has created and flees. God's abandonment of Adam and Eve is less obvious, for both Milton and his sources want to 'justify' God's behavior. Yet the skeptical reader cannot help but notice that God, knowing full well that Adam and Eve have a propensity toward sin, nevertheless leaves them to their own devices – with the unsurprising consequence that they do in fact sin. And the similarity between God and Frankenstein extends one step further yet. Having created a helpless and flawed creature and having then abandoned this creature in disgust, Frankenstein nevertheless insists upon holding the Monster morally accountable for all the crimes he commits in his desperate attempts to claim from his parent the self that has been denied him. So too God, having created in Adam and Eve a propensity to sin, and foreknowing that they will sin, nevertheless holds both them and their descendants solely accountable for the consequences of their sin. Indeed, both God and Frankenstein place their creatures in an intolerable and insoluble double bind. Denied the knowledge that would enable them to choose responsibly, Adam and Eve and their descendants are nevertheless held accountable by God for the consequences of their sins, just as Frankenstein holds the Monster responsible for the murders of William, Clerval, and Elizabeth. In both instances the creature, launched upon the world as a 'free' being with the power to shape his own destiny, is nevertheless expected to do nothing contrary to the will of his creator. The creature is in fact simultaneously an autonomous self and an extension of his creator, and these two dimensions of his existence are absolutely incompatible. Caught in this dilemma, the creature twists and turns. And this dilemma is, Mary Shelley reveals to us, the dilemma of patriarchy itself. The patriarchal creator is driven to create by the will to exercise authority over his Other, and yet as long as he sees the Other as merely an extension of himself he and his creature remain locked in a sterile combat. Is there a way out of this dilemma?[39] □

What Hatlen identifies as 'the patriarchal mythos of creation' perpetuates itself by systematically infantilising, ostracising and – if necessary – eliminating women and (potential) mothers especially. Hence, it seems tempting to speculate that a powerful return of 'the mother, the generative female',[40] might be able to remedy the damage done by centuries of hierarchical oppositioning and paternal failure. Inspired by this curative potential of the maternal, Hatlen writes in the third and last extract from his essay in this Guide:

■ If the 'horror' of [Shelley's] book arises in part from Frankenstein's unnatural usurpation of the prerogatives of woman, then this horror is compounded by the systematic elimination from the novel of all women who might potentially assert the claims of the generative female. Frankenstein's mother dies just before he leaves for the university. The servant Justine, who fills the place of a mother in the lives of Victor's younger siblings, is hanged for the supposed murder of William, and Victor's beloved Elizabeth dies at the hands of the Monster a few hours after her marriage to Frankenstein. All these deaths, the last in particular, suggest that the exigencies of Mary Shelley's fable demand the exclusion from the novel of the genitally and generatively potent female. No less important in this respect is a female who, rather than dying, is never born: the female Monster that Victor Frankenstein first agrees to create and then refuses to create. Indeed, Frankenstein's refusal is in some ways the pivotal moment of the plot. Milton's God, faced by Adam's request for a mate, accedes, and the creation of Eve initiates the 'countermovement' within *Paradise Lost* – a movement away from hierarchy and obedience toward freedom and equality. No similar countermovement occurs within Mary Shelley's grotesque parody of *Paradise Lost*, and this difference between the two texts seems to me no less significant than the similarities noted above. The generative female succeeds in subverting the hierarchical perfection of Milton's patriarchal cosmos, and as a consequence the poem can end in a vision of fruition and hope. But no similar rupture occurs in *Frankenstein*, simply because the creator here refuses to allow the female to exist. As a consequence, the sterile struggle between the patriarchal creator and his creature must here proceed to its terrible end.

. . . . . . *Frankenstein* strains to bring into being . . . the generative, nonpatriarchal creator – free of all dependence upon an exterior creator, freely creating in her own right, and claiming no residual rights of possession over the beings she creates. In pointing beyond itself to this possibility of freedom and creativity, *Frankenstein* opens up to us a new awareness of our birthright – a birthright we have as yet scarcely begun to make our own.

. . . a resolution to the destructive effects of patriarchy must involve a liberation of a power which is, under patriarchy, suppressed: the power of free, unpossessive creation. For Mary Shelley, this power is, in the current order of things (i.e., in a society which demands that men be 'masterful'), found primarily in women – although as we shall see this power is not restricted to women. The mother whose absence from *Frankenstein* speaks to us so eloquently is the principal exemplar of the creative power. Indeed she is a Trojan Horse within the bastion of patriarchy, for her concern with the organic growth of the child can counterbalance the patriarch's demand for obedience. Scattered through *Frankenstein* are several images of nutritive parent/child relationship. Invariably these nutritive families include both a father and a mother. An important example is Frankenstein's own family during his early years:

> My mother's tender caresses and my father's smile of benevolent pleasure while regarding me are my first recollections. I was their plaything and their idol, and something better – their child, the innocent and helpless creature bestowed on them by heaven, whom to bring up to good, and whose future lot it was in their hands to direct to happiness or misery, according as they fulfilled their duties towards me. With this deep consciousness of what they owed towards the being to which they had given life, added to the active spirit of tenderness that animated both, it may be imagined that while during every hour of my infant life I received a lesson of patience, of charity, and of self-control, I was so guided by a silken cord that all seemed but one train of enjoyment to me. (*F* 1831, p. 33)

And while he is living in the De Laceys' shed, the Monster develops a similar image of the 'normal' family:

> I heard of the difference of sexes, and the birth and growth of children, how the father doted on the smiles of the infant, and the lively sallies of the older child – how all the life and cares of the mother were wrapped up in the precious charge, how the mind of youth expanded and gained knowledge, of brother, sister, and all the various relationships which bind one human being to another in mutual bonds. (*F* 1831, p. 117)

What the mother brings to the family, it would appear, is a concern for the child not as possession, as object, but rather as an emergent, autonomous self. In the 'normal' family, the mother's nutritive concern for the child can in practice counterbalance the theoretically absolute rights of the father. But if the mother is removed from the family, the patriarchal social structure that reduces the child to the status of object reasserts itself – and the struggle between Frankenstein and his Monster graphically demonstrates the consequences. The alternative to patriarchy, it should now therefore be clear, is not matriarchy: the substitution of the powerful, controlling female for the powerful, controlling male. For if woman too creates only in order to possess her creation, she loses the very quality that establishes her as an alternative to the patriarch: her willingness (a willingness we cannot find either in God or in Frankenstein) to nurture her creatures as long as they need nurture, and to let them go (again unlike the patriarchal creator) when they are ready to assume responsibility for their own lives. Nor are the qualities that define the mother as an alternative to the patriarch generically female. After he gives birth to his Monster, Frankenstein experiences an episode of brain fever. Henry Clerval nurses Victor through this illness, becoming in effect a kind of surrogate 'mother' (in a positive sense of the word this time) who gives new life to his friend:

> Clerval called forth the better feelings of my heart; he again taught me to love the aspect of nature and the cheerful faces of children. Excellent friend! How sincerely did you love me and endeavour to elevate my mind until it was on a level with your own! A selfish pursuit had cramped and narrowed me until your gentleness and affection warmed and opened my senses; I became the same happy creature who, a few years ago, loved and beloved by all, had no sorrow or care. (*F* 1831, p. 68)

Clerval can nourish and regenerate Victor because he and Victor perceive each other as equals. As Mary Wollstonecraft insisted, the key to a nutritive relationship between two human beings (whether these individuals are male or female is irrelevant) is a mutual respect for the independence, the selfhood, the 'subjecthood' of the other. So too the good parent sees her/his child from the beginning as a person, not as a possession. Patriarchy denies the possibility of mutual relationships between equals, demanding instead that in every human relationship one person must be the master while the other must be a slave, that one must give orders while the other obeys, that one must be a subject while the other is an object. It is this system of patriarchy – not John Milton or William Godwin or Percy Shelley or any other individual male – that Mary Shelley here summons to the bar of judgment – and finds guilty.[41] ☐

Making an equally incisive distinction between the system of patriarchy on the one hand and the psychological disposition of the individual male on the other, Bette London takes Hatlen's observations yet another groundbreaking step further. London's argument in 'Mary Shelley, *Frankenstein*, and the Spectacle of Masculinity', first published in the *PMLA* in 1993, signals the beginning of an entirely new approach to the representation of gender in Shelley's novel. Like Hatlen, if perhaps more resolutely, London dismisses Mellor's emotive attack on the allegedly incorrigible individual male and instead launches into an interrogation of the insidious representational dynamics by which the patriarchal system continues to inscribe itself, oppressing women while at the same time brutalising and deforming men. According to London, *Frankenstein*'s emphatic marginalisation of women, as well as literary criticism's conspicuous omission to pay any closer attention to the men at the narrative's centre, are equally symptomatic of patriarchy's exploitation of the female as a spectacular supernumerary, whose foregrounding enables the male to maintain his invisibility and thus escape the deconstructive gaze of a detailed critical analysis. London seems determined to turn the table not on men as individuals but on masculinity as an iconographic effect or systemic mechanism. Far from endorsing the text's strategic employment of woman as some kind of theatrical prop sustaining the centre-stage performances of man, London sets out to unveil what she boldly designates as man's own spectacularity.

Following the detailed analysis of a sculpture and a painting capturing ostensibly characteristic elements of the Shelleys' relationship as a couple,[42] London moves on to a discussion of James Rieger's famous scholarly edition of the 1818 text of *Frankenstein*, first published in 1974. According to London, Rieger's criticism resembles other male-authored scholarly works and artefacts in that it implements the principles of a masculinist aesthetics of absence that simultaneously foregrounds and marginalises the female. In the first of two extracts from her essay reprinted in this Guide, London explains:

■ By making the male body my starting point, I insist on its tangibility in both the representational economy of *Frankenstein* and the cultural production of Mary Shelley's literary authority; and by reading *Frankenstein* against some specific literary and nonliterary constructions of Mary and Percy Shelley, I suggest the ways conventionalized operations of gender have foreclosed access to *Frankenstein*'s explorations of masculinity – so much so that an approach to the subject now requires the dismantling of elaborate critical edifices. As the Shelley monuments suggest, the documents that would secure or obscure *Frankenstein*'s place in literary history typically stage male anxieties across the body of the female subject. And in Mary Shelley scholarship, the relentless concern with questions of authority and bodily limits would seem to have taken its cue from the novel. In a pattern, then, for which James Rieger's edition of the 1818 text of *Frankenstein* may be only the most explicit instance, these works characteristically invest in versions of female monstrosity – practiced on the figure of Mary Shelley. But a critical re-reading of these formative texts might initiate discussion of what they repress: stories of the fractured foundation of masculine privilege.

'Mary Shelley's Life and the Composition of *Frankenstein*,' for example, the introduction to Rieger's critically indispensable text, contrives a biographical portrait of Mary Shelley that reproduces – in her own person – the figure of monstrosity that haunts her tale, a figure marked, like the novel's male creation, by unnatural bodily extension. Framed by her scandalous mother (kept alive, posthumously, by the defamatory reports of the reactionary press) and by the contamination of her own 'final adventure' (an amorous liaison ending in bribery and blackmail), Mary Shelley enters this account circumscribed by the scandal of the female body – a body even death cannot obliterate. And she remains, in Rieger's reconstruction, the emblem of a too substantial existence: 'the stiff, humorless and self-dramatizing woman she had always been.'[43] Like the novel's celebrated invention, this 'composite figure' troublesomely combines a mechanical body (stiff and humorless) with self-proliferating energy.

But as Rieger tells the story of *Frankenstein*'s entry into literary history, Mary Shelley's presence begins to diminish. Always 'Mary' to Percy's 'Shelley,' always modeled on or embodying a husband's or father's literary interests, Rieger's 'Mary' fulfills the condition of 'proper' secondariness. This truncated figure, however, remains riddled by contradiction. For it is *Frankenstein*'s claims to preeminent originality that support Rieger's effort at literary resuscitation – the reproduction of the very text, unavailable for over a century, reconstructed in his contribution to the *Library of Literature*. This effort, moreover, serves to bolster the authority of the woman artist. Indeed, Mary Shelley's authorship can be reconciled to Rieger's textual history only by the hypothesis of female monstrosity – a hypothesis supported, as in the movies, by the invention of the creator's accomplice: the physician's assistant.[44] Perhaps not surprisingly, then, Rieger's narrative uncovers another scandal of the body, a scandal of textual impurity that turns on the discovery of Percy Shelley's pervasive 'assistance at every point in the book's manufacture,' assistance so extensive that 'one hardly knows whether to regard him as editor or minor collaborator.'[45]

In Rieger's representation, then, 'the life' and 'the composition' enact the same scene: the exhibition of the female body with its paradoxical display of excess and lack; its insistently visible demonstration of the horror of having nothing to see. Moreover, in reconstituting the 'original' text of *Frankenstein* (the 1818 edition) with the aid of modern technologies, Rieger replicates this overdetermined configuration, exposing as feminine the text's monstrous lack of unity. For despite his somewhat jocular admission that 'there [were] moments in the preparation of this edition when [he] felt like Frankenstein himself,'[46] Rieger shies away from the implications of this analogy. Nonetheless, the identificatory structure of male auto-biographical creation resonates in his undertaking.

Glossing quotations and allusions as well as some of Percy Shelley's 'additions,' interpolating 'autograph variants' from the 1823 Thomas copy of the text, and appending (as a supplement) the collation of the 1818 and 1831 editions, Rieger manufactures a radically discontinuous text that displays the seams and sutures of its composition, decomposition, and recomposition. Rieger overreaches Frankenstein, however, insisting on the feminine signature of the (textual) body he brings into existence. Excusing his own violation of professional propriety ('I have violated another editorial convention, which prescribes either a clear or a diplomatic text'[47]) on the grounds that 'this mode of presentation shows the author's mind at work,' he locates the source of his editorial difficulties in Mary Shelley's 'feminine' incapacity – incapacity marked in the 'fussiness of her second thoughts' and her amateurish 'tinker[ing] with a completed imaginative act.'[48] In what seems an urbane, unobtrusive, and even critically sanctioned misogyny, Rieger's 'production' thus participates in and reproduces conventional gendered readings, upholding the feminine as the locus of spectacle.

This cultural production – surely one of Frankenstein's most enduring legacies – does not confine itself to the masculine academy; it surfaces conspicuously in Mary Shelley's preface to her own recomposing effort, her introduction to the third edition. Asked to account for the 'origin of the story,' Mary Shelley frames her response in the terms of a question often put to her: 'How I, then a young girl, came to think of, and dilate upon, so very hideous an idea?' (F 1831, p. 5). The question positions her as 'a young girl' in the place of spectacle; and, as Mary Poovey has ably illustrated, the ensuing explanation, with its elaborate rhetoric of modesty, reproduces the paradoxical alignment of monstrous exhibitionism and demure self-effacement that conditions the nineteenth-century construction of gender – a construction Rieger's introduction reinvents.

Moreover, as much feminist criticism has demonstrated, this spectacle of the woman writing, strikingly evoked by Mary Shelley, can be appropriated for feminism in a new deployment of (auto)biography. But the recovery of the female author behind the male-dominated text frequently involves a voyeuristic mechanism that leaves criticism fixed on the self-display of the woman, on what Barbara Johnson calls the 'my monster/my self' syndrome. Consequently, as Mary Jacobus insists, such biographical investments inevitably reduce the text to 'a monstrous symptom.'[49] And insofar as this is true, feminism might do well to alter its perspective, reexamining the structure of spectacle and the positions spectacle engenders.[50]

Such an examination might suggest that the place of spectacle is not unique to women, and from this perspective, the 'impropriety' of Mary Shelley's authorship need not be read as scandalous; the scandal, at least, does not necessarily inhere in a single body. If one turns Rieger's allegations back on themselves, Percy's presence in every stage of 'the book's manufacture' implicates the masculine in the production of monstrosity. And the scandal of Mary Shelley's fractured text may discredit the female author less than it does her masculine authorities, who have their own uneasy relations to textual originality. For like her excessively deferential acceptance of her husband's editing, Mary Shelley's unorthodox citational strategies – her insistent literary allusions and indiscriminate textual borrowings – may expose not so much her lack of originality as the material conditions that constitute textuality as a form of grafting. Writing in a hand not distinctly her own, Mary Shelley opens to question the copied status of the text she copies into her own. Bearing the word, as Margaret Homans suggests, *Frankenstein* (creature, creator, text) bares the underpinnings of the male romantic economy, '[literalizing] the literalization of male literature'.[51] The joins in *Frankenstein*'s textual anatomy thus demonstrate that composition, even in male hands, is always of the body. Accordingly, the spectacle of the text – of the text's irregular body – prompts with new urgency the question of gender at the novel's source: whose body does the text display?[52] □

In the second half of her essay, London reads *Frankenstein* intriguingly as a novel about 'man-making' in two closely interrelated respects. Finding himself under acute pressure to live up to the iconographic imperatives of patriarchal masculinity, Victor sets out to make a man of himself by creating a man, thus 'opening to view the inevitable gap between image and ideal that structure male self-representations'.[53] Not only does Victor's disastrous creation of the Monster, whom he fashions after an impossibly idealised heroic prototype, expose the masculine gender role as a monstrous distortion of the individual male self. By disclosing the ideal patriarchal subject's in(di)visibility as an unrealisable fantasy, it also brings to light a more general and deep-rooted problem of masculine embodiment. Ironically, so London elaborates, Frankenstein's desire for absolute coherency, integrity and perfection results in the precarious assemblage of the Monster, that is, a fragmented, outsize figure composed of an unmanageable multiplicity of abject differences:

■ Although the novel admittedly 'presents not one but three autobiographies of men,' feminist criticism has made a compelling case for reading *Frankenstein*, against all odds, as 'the autobiography of a woman'.[54] Strong feminist interpretations have virtually reconstructed the text to put its gender beyond question, teaching readers to privilege the novel's inscription of its absent women and to see in the very repression of the feminine the powerful marks of Mary Shelley's presence.[55] But now . . . a feminist critique might best fulfill its project by reversing this direction, reading the presence of the novel's self-consciously male texts to illuminate the absences they cover, to expose the self-contradictions they repress. Exceeding the text's self-proclaimed limits, such a reading might even name *Frankenstein*'s dreadful secret: the repression of masculine contradiction at the heart of dominant cultural productions.[56]

This attention to the production of masculinity has important implications for feminist inquiry, especially for studies of *Frankenstein*, a novel structured around this central allegory (the making of a man). Such critical rethinking demands, among other things, a renewed attention to the historical specificity of the construction of masculinity and a recognition that masculinity, as much as femininity, is created by cultural negotiations and contestations. It insists that brokenness has no necessary or exclusive connection to the feminine – witness Frankenstein's self-exhibition as 'a miserable spectacle of wrecked humanity.' And it brings to light the constitution and distribution of the male body in the making of cultural identity. Recontextualizing the cultural production of femininity, it suggests the way versions of the feminine reflect and illuminate a fractured masculinity.[57]

But the *Frankenstein* that emerges from such a redirected scrutiny is an entirely different creature from that produced by traditional scholarship and new feminist autobiography. For insofar as *Frankenstein*'s male bodies have claimed critical attention, criticism has resorted to one of two strategies, reading the bodily markings as the secret code for covert female presence or marginalizing them as signs of effeminacy. Either way, the male body drops out of sight, consigned to a condition of aberrancy. But the approach I have been proposing would make it possible to read Frankenstein's self-display in and as the writing of his body – a project foreclosed by a criticism that aligns the body exclusively with women. And it would permit the novel's critical operation to be seen as something more than the solitary production of an aberrant masculinity. For if *Frankenstein*'s insistent articulation of the male body would seem to challenge the pieties of masculinity, it may be the common understanding of masculinity that requires reconsideration and not *Frankenstein*'s position in it.

Indeed, the text of *Frankenstein* that criticism has sublimated reveals that male spectacle is an integral part of masculinity. Frankenstein himself illustrates the point: the novel relentlessly highlights the body of this exemplary man even where other bodies seem to be in question. Thus while the novel's most sensational moments – the animation of the monster, the destruction of the monster's 'bride,' the discovery of Elizabeth's death – point to specular objects other than Frankenstein, the narrative witnesses these dramatic passages on Frankenstein's body and replays them in his broken utterances. In the account of the monster's composition, for example, Frankenstein decomposes himself; anticipating his inventory of the creature's parts, he deanimates and divides – and thus opens to view – his own body, now seen as an object made up of component parts: 'my eyeballs were starting from their sockets' (*F* 1818, pp.36–37); 'my voice became broken, my trembling hands almost refused to accomplish their task; I became as timid as a love-sick girl' (autograph variant from the Thomas copy).[58] Frankenstein's transgression thus associates him with the 'feminine' scandal of discontinuous bodily materiality, a gendered position imprinted in the parodic catalogue of the monster's 'beauties':

> Beautiful! – Great God! His yellow skin scarcely covered the work of muscles and arteries beneath; his hair was of a lustrous black, and flowing; his teeth of a pearly whiteness; but these luxuriances only formed a more horrid contrast with his watery eyes, that seemed almost of the same colour as the dun white sockets in which they were set, his shrivelled complexion . . . straight black lips. (*F* 1818, p.39)

Normative readings of this scene, focusing on its horrific aspects, disguise its participation in the Petrarchan convention of (female) dismemberment: in the representation of the loved one as a composite of details, a collection of parts [following the style characteristic of the poetry of Petrarch, 1304–1374, Italian sonneteer]. But Mary Shelley's deployment of this technique at this climactic narrative intersection suggests its 'natural' function in the construction of an idealized masculine image . . . Inverting the traditional blazon (whose gender specificity has been powerfully articulated by Nancy Vickers and, more recently, by Patricia Parker[59]), *Frankenstein*'s creation scene thus doubly performs its male anatomy, on the body of the creature and on the body of the creator.

If, then, the question of how to 'compose a female' (*F* 1818, p.124) becomes the one on which both Frankenstein and the novel stall, the novel insists nonetheless on the discomposure of masculinity, on the troubled and troubling representation of the male body. Thus even when the monster is not corporeally present, the memory of its animation disturbs Frankenstein's equilibrium. Possessed by an 'excess of sensitiveness' and activated by Clerval's gaze, Frankenstein's body becomes a notable site of hysterical self-display. For in Clerval's presence, Frankenstein finds that he cannot 'contain' himself – that he cannot be stilled: 'I was unable to remain for a single instant in the same place; I jumped over the chairs, clapped my hands, and laughed aloud' (F 1818, p. 42). A kind of divertissement – a *danse macabre* that induces a dead faint – this mortifying performance earns Frankenstein the monster's specular place, turning Clerval's gaze from the signs of the absent creature to the creator's now 'lifeless' body. After restoring Frankenstein to life and nursing him back to health, Clerval asks only that he 'not discompose [himself]' (F 1818, p. 44).

Even here, however, Frankenstein's aberrant behavior exists within the normative construction of masculinity. For the dispersal of the male body that this scene strikingly demonstrates conforms to a construction of the body familiarly produced in eighteenth-century medical discourse: hypochondria, or male hysteria. Embodying a condition so prevalent as to be dubbed 'The English Malady,' Frankenstein betrays all the textbook signs of susceptibility: refinement of intellect, extraordinary 'understanding' or 'imagination,' solitary study, single-minded fixation, cloistered nocturnal reflection.[60] In fact, distributed across the male body, hysteria was frequently read, in the years before *Frankenstein* appeared, as a sign of privilege and superiority. Thus, *Frankenstein*'s engagement in male spectacle – in the production of a grotesque male body – participates in a culturally specific reconfiguration of the problems of masculine idealization. In the chain of idealized male figures that inhabit the novel, the monster represents only the most evident distortion.

From this perspective, it is easier to understand why, in the novel's monstrous logic of reciprocity, the termination of Frankenstein's effort to conceive and execute a female creature produces as its first embodiment not the much noted and symmetrically satisfying exchange of corpses – a bride for a bride – but the disconcerting self-image of male disfigurement: the shattered corpse of Clerval. For the novel turns on male mirrors, and the male body remains the privileged site of inscription. Whereas the murder of Elizabeth prompts Frankenstein to purposeful, if frenzied, action, the sight of the prostrate man ('I saw the lifeless form of Henry Clerval stretched before me' [F 1818, p. 148]) stops Frankenstein completely: 'The human frame could no longer support the agonizing suffering that I endured, and I was carried out of the room in strong convulsions' (F 1818, p. 148). Even recalling the 'anguish of the recognition' (F 1818, p. 148) subjects his body to disintegration, and he recovers himself – in the narrated events and in the narration – only to reenact this male spectacle, to find himself figuratively as well as literally 'stretched on a wretched bed, surrounded by . . . all the miserable apparatus of a dungeon' (F 1818, p. 149). Frankenstein thus lives to prove on his body his 'unnatural' elasticity, to exhibit in his prolonged self-reckoning 'the hideous phantasm of a man stretched out.'[61]

In the scenes of horror catalogued in the narrative, Frankenstein thus remains the prime representational stage – experiencing in himself all the wrackings of the body and the tortures of the unsolicited gaze, displaying an imagination acutely sensitized to the martyr's fate, claiming, at the last, preeminence in suffering: 'no creature had ever been so miserable as I was; so frightful an event is single in the history of man' (F 1818, p. 167). Even Elizabeth's death (the horror most insistently gender-marked) is anticipated on Frankenstein's frame, first in his premonitory imaginings and then in his act of narration. For in Frankenstein's distorted view of history, *man* is single in his capacity for feeling and suffering. Frankenstein's maddening inability to comprehend, for example, the obvious meaning of the monster's claim 'I shall be with you on your wedding-night' suggests an imagination exclusively bound to male theatricals, an imagination in which the man always occupies center stage. Imagining his own death at the monster's hands, Frankenstein enjoys both positions of the specular exchange: spectator and spectacle. Elizabeth functions merely to facilitate this self-display; as the ostensible object of Frankenstein's interest, she preserves the place of his gaze, permitting the thought of his own absent body to excite his sympathy: 'when I thought of my beloved Elizabeth, – of her tears and endless sorrow, when she should find her lover so barbarously snatched from her, – tears, the first I had shed for many months, streamed from my eyes . . .'(F 1818, p. 141). Similarly, when Frankenstein records the actual murder scene, he registers Elizabeth's death throes first on his own body: 'my arms dropped, the motion of every muscle and fibre was suspended; I could feel the blood trickling in my veins, and tingling in the extremities of my limbs.'[62] Moreover, the scream that signals the monster's offstage consummation of his deed proceeds ambiguously from either Elizabeth's or Frankenstein's mouth: 'the scream was repeated, and I rushed into the room' (F 1818, p. 165). Expressly arranged for Frankenstein's scopic regime, the haunting sight of Elizabeth's 'lifeless and inanimate' body ('Every where I turn I see the same figure – her bloodless arms and relaxed form flung by the murderer on its bridal bier' [F 1818, p. 165]) consequently appears doubly as an afterimage.

Frankenstein's text thus displays the drama of what D. A. Miller calls the 'sensationalized body' – a body culturally coded as feminine, particularly in the later nineteenth century, but subject to discursive appropriation in the masculine domain.[63] Such a body renders visible the culture's sexual codes and mechanisms of identification – mechanisms that would seem to provide little space for women. For even if, as Walton's framing suggests, the ultimate recipient of 'this strange and terrific story' is female (the reader embodied in Walton's sister, Margaret), the story's horror is dramatized in the experiences of men, in the exchange of sensations between male bodies. Thus when Walton testifies, in his appeal to his sister, to his own somatic sensations of horror ('do you not feel your blood congealed with horror, like that which even now curdles mine?' [*F* 1818, p. 178]), his representational practices bear the imprint of Frankenstein's body. While the absence of signature leaves the reception of Walton's 'tale of horrors' uncertain, his testimonial seals Frankenstein's narrative exchange. The blood-curdling secret withheld from Elizabeth – 'I have one secret, Elizabeth, a dreadful one; when revealed to you, it will chill your frame with horror' (*F* 1818, p. 160) – finds its destination in Walton's frame; the 'tale of misery and terror' Frankenstein promises to confide to Elizabeth 'the day after [their] marriage shall take place' passes instead to Walton's pen in an act that stands as the thrilling consummation of confidential vows between men.

Excluded from the sensations of horror, Elizabeth is simultaneously excluded from the field of pleasure the novel fantasizes. And Walton's narrative, for all its assertions of fraternal devotion, promises to reinscribe this exclusionary logic. Relinquishing the reciprocity of letter writing for the journal's narcissistic investments, Walton readily accommodates his sister to a functional position – the pretext for his pleasure. The question of woman's pleasure, in fact, enters Walton's text at precisely the moment it is precluded by the union of male bodies, the moment when Walton becomes Frankenstein's amanuensis [scribe]:

> I have resolved every night, when I am not engaged, to record, as nearly as possible in his own words, what he has related during the day. . . . This manuscript will doubtless afford you the greatest *pleasure*: but to me, who know him, and who hear it from his own lips, with what interest and sympathy shall I read it in some future day! (*F* 1818, p. 18)

For Walton – who lacks the signature of self-identity, who signs himself differently in each recorded instance – the text becomes the unnatural extension of Frankenstein's hand writing. Writing to and from Frankenstein's body, Walton declares his work the paradigmatic autobiography: a vehicle for anticipating and replicating male self-bonding. It is perhaps not surprising, then, that in the copy of the text presented to Mrs. Thomas, Mary Shelley underlines the word *pleasure* and adds a marginal note, 'impossible,' for here especially pleasure is proscribed by sexual difference.

If, however, such a reading seems to repeat the novel's marginalization of the feminine, leaving women readers no unappropriated space for gender-specific identification, it does not for that reason fore-close the possibility of other sites of pleasure – the pleasure, for example, reserved for the spectator of such male spectacles. For in its turn on the fetishistic mechanism, *Frankenstein* records the pleasure of seeing what is prohibited in relation to the broken male body. While within the novel's theater of representation the spectator continues to inhabit the male body, his spectatorial pleasure is construed as a form of mortification. But this representation leaves open to investigation the way the performance of masculinity solicits and engages a reader outside the frame – a reader whose response is not preenacted. For the woman reader, for example, seeking a site for feminist intervention, the novel's male theatricals register differently on the body. For what they reveal is not the exhibition of masculine difference – the pleni-tude of phallic power and possession – but the emptying out of the masculine center. The novel can thus be read as putting into question the singular authority of masculinity and, with it, the fixity of sexual positions and the determinateness of gender privileges.

In its fixation on masculine spectacle, then, *Frankenstein* unsettles the positions of the specular relationship, but the corollary to this gen-der transposition is the space opened up to the possibilities of female spectatorship. And this perspective invites a reconsideration of the way Mary Shelley represents herself in the scene of original creation: the 'devout but nearly silent listener' to male literary and scientific speculations (*F* 1831, p.8). For in view of *Frankenstein*'s exposure of masculine discourses and bodies, one might question the convention-ality of Mary Shelley's position behind the scenes – a position from which the female spectator, unobserved, can illuminate and mobilize the skeletal structure of masculinity. In such a model, then, the repre-sentation of women is not without its interest, but that interest may lie less in the construction of woman as a self-empowering agency than in the understanding of the woman's position in the arrangement of male exhibitions, in the staging of male spectacle. For the woman silenced at the margins of the male imagination can do more than demonstrate masculine preeminence. Like the figure of Mary Shelley produced in the reconstruction of her story's origins (the 1831 introduction) or the sacrificial figures cast up in her novel, the woman at the extremities can point to the fractures in the unified male image: the excesses and deficiencies that disturb the surface of masculinity. From such a posi-tion she can carve out a space for reading differently, opening to view the inevitable gap between image and ideal that structures male self-presentations, that renders male literature – and literary criticism – autobiographical confession.

If the novel's performance of gender, then, can solicit readers dif-ferently, I would like, by way of conclusion, to pursue one of the text's unacted configurations. When Walton introduces Frankenstein into his narrative, it is as someone who 'make[s] a figure in a letter'; at the same time, Walton retreats from the space of masochism opened up by his investment in this (male) spectacle, from the figural possibilities invoked by an object that excites in him the most 'painful interest.' 'Will you laugh,' he entreats his sister, 'at the enthusiasm I express concerning this divine wanderer? If you do, you must have certainly lost that simplicity which was once your characteristic charm' (*F* 1818, p. 17). A performative utterance, this speech would preempt the response Walton fears by raising the specter of female monstrosity – the loss of the characteristic charm of femininity. For the uncharming woman, simultaneously produced by and producing masculine instability, spells the end of representational transparency. She suggests the precarious grounds on which the male escapes the position of spectacle. The male body, it would seem, can be protected from disarming scrutiny only if . . . it is propped by the image of feminine propriety: the figure of woman that, confirming the text's iconographic meaning, allows us to see and not to see the component parts of masculinity. But if, as Walton intimates, we refuse the position allocated for woman, the laugh of the Medusa will echo in our reading. [*Editor's note:* This appears to be an allusion to the French feminist Hélène Cixous's seminal essay, 'The Laugh of the Medusa', first published in *Signs*, 1:4 (1976), pp. 875–93, in which she introduces her influential concept of a female 'writing from the body' or *écriture féminine.*] In *Frankenstein*, this laughter might produce a new mythology, focusing not on the spectacle of female monstrosity but on the extravagant fantasies of a deficient masculinity. Reading *Frankenstein*'s spectacle of masculinity, we might turn the Medusa story on its head; for in the version I am constructing, the laugh of the Medusa would animate the novel's lifeless male bodies to reveal the conditions of their articulation.[64] □

As London's account suggests, recent feminist perspectives on *Frankenstein* have begun to detach themselves from Anne Mellor's characterisation of Victor as a masculine stereotype of destructive, phallic aggression. According to London, for example, it is not so much Victor himself who gives birth to the Monster as the representational economy of the patriarchal system as a whole. In 'Reading the Symptoms: An Exploration of Repression and Hysteria in Mary Shelley's *Frankenstein*', an essay whose argument intriguingly complements London's, Colleen Hobbs interprets Victor's monstrous split as an immediate corollary of 'problems in the cultural orthodoxy of masculinity'.[65] Like London, Hobbs reads Shelley's novel primarily as a female-authored case study of the masculine psyche under patriarchal pressure. Rather than viewing him as a perpetrator of systemic oppression, both Hobbs and London present Victor as a victim of insidious processes of ideological manipulation, that is, as someone who has been coerced into an extreme kind of normative behaviour that damages him as much as it harms others. While London regards Victor's hyperbolic creation as emblematic of patriarchy's project of 'unnatural' man-making, Hobbs outlines the deleterious impact such monstrous masculine self-fashioning has on the individual man's emotional equilibrium. Unfortunately, so Hobbs explains, the spectacularly revolting physiognomy of the Monster has so far deflected critical attention from the representational subtleties of Victor's emotional collapse that manifests itself on, and through, his increasingly emasculated and hysterical body. Nobody hears 'Victor's somatic cries of distress',[66] Hobbs writes. Torn between the mutually exclusive imperatives of allegedly correct masculine and feminine behaviour, the hero is reduced to a state of utter inarticulacy that 'expresses' itself in nervous bodily agitation. As Hobbs concludes, 'Shelley's characters must articulate their most essential needs with only the vocabulary of their bodies', adding that 'in the silence that results, many monsters will be formed'.[67]

In their innovative interpretations London and Hobbs regard Shelley's images of monstrosity as illustrative of a masculine quandary that leaves the individual male divided between an impossible ideal and its inevitably self-annihilative realisations. However, this is only one possible way of making sense of Shelley's 'hideous progeny'. Apart from adumbrating and giving voice to anxieties that afflict the individual psyche, the paranoid horror of *Frankenstein* can also be read as symptomatic of both specifically nineteenth-century and generally modern tensions in the communal spheres of the cultural, socio-political and economic. This latter aspect of Shelley's demonic imagery is explored in the next chapter of this Guide.

CHAPTER FIVE

Pregnant with an Idea: Discourses of Monstrosity in *Frankenstein*

WHEREAS FROM a feminist perspective Frankenstein's monster tends to be read as a metaphor of the self-destructive disintegration of the traditional masculine subject, historicist and Marxist critics usually regard the Creature as an allegorical herald of the definitive break-up of Europe's old feudal order. As Fred Botting indicates in *Making Monstrous*, in times of crisis images of monstrosity remind people of the precarious instability and ultimately unmanageable diversity of the society in which they live. Like Frankenstein's monster, nation states find their origin in a volatile assemblage of often incongruous and intrinsically incompatible parts highly susceptible to friction, dissent and counterdiscursive devolution. Botting writes:

■ Most evident in periods of social, political and economic crisis, monsters appear as the marks of division and difference that cannot be held together and fixed within the hierarchical relations of a social order which sustains the illusion of itself as unified.[1] □

Works of literature written in an era of revolution are often rife with images and motifs of monstrosity. Thus, as a genre endemic to English literature of the late eighteenth and early nineteenth centuries, the Gothic novel appears to reflect the British aristocracy's paranoid horror of ending up on the scaffold like their French counterparts and seeing their cherished isle fall into the hands of the unwashed masses. Commenting on the obtrusively allegorical qualities of the Gothic mode, Ronald Paulson writes in 'Gothic Fiction and the French Revolution':

■ precisely what was being destroyed [in the French Revolution] was the beautiful, passive, feminine, chivalric, pastoral world that is embodied in the maiden fleeing down dimly lit, tortuous corridors, followed by the active, masculine, sublimely aggressive force of the French revolutionaries who threatened the queen and abducted, humiliated, and overthrew her husband, the father of his people, the king.[2] □

With respect to *Frankenstein*, Paulson notes that its allegorical scope and political insight significantly surpass those of other famous works written in the Gothic mode such as, for instance, Ann Radcliffe's *The Mysteries of Udolpho* (1794) or Matthew Lewis's *The Monk* (1796). Rather than comprising a directly contemporary response to the revolutionary scenario in France, Shelley's novel has the advantage of constituting 'a retrospect on the whole process through Waterloo, with the Enlightenment-created monster leaving behind its wake of terror and destruction across France and Europe, partly because it had been disowned and misunderstood and partly because it was created unnaturally by reason rather than love'.[3] According to Paulson, *Frankenstein* makes such a fitting allegory of the French Revolution because both the novel and the historical event tell the story of an 'attempt to *re*create man and the disillusionment and terror that followed'.[4] The havoc wreaked by Victor's monster among its creator's family and friends, as well as the embittered pair's final tragic trajectory across the deserts of the Arctic, could be regarded as a metaphorical rendition of 'the swath of devastation cut across France by the Russian troops following Napoleon's retreat from Moscow'.[5] Indeed, to many an outraged European aristocrat, Napoleon himself – as a commoner wearing the insignia of an emperor – must have epitomised the full apocalyptic horror and monstrous perversity of the French revolutionary project.

In 'Mary Shelley's Monster: Politics and Psychology in *Frankenstein*', published in Levine and Knoepflmacher's *The Endurance of Frankenstein*, Lee Sterrenburg makes the first attempt at a historical contextualisation of the demonic imagery that informs Shelley's novel. The essay, of which an edited version is reprinted below, discusses *Frankenstein*'s monstrosity in relation to the rhetorical strategies and devices deployed in contemporaneous debates on the causes and effects of the French Revolution. Apart from the general ubiquity of spectral and demonic imagery in the political and philosophical literature of the time, Sterrenburg is particularly interested in the demonisation campaign that reactionary conservatives launched against Mary Shelley's parents. Intent on conjuring up a chilling image of the dangers of radical reform and the unspeakable horror of revolutionary insurrection, Edmund Burke (1729–1797) and other prominent representatives of the anti-Godwinian backlash furnished their lectures and pamphlets with an abundance of parricidal monsters and grave-robbing ghouls. Quite evidently, the chief objective of these orators and writers was not to enlighten but to petrify their readers and audiences.

Sterrenburg's essay begins by asserting that, although Shelley was beyond doubt greatly inspired by her parents' revolutionary ideas and commitment, she was never a fervent supporter of the French Revolution and clearly horrified by the Reign of Terror that succeeded it. In fact, after her husband's untimely death in 1822, Shelley increasingly distanced herself from her youthful radicalism. Famously, in 1838, at the age of 41, she wrote in her journal:

■ since I lost Shelley I have no wish to ally myself to the Radicals – they are full of repulsion to me. Violent without any sense of justice – selfish in the extreme – talking without knowledge – rude, envious & insolent – I wish to have nothing to do with them.[6] □

However, while definitely not a radical revolutionary, Shelley cannot truthfully be labelled a conservative either. Indeed, both her fiction and political position seem unique in that they aim to find some kind of compromise between the orders of the old and the new. According to Sterrenburg, already *Frankenstein* contains certain traits that would suggest the novel reaches conceptually 'beyond both the radical and conservative traditions it appropriates. Though relying on images drawn from these traditions, Mary Shelley writes a novel that is, in many ways, a subversion of all ideology'.[7]

Even in her most prominent use of demonic imagery, Shelley's representation eschews a definition of unequivocal clarity. Both Victor and his monster are endowed with tragic potential which means that, however repelled we may be by their thoughts and actions, we continue to sympathise with them due to their inalienable heroic stature. Discussing this ambivalence, Sterrenburg suggests that Shelley may actually have modelled the character of Victor Frankenstein on her father whose well-intentioned, if perhaps too starry-eyed ideas she thought at risk of causing cataclysmic chaos if they were ever rashly put into practice. The Monster embodies this alleged volatility of Godwin's utopian thinking as well as his work's ominous alignment with the aims and objectives of the French Revolution. However, despite the Creature's explicit monstrosity, which by the rhetorical conventions of the time signalled evil and moral depravity, Shelley does not categorically condemn him. He is dangerous no doubt, yet his wickedness is described as circumstantial rather than innate, caused by human failure compounding an already highly unfortunate combination of damaging socio-political factors. If these could be repaired, and the allegedly incorrigible Creature were taken into proper parental care, there is a chance that the Monster might eventually shed his monstrosity again and revert to his original benevolent disposition.

As noted above, Sterrenburg claims that *Frankenstein* reaches beyond both the radical and conservative traditions of political representation.

Shelley's monster stands for hybridity. At once both a perpetrator of violence and a victim of structural coercion, he constitutes a perfect mixture of republican hopes and conservative anxieties, an amalgamation of utopia and apocalypse. Moreover, while intensely political in his implications, Frankenstein's monster also incorporates an intimately personal conflict. As Sterrenburg indicates, 'Mary Shelley translates politics into psychology'.[8] The creature becomes the emblem of a new postrevolutionary subjectivity engendered by a tragic split of the individual between his desire for heroic self-authentication and the mundane responsibilities of a given social role, that is, between the alluring freedom and adventure of progress on the one hand and the intellectual and emotional compromise necessitated by tradition on the other. Sterrenburg writes:

■ The symbolic association between Godwin and monsters was forged in the years 1796–1802, when the conservative reaction against him reached its peak.[9] During those years demonism and the grotesque were frequently used to deflate Godwin's theories about the utopian regeneration of humanity. Conservatives depicted Godwin and his writings as a nascent monster that had to be stamped out, lest England go the way of revolutionary France.[10] The demonic style of these attacks against radical philosophers was established in part by Edmund Burke, who wrote in 1796 of 'metaphysical' social theorists:

a more dreadful calamity cannot arise out of hell to scourge mankind. Nothing can be conceived more hard than the heart of a thoroughbred metaphysician. It comes nearer to the cold malignity of a wicked spirit than to the frailty and passion of a man. It is like that of the principle of evil himself, incorporeal, pure, unmixed, dephlegmated, defecated evil.[11]

William Godwin served as a chief example of this evil reforming type. Burke called Godwin's opinions 'pure defecated atheism . . . the brood of that putrid carcase the French Revolution.'[12] Horace Walpole called Godwin 'one of the greatest monsters exhibited by history.'[13] The *Anti-Jacobin Review* [*Editor's note:* 'Jacobins' was the name given to the English sympathisers of the French Revolution.], which championed the attack upon William Godwin and Mary Wollstonecraft, denounced the couple's disciples in 1800 as 'the spawn of the monster.'[14] The previous year, the *Anti-Jacobin* published a print and an accompanying poem entitled 'The Nightmare,' a take-off on Fuseli's famous painting.[15] The print shows the opposition Whig leader Charles James Fox [1749–1806] asleep on his bed, while a grinning French Jacobin monster, resurrected from the dead, replete with revolutionary cap and grinning skeletal face, rides the horse of death across the sleeper's chest. And the cause of Fox's nightmare is not hard to find. At the foot of the bed lies a copy of his nighttime reading, William Godwin's *Political Justice*. Long before Mary Shelley wrote her novel, Godwin's utopian theories were symbolically reviving the dead. Looking back at the reactionary 1790s, Thomas de Quincey [1785–1859, English critic and essayist] later declared, somewhat anachronistically, that 'most people felt of Mr. Godwin with the same alienation and horror as of a ghoul, bloodless vampyre, or the monster created by Frankenstein.'[16]

. . . . . . *Frankenstein* might well be described as a descendant of the anti-Godwinian novel of the 1790s. Although Mary Shelley dedicated her novel to William Godwin, her dedication . . . was secretly invidious. If her novel surreptitiously criticizes Godwin in personal and autobiographical terms, it also mounts a critique of Godwin's philosophical ideas – especially his schemes for regenerating the human race. As some critics have pointed out, Victor is a latter-day Godwinian. Victor's attempts to regenerate human life echo both Godwin and the conservative critique of Godwin's ideas. It is as if Mary Shelley has appropriated the standard conservative portrayal of Godwinianism, and then added her own private and domestic perspective to it. Godwin entertained millennial expectations in *An Enquiry Concerning the Principles of Political Justice* (1793), where he exulted in nothing less than the coming of a new human race. This race, to emerge once overpopulation had been scientifically brought under control, was to be produced by social engineering, not sexual intercourse. Godwin's scheme summarily dispenses with sexual reproduction, mothers, and children. In his famous chapter on population, Godwin envisions a future form of humanity. He writes:

> The men . . . who exist when the earth shall refuse itself to a more extended population, will cease to propagate, for they will no longer have any motive, either of error or duty, to induce them. In addition to this they will perhaps be immortal. The whole will be a race of men, and not of children. Generation will not succeed generation, nor will truth have in a certain degree to recommence her career at the end of every thirty years. There will be no war, no crimes, no administration of justice as it is called, and no government.[17]

Viewed in the revolutionary context of the 1790s, these utopian speculations on human immortality may have seemed plausible, at least to their author. Many people at the time were talking about the regeneration of society and humanity. Godwin simply took the matter more literally than most. But his abstract, overly philosophical, and thoroughly male-oriented vision of the coming utopia is hardly something his daughter could have been expected to embrace.

Godwin's utopia is public, political, and messianic. It foresees the salvation of the human species as a correlative of the coming state of anarchism. Restraining institutions will be dissolved and oppression will come to an end. Humanity will be reborn socially and physically. Mary Shelley parodies these heroic hopes in the quest of Victor Frankenstein. But she also shifts the emphasis from politics to psychology. Godwin's disinterested utopianism is parodied through Victor Frankenstein's self-centered creation of a new Adam of 'gigantic stature.' In Godwin's paternalistic utopia, children were eliminated entirely. Victor does seem to want offspring, but only as a glorification of himself. He anticipates:

A new species would bless me as its creator and source; many happy and excellent natures would owe their being to me. No father could claim the gratitude of his child so completely as I should deserve their's. (*F* 1818, p. 36)

Victor foresees a utopia that reflects his own subjective desires. What was previously a form of social millenarianism [(in Christianity) the belief in a future millennium following the Second Coming of Christ] has been reduced or narrowed to the status of a psychic obsession.

To a large extent, the sections of the novel narrated by Victor Frankenstein concern themselves with his subjective hopes and fears, his millenarian expectations and his demonic sufferings, and his emotional inability to cope with the Monster he has unleashed. In representing Victor's psychology, Mary Shelley deliberately draws on the features of earlier political literature. Conservative writers had parodied Godwin's bloodless, 'incorporeal' theories by rendering them into something demonic, grotesque, and ghoulish. Where Godwin foresaw the triumph of mind over matter, and the banishment of death and disease from the human frame, his conservative opponents saw something promiscuous, perverted, and unnatural. They denounced Godwin's theories as a virtual invitation to grave-robbing and trafficking with the dead.

. . . . . . If the characterization of Victor Frankenstein owes much to Godwin's utopian writings and to the body of literature that grew up in response to him, Frankenstein's Monster, in contrast, rises from the body of writings on the French Revolution. Mary Shelley's reading was by no means confined to the philosophical tradition of her father. As Gerald McNiece has shown, Mary and Percy Shelley were ardent students of the literature and polemics written about the French Revolution, the Reign of Terror, and the meteoric career of Napoleon [Bonaparte, 1769–1821, French emperor (1804–1815)].[18] During their trip to the continent in 1816, the year she began writing *Frankenstein*,

Mary and Percy toured various revolutionary landmarks, noted the spot where the King and Queen had appeared before the Paris insurrectionaries, and even tried to find the chambers where the demonstrators had allegedly burst in upon and captured the royal pair. In their attempts to understand the Revolution and how it had issued forth into Napoleonic despotism, Mary and Percy systematically studied the works of the radicals, including Thomas Paine, Mary Wollstonecraft, and William Godwin. But they also read widely in the works of the conservatives and anti-Jacobins, including Edmund Burke [and the] Abbé [Augustin de] Barruel [1741–1820, French Jesuit writer] . . . In all these latter works appear metaphors that depict the revolutionary crowd as demons and monsters. These monsters are the precursors of Mary Shelley's creature in *Frankenstein*, although she again internalizes the metaphor and adapts it to new ends.

According to the conservative myth of the French Revolution, that event was the result of sinister external influences. In fact, the 'revolution' itself is often rhetorically rendered as an external influence that has invaded and altered the human mind, thereby giving rise to unprecedented evils and monstrous horrors. The stylistic focus on externals is by no means confined to the psychology of single fictional characters . . . It also serves to depict the collective psychology of revolutionary France. . . . the French revolutionaries are depicted as the victims of a twofold attack from without. First they are invaded and infected by 'revolution' or radical philosophy. Then they set about rebelling, robbing graves, tampering with the dead, and calling forth deadly monsters. The resurrected dead constitute a second attack from without, which descends upon those who succumbed to revolution in the first place. This etiology of political demonism informs Edmund Burke's passage on grave-robbing in his *Letter to a Noble Lord* (1796). Burke haughtily warns:

Before this of France, the annals of all time have not furnished an instance of a *complete* revolution. That revolution seems to have extended even to the constitution of the mind of man. . . . They [the French Revolutionaries] have so determined hatred to all privileged orders, that they deny even to the departed the sad immunities of the grave . . . they unplumb the dead for bullets to assassinate the living. If all revolutionists were not proof against all caution, I should recommend it to their consideration, that no persons were ever known to history, either sacred or profane, to vex the sepulchure [*sic*], and, by their sorceries, to call up the prophetic dead, with any other event, than the prediction of their own disastrous fate.[19]

Burke echoes the standard conservative melodrama of invading externals. He himself views the Revolution from the outside and without sympathy. It is a drama happening to foreigners, who are the pawns of alien, external forces. The social revolution has 'extended' itself into the minds of the French, thus revolutionizing their mental economy as well. They have been turned into a new and unprecedented race of grave-robbers. But Burke caustically warns these revolutionaries that their demonic nemesis is near at hand. The prophetic dead will awaken, and turn upon the sorcerers of the revolutionary tribunal.

Burke also develops an externalized, Gothic melodrama in his *Reflections on the Revolution in France* (1790). He denounces armed insurrection as a pernicious monster, set free by experimenters and reformers. He pointedly warns that military democracy is 'a species of political monster, which has always ended by devouring those who have produced it.'[20] For Burke, even resurrected monsters and the prophetic dead are animated by external forces, 'radical and intrinsic' evil.[21] He uses a Gothic symbolism of transmigrating spirits to suggest the new, unexpected shapes rebellion can assume once it begins its rampages. As history moves forward, he suggests, the spirit of evil invades new bodies and works in new ways. Now, during the French Revolution,

> vice assumes a new body. The spirit transmigrates; and, far from losing its principle of life by the change of its appearance, it is renovated in its new organs with the fresh vigour of a juvenile activity. It walks abroad; it continues its ravages; whilst you are gibbeting the carcass, or demolishing the tomb.[22]

Burke's personifications are effective. It is difficult to sympathize with a revolution that springs forth from the tomb and stalks abroad like some evil monster, specter, or phantom haunting its hapless victims.

. . . . . . In its most extreme form, the melodrama of external influences emerges as a full blown theory, which holds the French Revolution to be the result of a vast, organized international conspiracy. This theory emerges most overtly, perhaps, in Abbé Barruel's lurid *Memoirs Illustrating the History of Jacobinism* (1797), which . . . was a favorite work of Percy Shelley's during his days at Oxford. . . . Shelley read all four volumes of Barruel again and again, and . . . he was particularly taken with the conspiratorial account of the Illuminati. [*Editor's note:* According to Ronald Paulson, Shelley's choice of Ingolstadt as Victor Frankenstein's university town constitutes a clear reference to the Illuminati. 'Munich or Heidelberg would have been closer to his home in Geneva', Paulson writes, 'but Ingolstadt (as Shelley knew from [Barruel's Memoirs]) was where Adam Weishaupt, the symbolic arch-demon of revolutionary thought, founded the Bavarian *illuminati* in 1776, and from this secret society supposedly grew the French Revolution'. Paulson adds that 'the *illuminati* were sworn to further knowledge for the betterment of mankind, no matter what the costs or the means'.[23] We know that Mary and Percy both studied Barruel during their continental tour of 1814, and that Percy read parts of the *Memoirs* to her out loud at that time.[24] Barruel sets out to expose the secret conspiracies he sees lurking behind the French Revolution. He uncovers a vast, proliferating cabal, which originates with the Illuminati in Ingolstadt, and descends downward through the Freemasons, the *philosophes*, the Jacobins, and finally reaches the revolutionary crowds in the streets. He depicts the Jacobins and the revolutionary crowds as a monster incarnate. This monster is an offspring of the Illuminati, whose reforming philosophies have brought it into being. At the end of his third volume, Barruel looks forward to his fourth with an ominous warning to the reader:

> Meanwhile, before Satan shall exultingly enjoy this triumphant spectacle [of complete anarchy] which the Illuminizing Code is preparing, let us examine how . . . it engendered that disastrous monster called Jacobin, raging uncontrolled, and almost unopposed, in these days of horror and devastations.[25]

The international conspiracy theory here takes the form of a sexual or parenting metaphor. The secret code of the Illuminati has 'engendered' a 'monster called Jacobin,' who now rages out of control across Europe. Barruel makes extensive use of the parent-child metaphor. He writes: 'the French Revolution has been a true child of its parent Sect; its crimes have been its filial duty; those black deeds and atrocious acts the natural consequences of the principles and systems that gave it birth.'[26] The symbolic projection of external causes and external agents could hardly be more extreme. Without the parent philosophical sect, there would be no childlike monster arising to terrorize Europe. Without the secret conspiracy of the Illuminati at Ingolstadt, there purportedly would have been no French Revolution, either. For Barruel reforming philosophies lead directly and inevitably to the production of rebellious monsters.

There is reason to assume that Mary Shelley had Barruel in mind when she composed *Frankenstein*. Victor Frankenstein of course does not produce a real Jacobin monster. But he does create his Monster in the same city, Ingolstadt, which Barruel cites as the purported secret source of the French Revolution – and as the place in which the 'monster called Jacobin' was originally conceived. Victor, in effect, is producing the second famous literary monster to issue forth from the secret inner sanctum of that city. This second coming differs significantly from the first. Even though the demonic personification remains intact and though the story is nominally set in the 1790s, the French Revolution has simply disappeared. Mary Shelley retains the monster metaphor, but purges it of virtually all reference to collective movements. Her monster metaphor explains the coming of a domestic tragedy. Political revolution has been replaced by a parricidal rebellion within the family. And . . . that family is essentially bourgeois.

The form of Mary Shelley's novel further serves to depoliticize the monster tradition. Instead of watching the birth and career of the monster from without, as we do in Burke and Barruel, we watch it from within, from the personal viewpoint of the participating parties. This shift within opens up subjective perspectives left untapped in the political milieu of the 1790s. Mary Shelley's new formal subjectivity does more than efface and replace politics. It also subverts the clear, definable melodrama of external ideological causes that informed writings of the 1790s. The world is now much more problematic. Monsters are still abroad, but we are no longer quite sure why. In order to find out, we have to piece together and compare the various subjective explanations offered by Victor, by the Monster, and even by the frame narrator, Robert Walton. But these narratives are patently at odds with one another, especially when it comes to explaining causes. Mary Shelley's world-view is less political than Godwin's or Burke's; it is also far more labyrinthine and involuted when it comes to telling us why things fall apart.

For writers of the 1790s, the world could be improved, saved, or destroyed by manipulating external and environmental influences. William Godwin thought that humans might become immortal, once the pressures of overpopulation were brought under control. Edmund Burke was Godwin's political enemy and a bitter opponent of Enlightenment philosophies. But he too used social and environmental explanations, at least when it came to dealing with the threat of revolution. Godwin wanted to eliminate misery, and he thought this could be done by eradicating excess population. By the end of his career, when Burke actively wanted to eliminate the international revolutionary menace, he thought (or hoped) this could be done by locating and eradicating revolutionaries at home and abroad. Both writers were thus the heirs of Enlightenment thinking, at least rhetorically, in the sense that they held forth the practical hope of isolating and doing away with a social cause of suffering.

To put the matter in moral terms, both Godwin and Burke presumed to know where evil resided. For Godwin, it was in social institutions that maintained arbitrary inequality, oppression, and want. For Burke, evil resided in those philosophers and rebels who wanted to strip away the protection of social hierarchies and institutions. Both these world-views contain an element of melodrama. They are also typical expressions of the polarized thinking which emerged, during the revolutionary 1790s, as a political extension of the Enlightenment world-view . . .

Viewed in its wider cultural context, Mary Shelley's shift from politics to psyche in *Frankenstein* should be seen, not merely as a reaction against the utopianism of Godwin, nor against the conservatism of Burke, but rather as a reaction against this entire world-view of the revolutionary age. Mary Shelley does not escape from the schisms of that polarized world. Hers is still a world of good versus evil, men versus monsters. But she does set about internalizing those dualisms. Instead of depicting the vast political dramas of the revolutionary age, she narrows the focus to a few isolated characters, who are often too subjectively rendered to conform neatly to the old political labels. In *Frankenstein*, the very act of perceiving and defining a monster has become problematic.

The confessional structure of *Frankenstein* pulls our attention away from the world of politics. We shift our attention from the social object to the perceiving subject. The novel often deals with the problems of the subjective viewer, who is projecting upon others a private vision of demonic persecution. Mary Shelley pays a good deal of attention to how characters misperceive or half invent the social forces aligned against them. For example, she goes to great lengths to portray Victor's subjective fantasies of the Monster he has created. Subjective images of the fiend intrude upon Victor's nighttime dreams; they also appear during his waking hours as a kind of spectral hallucination. . . . . . .

. . . Victor's account is complicated by the fact that he often perceives the creature as an imago of his own blasted hopes. Victor continually talks in terms of dualistic reversals. Within the space of a single disjunctive sentence, he can pass from utopian hope to demonic suffering and catastrophic failure. Victor recalls the moment the creature opened his eyes for the first time: 'now that I had finished, the beauty of the dream vanished, and breathless horror and disgust filled my heart' (*F* 1818, p.39). Victor's dualistic sentences chart emotional convulsions that take place within his own psyche. *He* is the focal point of his own narrative. *His* utopian expectations have been blasted by failure. . . . Hells and demons are, for Victor, the symbolic reversals of his extravagant hopes and desires.

When Victor finally meets and speaks with his Monster, we are implicitly witnessing a clash of rival world-views. Victor speaks in his typically subjective and self-reflexive manner. The Monster retains much more of the Enlightenment political style. He talks analytically about the social influences that have shaped his life. The Monster speaks like a *philosophe*, while Victor rages in Romantic agony. The first time Victor ever speaks with his creature, he breaks out in a fit of wild imprecations, and the Monster replies: 'I expected this reception. . . . All men hate the wretched; how then must I be hated, who am miserable beyond all living things' (*F* 1818, p. 77). There is considerable irony in this stylistic reversal. The novel assigns to Victor the conventional role of the experimenting *philosophe*-scientist; but he raves like a mad demon. Conversely, the novel assigns to the creature the role of the mad, Jacobin demon, risen from the grave to spread havoc abroad. But he talks like a *philosophe*, indicting the social system for the suffering it causes individuals. Mary Shelley does not always escape from the stereotypes of the revolutionary age, but she does conflate and mix them in new and subversive combinations.

The confrontation of world-views continues. Oblivious of his own cruel neglect, Victor remains fixated on the crimes and innate evils of his adversary and continues to rave in a dire, apocalyptic style ('Abhorred monster! fiend that thou art! the tortures of hell are too mild a vengeance for thy crimes' [*F* 1818, p. 77]). Yet the Monster's rhetorical style tells us that his identity as a rebel was learned, not innate. In direct contradiction to the Burkean tradition of the monster as evil incarnate, the creature tells Frankenstein: 'I was benevolent and good; misery made me a fiend' (*F* 1818, p. 78). This disjunctive rhetoric itself reenacts a passage from benevolence to rebellion. In part, the Monster has been converted to his demonic identity, and does not deserve Victor's reactionary labeling, which assumes that he is the principle of evil incarnate. And Victor's rejection is all the more ironic because the utopia projected by the monster is highly paternalistic: he wants to be cared for by Victor, whom he calls his 'natural lord and king' (*F* 1818, p. 77).

The Monster proves a very philosophical rebel. He explains his actions in traditional republican terms. He claims he has been driven to rebellion by the failures of the ruling orders. His superiors and protectors have shirked their responsibilities toward him, impelling him to insurrection. He says of the De Laceys: 'My protectors had departed, and broken the only link that held me to the world. For the first time feelings of revenge and hatred filled my bosom, and I did not strive to control them' (*F* 1818, p. 113). This rebellion against irresponsible superiors soon turns against Victor, who has rejected the creature from the moment of its awakening. The Monster's rebellion is parricidal; he rises against his own creator. He defiantly tells Victor: 'I will revenge my injuries: if I cannot inspire love, I will cause fear; and chiefly towards you my archenemy, because my creator, I do swear inextinguishable hatred' (*F* 1818, p. 119). This imprecation echoes a motif in the political literature of the 1790s. Especially for republican historiographers, parricidal monsters serve as emblems of the consequences of misrule. For republicans, monsters rebel not because they are infected by the evils of radical philosophy, but because they have been oppressed and misused by the regnant order. In the language of *Frankenstein*, social misery turns them into fiends.

...... Still, Mary Shelley's Monster would have been unique and isolated even in the 1790s. He is a hybrid, a cross between two traditions that produces a unique third. From the Burkean tradition of horrific, evil, and revolutionary monsters, he seems to have derived the grotesque features that physically mark him and set him apart; he has risen from the tomb like a revolutionary monster, and the mark of death is still upon him. All men flee from such ugliness and apparent evil, as the Monster knows only too well. From the republican tradition of social monsters, he seems to have derived his acerbic, verbal critique of poverty and injustice, which serves as his stated rationale for insurrection. As he tells us with pointed eloquence, monsters are driven to rebellion by suffering and oppression. People flee from this monster, and they try to kill him as well. The Monster in *Frankenstein* thus suffers the consequences of two symbolic traditions.

But Mary Shelley does more than conflate two traditions. She molds them into a unique third. She moves inside the mind of the Monster and asks what it is like to be labeled, defined, and even physically distorted by a political stereotype. The Monster in *Frankenstein* is the victim of Burkean circumstances: he is resurrected from the grave. He is also the victim of circumstances a republican might single out: he is oppressed and misused by the social orders above him. Mary Shelley is able to represent the consequences of these influences subjectively, through the eyes of a victim who is also a rebel. This is a new perspective. It is something her Enlightenment forerunners could not see, preoccupied as they were with charting, explaining, and debating the external influences that enkindle revolution.

...... In *Frankenstein* Mary Shelley relies on political symbols to depict a psychological struggle. She could therefore animate what, in the political writings from which she drew her symbolism, had hardened into stereotype and rhetoric. Victor Frankenstein is more than a Godwinian theorist; the rebellious Monster, the offspring of utopian ideas, is more than the vindictive and 'hideous phantom' envisioned by Burke. The earlier stereotypes are nonetheless encrusted in the novel. Like the monsters depicted in conservative writings, the nameless creature arises from the grave and perishes in flames. He acts out the apocalyptic paradigm when he destroys his formerly benevolent creator and consigns himself to a fiery holocaust. Mary Shelley can imagine a positive side to radical hopes for reform, yet she also sees their degeneration into carnage and disaster. Unlike the polemicists who assailed her father and the French Revolution, however, she can go beyond ideology, from the world at large to the quarrel within.[27] □

In 'An Issue of Monstrous Desire: *Frankenstein* and Obstetrics', an essay that first appeared in the *Yale Journal of Criticism* in 1988, Alan Bewell approaches Shelley's monstrous imagery from an angle entirely different to Sterrenburg's. According to Bewell's argument, of which an abridged version is reprinted here, the discourse that had the most significant impact on the composition of *Frankenstein* was not the discourse of reactionary politics but the socio-medical discourse of eighteenth-century obstetrics. Inspired, if not quite convinced by Ellen Moers's reflections on the correlation between authorship and motherhood in Shelley's novel, Bewell embarks on a detailed historical investigation of obstetric knowledge. In his view, *Frankenstein* represents a woman writer's powerfully subversive appropriation of what has perhaps always potentially been patriarchy's most deeply misogynous discourse.

Bewell's research shows that, while a pregnant woman's body was traditionally regarded as a mere incubator for her husband's formative and ensouling seed, her imagination was assumed to possess the power to interfere with the unborn baby's development. Hence, it was not only common but perfectly legitimate to blame mothers for miscarriages, still-births, as well as all kinds of birth defects and bodily malformations that affected the newborn infant. According to Bewell, Shelley shrewdly deconstructs this discourse. Not only does the female-authored achievement of *Frankenstein* testify to the fact that, rather than debilitated by the treacherous antics of a hyperactive mind, women find themselves in actual fact greatly empowered by the strength and vividness of their imagination. More importantly, the novel also demonstrates that it is clearly the male – and *not* the female – whose (pro)creative faculties need to be policed more rigorously by subjecting them to a strict regulatory agenda of familial, and especially maternal, control. Bewell explains:

■ Mary Shelley's experience of pregnancy and loss was not simply a biological matter, but also a social and discursive event, which made her familiar, in ways that critics have not been, with the language of obstetrics and its extensive and long-standing discourse on the causes of monsters and abortions. Moers takes the presence of this language in *Frankenstein* as a sign that the novel is autobiographical; I would argue in addition that it represents Mary Shelley's deliberate attempt to introduce an ambiguously female-based theory of creation into the Romantic discourse on the imagination. Using sexual reproduction as a model for all modes of creation, she made obstetrics the master-code of her aesthetics and applied its concrete arguments, about the creative power of a mother's psyche upon the fetus and the proper environ-ment for human reproduction, to criticize and to curb the excesses of male Romantic imaginations, particularly her husband's.

The period between 1650 and 1800 saw a massive increase in the publication of books on midwifery. This spate of books is largely attributable to the appearance of man-midwives, who asserted their dominance over traditional midwives, first, by claiming that the pro-fession required extensive medical expertise, and second, through their exclusive right to use surgical instruments, such as hooks, crotchets, extractors, and crutches, in delivery. Leaving this issue aside for the moment, I would note that the books generally follow a fairly standardized pattern. They all stress the importance of a knowledge of anatomy and physiology, so the structure and function of the organs of generation receive a good deal of attention. By the middle of the eighteenth century, artists and engravers . . . were commissioned to do high-quality anatomical plates. Most of these books also give advice on the symptoms and diagnosis of pregnancy, the disorders peculiar to pregnant women, and various ways to determine the sex of an unborn child. Delivery methods are frequently dealt with in detail, often with plate illustrations of the different kinds of births that a midwife may confront. Remarks on the lying-in period and on the diseases that women and newborn infants are subject to during this period some-times appear as well, and earlier books often include advice on choosing a midwife. For my present purposes, I want to stress that these books tend to be very much concerned with discipline, with establishing rules of conduct for pregnant women who wished to be delivered of healthy and well-formed children. They are explicitly books on the 'management' or 'government' of pregnant wives. Where normally a woman's behavior was guided by moral, religious, famil-ial, and economic restraints, pregnant women found themselves – then, as now – the subject of intensive medical scrutiny and advice. A brief mention of the titles of a few of these books will suffice to indi-cate their disciplinary character. The seventeenth-century midwife Jane Sharp wrote *The Midwives Book. Or the whole Art of Midwifery Discovered. Directing Childbearing Women how to behave themselves; In their Conception, Breeding, Bearing, and Nursing of Children.* James Guillemeau's is entitled *Childbirth; or, The Happy Deliverie of Women. Wherein is set downe the Government of Women. In the Time: Of their Breeding Childe: Of their Travaile, both Naturall, and Contrary to Nature: And Of their Lying in.* The book includes two chapters, one entitled, 'What dyet and order a woman with child ought to keepe,' and another, 'How a woman must governe her self the nine months she goeth with child.' One of the most popular handbooks of the eighteenth century, *Aristotle's Compleat Master-Piece, In Three Parts; Displaying the Secrets of Nature in the Generation of*

Man (1694?), includes a chapter on 'How a woman should order herself that desires to conceive, and what she ought to do after conception,' and another on 'How child bearing women ought to govern themselves during the time of their pregnancy.' The London physician John Clarke, who was summoned when Mary Wollstonecraft developed complications at the birth of her daughter, and who also arrived five minutes late for the birth of Mary's first child (in 1815), was famous for *Practical Essays on the Management of Pregnancy and Labour*, published by the radical bookseller Joseph Johnson.

This antenatal regimen generally revolved around the right use of the classical six 'non-naturals': air, meat and drink, exercise and rest, sleeping and waking, fulness and emptiness, and the passions of the mind. Alexander Hamilton, in *Outlines of the Theory and Practice of Midwifery*, in the section entitled 'Management during Pregnancy,' sets down a typical list of rules of conduct. 'The strictest temperance and regularity in diet, sleeping, exercise, and amusement,' he argues, 'are necessary to be observed by those who have reason to dread abortions,' 'Overheating, irregular passions, and costiveness' are also to be avoided, as are 'the hazards of shocks, from falls in walking or riding, from bruises in crowds, or frights from bustle.'[28] No extreme cures or actions regarding complaints are to be taken. The dress is to be loose and easy. Women are advised to frequent places where the air is pure and tempered. For this reason, as Hamilton argues in a later book, *The Family Female Physician*, they 'should be strictly prohibited from crowded companies and public places. The impurity of the air, on such occasions, is sufficient, in the irritable state of pregnant women, to induce many very disagreeable complaints.' Nevertheless, he stresses the equal importance of their avoiding being alone, because in solitary situations 'they are apt to become melancholy; and it is well known that the depressing passions sometimes prove the source of the most dangerous disease which can occur during pregnancy.'[29] The proper psychological environment for pregnant women, then, is neither public, nor private, but a domestic one, in which, through 'cheerful company and variety of objects . . . their minds may be always composed and happy.'[30] Eighteenth-century obstetric theory did not simply reflect the emerging ideological importance of the idea of domestic family life. It helped to shape it. It was a major element in the 'entire medico-sexual regime' that, in Michel Foucault's words, 'took hold of the family milieu.'[31]

There remains another aspect of the obstetric management of pregnant wives, which is of major importance to *Frankenstein*: the striking emphasis placed on the power of a pregnant woman's imagination and desires to mark or deform a developing fetus. The midwifery books constituted an important early discourse on the female imagination, one that accorded it extraordinary powers. Central to this theory was the notion that a woman's imagination functioned mimetically: an image placed before her eyes and strongly impressed on her imagination would be reproduced on the body of the child. 'The strong Attention of the Mother's Mind to a *Determined* Object,' James Augustus Blondel comments, in summarizing this tradition, 'can cause a *Determined* Impression upon the Body of the Child: As for Instance . . . her strong Desire of a *Peach*, or of an *Apricock* can cause the Colour and shape of a *Peach*, or of an *Apricock* upon a *Determined* part of the Child's Body.'[32] . . . . . .

Ambroise Paré, in his account of the origin of monsters, supplies two other famous examples, in which an image brought before the eyes of a conceiving woman is transferred directly to the fetus:

> The Ancients having diligently sought into all the Secrets of Nature, have marked and observed other causes of the generation of Monsters: for, understanding the force of imagination to be so powerful in us, as for the most part, it may alter the body of them that imagine, they soon persuaded themselves that the faculty which formeth the Infant may be led and governed by the firm and strong cogitation of the Parents begetting them (often deluded by nocturnal and deceitful apparitions) or by the mother conceiving them; and so that which is strongly conceived in the mind, imprints the force into the Infant conceived in the wombe. . . . We have read in *Heliodorus*, that *Persia*, Queen of *Aethiopia*, by her Husband *Hidustes*, being also an Ethiope, had a daughter of a white complexion, because in the embraces of her husband, by which she proved with child, she earnestly fixed her eye and mind upon the picture of the faire Andromeda standing opposite unto her. Damascene reports, that he saw a Maid hairy like a Bear, which had that deformity by no other cause or occasion than that her Mother earnestly beheld in the very instant of receiving and conceiving the seed, the image of *St. John* covered with a Camels skin, hanging upon the posts of the bed.[33]

In both these instances . . . monsters are produced at the moment of conception when a mother's ardent gaze on an image overpowers the form-making power of the seed, which, from Aristotle's *De generatione animalium* onward, was usually believed to originate in the male. In these texts, sexual possession and conception ('in the embraces of her husband') are linked to *mental* possession and conception ('she *earnestly* fixed her eye and mind,' 'her Mother *earnestly* beheld') because the sexual act was not viewed simply as a biological event, but one in which volition was linked to pleasure through the womb's active grasping of the seed. As the ambiguous description of St. John 'hanging upon the posts of the bed' suggests, monsters are conceived when an image usurps the place of the biological father, if not in the bed, at least in the mind of his wife.[34] Traditional obstetric theory may have often allotted women a secondary or subordinate role in biological reproduction, their purpose frequently being that of a *tabula rasa* for the male seed, the 'nutriment' for the developing 'form' of the child. But a contrary, more feminist position, also developed, that reasserts the importance of the mother by admitting that the mother's imagination, if not fully satisfied with this arrangement, might intervene in this process, when not carefully regulated, to mar or deface the form provided by the father.

.. .. Women's longings and imaginings were generally considered dangerous, and this was especially true of pregnant women, because it was believed that pregnancy was an abnormal condition that gave rise not only to great bellies, but also to 'great Loathings and ... many different Longings.'[35] ... This abnormal intensity and irregularity of imagination was seen as a major threat to the child, for it suggested that 'the Marks and Deformities, Children bring into the World' were not only attributable to what a woman might have seen, but also were expressions of her unnatural desires, 'the sad Effect of the Mother's irregular Fancy and Imagination.' In short, pregnant women can and 'do breed *Monsters* by the Wantonness of their *Imagination*.'[36]

Concerned about the assumed intensity and abnormality of a pregnant woman's imagination as well as the enormous effect that her unsatisfied desires and inexplicable loathings might have on the child, the authors of midwifery books developed an extensive discourse on the nature and functioning of her imagination, aimed at regulating and normalizing not only what she did, but what she looked at, thought about, and desired while pregnant. In addition to advice about proper physical activities, they also developed a psychic regimen that sought to curb her imagination and desires from excessive or unusual activity. Blondel in his criticism of what he calls 'the imaginationists' summarizes what a woman in this condition should avoid:

1. A strong Longing for something in particular, in which Desire the Mother is either gratified, or disappointed. 2. A sudden Surprise. 3. The Sight and Abhorrence of an ugly and frightful Object. 4. The Pleasure of Looking on, and Contemplating, even for a long Time, a Picture, or whatsoever is delightful to the Fancy. 5. Fear, and Consternation, and great Apprehension of Dangers. 6. And lastly, An Excess of Anger, of Grief, or of Joy.[37]

This is a discipline that focuses on excesses. It matters little whether a desire is gratified or disappointed. And the indulgence in pleasurable sights or in the delights of Fancy can be just as damaging as the experience of horror. All sustained emotional or intellectual activities and any situation that might *impress* a woman in any way are to be avoided; pregnant women are 'to take great care, that their imagination be pure and clear, that their children may be well formed.'[38] Sheltered, yet limited by these rules of conduct, a woman's spiritual and physical life found its apt culminating expression in her literal 'confinement' during the ninth month of pregnancy. Little wonder, then, that pregnant women appear so rarely in early literature, except as a subject of comic or satiric control.

.... In most cultures, pregnant women are a marginalized population, dependent on others and frequently set apart from society. It should not surprise us then that they were subject to increased discursive and social control. And then, as now, it would have been hard for them to ignore medical advice, even when it had no experimental basis. It is difficult, then, to think of a more androcentric discourse, one more interested in the control of women's bodies and minds. One way of critically appraising this discourse might be to seek out female authors who were resistant to its dictates or who struggled to articulate a different sense of what it means to be pregnant. ...

.... Given the complex issues surrounding the employment of obstetric theory at the beginning of the nineteenth century, the simplest way of approaching a discussion of its role in *Frankenstein* is to analyze first its function in the novel, and then its significance in Mary Shelley's 1831 preface. As a cautionary obstetric tale that recounts how an individual who pays scant heed to either the biological or imaginative conditions of human reproduction gives birth to a monster, *Frankenstein* draws extensively on this discourse. Many readers have noted that Victor goes to great lengths, in Margaret Homans's words, 'to circumvent the normal channels of procreation.'[39] It should be added, however, that he also ignores the antenatal regimen proffered by midwifery handbooks. Irregular in diet, caring little for sleep as he engages in his 'midnight labours . . . with unrelaxed and breathless eagerness' (*F* 1818, p.36), taking in the dank and poisonous airs of graveyards, dissecting-rooms, and slaughterhouses, increasingly avoiding all contact with others because, as he says, 'Company was irksome to me' (*F* 1818, p.131), Victor shows by negative example what one should not do if one wants to create a healthy child. 'My cheek had grown pale with study, and my person had become emaciated with confinement,' Victor declares, as he unconsciously identifies himself with a woman in confinement (*F* 1818, p.36). 'Every night I was oppressed by a slow fever, and I became nervous to a most painful degree; my voice became broken, my trembling hands almost refused to accomplish their task; I became as timid as a love-sick girl, and alternate tremor and passionate ardour took the place of whole-some sensation and regulated ambition'[40] (*F* 1818, p. 38). In the 1831 edition, Victor's nervous condition increases his susceptibility to 'shocks' and 'frights': 'the fall of a leaf startled me, and I shunned my fellow-creatures as if I had been guilty of a crime.'[41] Yet, ever a pro-crastinator, Victor believes that this melancholy will be short-lived: 'exercise and amusement would soon drive away such symptoms; and I promised myself both of these, when my creation should be complete' (*F* 1818, p. 38). Any person with even a moderate know-ledge of contemporary obstetric theory might have told him that by then it would be too late.[42]

Shelley not only draws on obstetric recommendations regarding diet, sleep, exercise, and pure air, but also focuses explicitly on regu-lating the imagination in creation. Since monsters and monstrous markings constituted a document of the embryological conflicts caused by a mother's wanton or abnormal passion, Victor's monster can be read as the objectification of his own unregulated and contra-dictory desires. Victor Frankenstein draws our attention to this question when he attempts to recount the events that led up to the cre-ation of the monster. Interestingly, he links the onset of this passion with the onset of puberty, when, at the age of thirteen, while 'con-fined' to an inn, he discovered a volume of the works of Cornelius Agrippa [1486–1535, German scholar and alchemist]:

> When I would account to myself for the birth of that passion, which afterwards ruled my destiny, I find it arise, like a mountain river, from ignoble and almost forgotten sources; but, swelling as it proceeded, it became the torrent which, in its course, has swept away all my hopes and joys.
>
> Natural philosophy is the genius that has regulated my fate. (*F* 1818, p. 22)

Victor would claim that his imagination was 'regulated,' that natural philosophy was 'the genius,' or deity of generation and birth, govern-ing his actions. Yet his description of the 'birth' of this passion is of a 'swelling' that leads to an abortion, a 'torrent' sweeping away his 'hopes and joys.' Just as in Paré's account of how the image of St. John interposed itself between the conceiving mother and her proper object of desire, Cornelius Agrippa comes to stand between Victor and Elizabeth: 'she did not interest herself in the subject, and I was left by her to pursue my studies alone' (*F* 1818, p. 23). In his 'ardour' to create, a word emphasized repeatedly throughout the novel, Victor shows little concern for a regimen of the imagination. 'I had worked hard for nearly two years,' he confesses, 'for the sole purpose of infusing life into an inanimate body. For this I had deprived myself of rest and health. I had desired it with an ardour that far exceeded moderation' (*F* 1818, p. 39). Equally clear is his inability to turn his eyes away from this object of desire. 'I was . . . forced,' he says, 'to spend days and nights in vaults and charnel houses. *My attention was fixed* upon every object the most insupportable to the delicacy of the human feelings' (*F* 1818, p. 34, my emphasis). He describes how his 'eyeballs were starting from their sockets in attending to the details of my employment,' and yet how, with the strange mixture of 'loathing' and 'eagerness' so much a part of the discourse on pregnant women – he sought to bring his 'work near to a conclusion.' 'I could not tear my thoughts from my employment, loathsome in itself, but which had taken an irresistible hold of my imagination,' he declares. Obsessed with this single desire, he even begins to lose 'all soul or sensation' in his body. He becomes 'insensible to the charms of nature' and forgets 'those friends who were so many miles absent, and whom I had not seen for so long a time' (*F* 1818, p. 37).

Because Western culture has traditionally understood sexual reproduction as a mode of representation – the transmission of the image of the father to his children – obstetric theory, in its emphasis on and attempt to limit the powers of women's imaginations, implicitly constituted a theory of representation, dealing with the conception and production, the expression and revision, of living (rather than sculptural or literary) forms. *Frankenstein* distinctively appropriates and extends this discourse on bodily creation to all aspects of human knowledge, and especially to literary creation. Where [William] Wordsworth [1770–1850, English poet] speaks of the imagination as passing through an educative discipline that socializes it and leads it to see itself in the calm and enduring forms of external nature, Mary Shelley achieves a similar goal by applying the laws of biological creation to human thought, claiming (through Victor) that 'a human being in perfection ought always to preserve a calm and peaceful mind, and never to allow passion or a transitory desire to disturb his tranquillity. I do not think that the pursuit of knowledge is an exception to this rule. If the study to which you apply yourself has a tendency to weaken your affections, and to destroy your taste for those simple pleasures in which no alloy can possibly mix, then that study is certainly unlawful, that is to say, not befitting the human mind' (*F* 1818, p. 37). The link between literary activity and sexual reproduction among the male characters is quite clear. *Frankenstein* is ostensibly the published manuscript, 'the tale which I have recorded' (*F* 1818, p. 186), of the failed poet-cum-explorer Robert Walton. Because this narrative is composed over a nine-month period, between December 11th, the date of his first letter to his sister Margaret Saville, and September 12th of the following year, it can thus be seen as the monstrous product of his own isolation, of his inability to find what he claims he greatly needs at the very beginning of his journey – a friend with 'affection enough for me to endeavour to regulate my mind' (F 1818, p. 9). Victor also knows quite well that he is not only the creator of a monster, but also the author of 'the strangest tale that ever imagination formed' (F 1818, p. 179). Through the monster, we learn that he recorded in detail the events leading up to the creation of the monster. 'You minutely described in these papers every step you took in the progress of your work,' comments the monster (F 1818, p. 105). Further, when Victor discovers that Robert Walton is making notes concerning this history, 'he asked to see them, and then himself corrected and augmented them in many places; but principally in giving the life and spirit to the conversations he held with his enemy.' For readers who may have missed the analogy between Victor's endeavor to reanimate these dead conversations (that is, Robert Walton's already aborted record of them) and his earlier efforts at 'bestowing animation upon lifeless matter' (F 1818, p. 34), Mary Shelley adds the following comment. '"Since you have preserved my narration," said he, "I would not that a mutilated one should go down to posterity"' (F 1818, p. 179).

Mary Shelley's decision to write a novel in which creation takes the form of a birth myth should not be seen, then, as simply a form of personal therapy, a way of representing, as Moers first argued, maternal horror; nor is it simply an autobiographical depiction of the abstract notion of the self as monster. By drawing out the analogy between bodily and artistic reproduction, Shelley also found a way to argue for the importance of a domestic environment and a discipline of imagination in the creation of art. Agreeing with her mother that it was not women, but men who suffered most from excessive imaginations, from moral weakness, and from 'appetites . . . more depraved by unbridled indulgence and the fastidious contrivances of satiety,' Mary Shelley turns the discourse on the management of pregnant women back upon men, to argue that it is they who must learn to regulate their bodies and idealizing fantasies.[43] As William Veeder has suggested, Mary Shelley shares with nineteenth-century 'domestic' feminists the ideal of extending 'feminine virtues,' such as modesty, to men, in order to 'curb masculine excesses.'[44] By making Victor 'pregnant' with an idea, she is able to apply this complex discourse on the biological creation of monsters, one that had focused on female creation, to Romantic aesthetics. She was thus able to counter the prevailing idea of the poet, set forth by her husband in Alastor, as an isolated genius whose fixation on the ideal necessarily leads him into conflict with nature and society. By abrogating the laws of nature and reproduction, Victor destroys nature and himself.

I have so far restricted my comments to the manner in which Mary Shelley applied obstetric discourse to others, to the physical and psychic management of male Romantic conceptions. This still leaves the question of her own attitude toward this discourse unclear. To the extent that we read *Frankenstein* as an autobiography, we might see it as the expression of a contradictory sense of guilt on her own part and a reproach against her husband for his outright disregard of the emotional and physical needs of a pregnant woman. It is well known that the novel is closely bound up with Mary Shelley's intense anguish at the death of her first child, an unnamed daughter, born prematurely, who died shortly thereafter. It should be added, however, that it would have been difficult for any woman, having faced this painful loss, not to have also wondered whether her inability to carry this child for its full term was not caused by the physical, emotional, and financial strains that she had suffered from the moment she first eloped with Shelley. The death of this child, combined with the events surrounding the death of [one-year-old] Clara in 1818, not only suggest that her husband gave little thought to the needs of pregnant women and children, but also make it clear that Mary's insistence on the importance of a domestic environment for the delivery of healthy children was not for her a set of abstract principles, but was deeply rooted in personal experience.

In the preface of 1831, a more complex idea of the relationship between Mary Shelley's aesthetics and obstetric theory emerges. Though ostensibly written to provide biographical facts concerning the creation of *Frankenstein*, the preface is actually largely a fiction, explicitly addressing the question of literary authority. From the moment that Shelley, punning on the word 'dilate,' announces that she will answer the frequently asked question, 'How I, then a young girl, came to think of, and to dilate upon, so very hideous an idea?,' we are given notice that the preface will equate, as Marc Rubenstein has observed, conceiving or *'thinking of a story* . . . with producing a baby.'[45] Obstetric theory reappears as the language with which she explains, often using double-entendres [ambiguous phrasing], the birth of this monstrous text.[46] □

Despite their disparate approaches to *Frankenstein*, both Sterrenburg and Bewell manage to come up with persuasive, even plausible interpretations. However, a chapter on Shelley's use of demonic imagery would remain incomplete without at least mentioning a third possible reading that appears to transcend the two outlined above. Importantly, at the beginning of *In Frankenstein's Shadow*, Chris Baldick reminds us that the word *monster* etymologically derives from the Latin word *monstrare* and that hence 'a "monster" is something or someone to be shown'. As Baldick explains further, 'in a world created by a reasonable God, the freak or lunatic must have a purpose: to reveal visibly the results of vice, folly, and unreason, as a warning (Latin, *monere*: to warn) to erring humanity'.[47] Accordingly, monsters cease to terrify as soon as they have been shown to belong in the world, that is, as soon as they are proven to be 'natural'. As Alan Rauch suggests in 'The Monstrous Body of Knowledge in Mary Shelley's *Frankenstein*', first published in *Studies in Romanticism* in 1995, Frankenstein's monster remains ostracised, and violently repulses everyone who encounters him, simply because he represents 'a "species" of knowledge that has not been contextualised'.[48] Significantly, Frankenstein's monster makes numerous desperate efforts to integrate himself into society. According to Rauch, 'Shelley's monster, unlike Frankenstein, understands that there should be a way to situate himself in the discourse of relationships'; even in asking for a mate, he 'is merely trying to find a social context for his own existence'.[49] The Monster embodies the secret of a new scientific discovery that has to be explained to the wider public in order to be rendered less alien and frightening. This crucial task of the scientist is quite obviously being neglected by Victor, which is why everything begins to go so disastrously wrong in *Frankenstein*. Rauch writes:

■ Frankenstein opts to direct all of his science in the creation of a separate and distinct body of knowledge. The monster as the incarnation of that knowledge enters the world without introduction and without precedent.

New and unfamiliar knowledge, however 'good' or 'bad,' can only be troubling to those who are unacquainted with its origins. The scientist needs to recognize that all knowledge has a monstrous quality and the only way to introduce knowledge is to de-monstrate it, that is, to display it and in doing so, to demystify it.[50] □

In a chapter that seeks to explain the demonic imagery of *Frankenstein* by relating it to different aspects of Mary Shelley's real-life circumstances, it must seem ironic to conclude that ultimately the Creature's monstrosity may be defined by the very gratuity and utter meaninglessness of his creation. Rauch appears perfectly justified to call it the most frightening aspect of Victor's monster that he has come into the world without communal purpose, reference or value. Born 'useless', he remains 'useless'. Surely, considering the many deaths among his friends and family, it stands as one of the most perplexing features of *Frankenstein* that Victor consistently fails to make any practical use of his groundbreaking new discovery. 'It is indeed remarkable', so Rauch writes, 'that someone so obsessed by the force of life shows no insight into how to restore, lengthen, or preserve it'.[51]

CHAPTER SIX

'I'll Be Back!': Reproducing *Frankenstein*

EVER SINCE *Frankenstein*'s first publication, the Monster and the Mad Scientist have been conjured up in endlessly variegated configurations. Initially, the dualism of Victor and his creature was read as an allegory of British society which, throughout the nineteenth century, was caught up in a permanent state of crisis, riven by violent conflicts of interest between the rich and privileged on the one hand and the utterly disenfranchised on the other. However, as Lee Sterrenburg points out, even in the nineteenth century Shelley's metaphor was never confined to any one single historical event or socio-political circumstance; in fact, it soon turned out to be almost infinitely malleable, 'surfac[ing] during the revolutionary scares and reform agitation of the 1830s, the climax of Chartism in 1848–9, the enfranchisement of the working classes in the late 1860s, and the Irish troubles of the 1880s'.[1] Further testifying to its inexhaustible allegorical potential, the twentieth century saw the Frankenstein myth vanish almost completely from the socio-political realm only to witness its re-emergence in public debates on the ethical implications of technological and scientific progress. Be it human fertility treatment or the cloning of sheep, nuclear armament or the controversy surrounding genetically modified foods, even the most recent discussions of scientific breakthroughs cannot refrain from alluding at least in passing to the notorious prototype of Shelley's tragic overreacher. As a brief quotation from Ray Hammond's populist study, *The Modern Frankenstein: Fiction Becomes Fact*, first published in 1986, illustrates, such allusions still stand a fairly good chance of instilling irrational fear and disgust even in an otherwise discerning and perfectly enlightened readership. Couching his narrative in the insidiously suggestive mode of tabloid journalese, Hammond is evidently more interested in sensationalist scaremongering than the provision of any factual or genuinely useful information:

■ Modern Frankensteins are continuing the work Victor abandoned. One of the most spectacular recent acts of Frankensteinian science occurred on a summer's afternoon in December 1967 when Professor Christian Barnard cut into the chest wall of a patient called Louis Waskansky. He then sawed through his sternum and snipped out his failing heart. Within three hours, a new heart, one taken from the dead body of 25-year-old Denise Darvall, a car-crash victim, had been placed in Waskansky's chest and connected to the vital aorta and the pulmonary artery, and then, with microsurgery techniques ('the minuteness of the parts formed a great hindrance to my speed . . .' complained Victor in Chapter 4 of *Frankenstein*), to the lesser ducts. But, unexpectedly, the heart did not beat when it filled with blood – it remained 'dead'.

Christian Barnard and his assistants at the Groote Schuur Hospital in Cape Town, South Africa, then attached electrodes to the transplanted heart and, in true Frankensteinian tradition, delivered an electric shock to the lifeless muscle. The heart started to beat and continued to do so after the electrodes had been removed. Christian Barnard had turned fiction into fact.[2] □

Rather than tackling the impossible task of covering all cultural appropriations of *Frankenstein* in their totality, this final chapter concentrates on an exclusive investigation of different cinematic reproductions of the Frankenstein motif. The first three extracts reprinted here are taken from 'Production and Reproduction: The Case of *Frankenstein*', an essay by Paul O'Flinn first published as a journal article in *Literature and History* in 1983 and later included in Fred Botting's casebook collection of criticism on Shelley's novel. Inspired by Marxist techniques of literary analysis, the essay concentrates on the socio-political conditions and economic interests that motivate particular forms or strategies of reproduction. According to O'Flinn, a work of literature comes to life in the history of its reception, with its basic scenario endlessly reproduced by generations of readers who assess and renegotiate the work's relevance out of the specificity of their own cultural context. Most people in the western world would claim they 'know' the story of Frankenstein and his unfortunate creation, but how many have actually read Shelley's novel? Rather than firmly anchored in the alleged authenticity of an original text, so O'Flinn argues, the Frankenstein myth comprises an accumulative web of reproductions and appropriations that *per se* always already represent readings of other readings. Each reading becomes a text in its own right, thus instigating a secondary process of production that translates the original work into an infinite plurality of often mutually incompatible versions. O'Flinn asserts that *Frankenstein*'s enduring popularity mainly ensues from this exuberant diversification of Shelley's original, its resourceful ambivalence and overabundance of meaningful and, more importantly perhaps, *potentially* meaningful structures of signification. O'Flinn writes:

■ Mary Shelley's Gothic novel *Frankenstein* was published anonymously in 1818. In the same year, a couple of other novels – [Thomas] Peacock's *Nightmare Abbey* and Jane Austen's *Northanger Abbey* – appeared and their derisive use of Gothic conventions suggested that the form, fashionable for fifty years, was sliding into decline and disrepute. There seemed good reason to suppose that *Frankenstein*, an adolescent's first effort at fiction, would fade from view before its print-run was sold out. Yet several generations later Mary Shelley's monster, having resisted his creator's attempts to eliminate him in the book, is able to reproduce himself with the variety and fertility that Frankenstein had feared. Apart from steady sales in Penguin, Everyman and OUP editions, there have been over a hundred film adaptations and there have been the Charles Addams cartoons in the *New Yorker*; Frankie Stein blunders about in the pages of *Whoopee* and *Monster Fun* comics, and approximate versions of the monster glare out from chewing gum wrappers and crisp bags. In the USA he forged a chain of restaurants; in South Africa in 1955 the work was banned as indecent and objectionable.[3]

None of these facts are new and some of them are obvious to anyone walking into a newsagent's with one eye open. They are worth setting out briefly here because *Frankenstein* seems to me to be a case where some recent debates in critical theory about cultural production and reproduction might usefully be centred, a work whose history can be used to test the claims that theory makes.[4] That history demonstrates clearly the futility of a search for the 'real', 'true' meaning of a work. There is no such thing as *Frankenstein*, there are only *Frankensteins*, as the text is ceaselessly rewritten, reproduced, refilmed and redesigned. The fact that many people call the monster Frankenstein and thus confuse the pair betrays the extent of that restructuring. What I would like to offer is neither a naive deconstructionist delight at the endless plurality of meanings the text has been able to afford nor a gesture of cultural despair at the failure of the Philistines to read the original and get it right. Instead I'd like to argue that at its moment of production *Frankenstein*, in an oblique way, was in touch with central tensions and contradictions in industrial society and only by seeing it in those terms can the prodigious efforts made over the last century and a half to alter and realign the work and its meanings be understood – a work that lacked that touch and that address could safely be left, as Marx said in another context, to the gnawing criticism of the mice.

Frankenstein is a particularly good example of three of the major ways in which alteration and realignment of this sort happens: firstly, through the operations of criticism; secondly, as a function of the shift from one medium to another; and thirdly as a result of the unfolding of history itself. The operations of criticism on this text are at present more vigorous than usual. When I was a student twenty years ago I picked up the *Pelican Guide to English Literature* to find the novel more or less wiped out in a direly condescending half-sentence as 'one of those second-rate works, written under the influence of more distinguished minds, that sometimes display in conveniently simple form the pre-occupations of a coterie.'[5] *Frankenstein* may have been on TV but it wasn't on the syllabus. A generation and a lot of feminist criticism later and Mary Shelley is no longer a kind of half-witted secretary to Byron and Shelley but a woman writer whose text articulates and has been convincingly shown to articulate elements of woman's experience of patriarchy, the family and the trauma of giving birth.[6] □

After this brief introduction O'Flinn's essay continues with a detailed account of the specific socio-historical context in which *Frankenstein* was written. In particular, O'Flinn relates Shelley's novel to the Luddite uprisings of the 1810s (so called after Ned Ludd, an eighteenth-century Leicestershire workman) when English textile workers, horrified at the rapidly increasing commodification of their labour, mutinied and began to destroy the newly introduced industrial machinery that threatened to put a substantial fraction of their community out of work, thus condemning them to a life in misery and utter destitution. O'Flinn suggests, however, that a reader's knowledge of this historical framework of *Frankenstein*'s original composition, although no doubt pertinent and in many respects even indispensable, may ultimately distract him or her from the novel's full repertoire of possible meanings. Moving on to an interpretation of two classic screen versions of *Frankenstein*, O'Flinn asserts that the conditions facilitating the reception or creative reproduction of a cultural artefact are at least as important as the conditions that surround its original production. According to O'Flinn's comparative analysis of James Whale and Terence Fisher's films in the fourth and fifth sections of his essay, *Frankenstein* 'meant certain things in 1818 but meant and could be made to mean different things in 1931 and 1957, irrespective of authorial "intention"'.[7] O'Flinn explains:

■ there seem to me to be at least three different types of shift that need to be borne in mind when looking at the gap between Mary Shelley's book and twentieth-century films; those shifts concern medium, audience and content. In the case of *Frankenstein*, the shift of medium is particularly important because it must inevitably obliterate and replace what is central to the novel's meaning and structure – namely the patterned movement through three narrators as the reader is taken by way of Walton's letters into Frankenstein's tale and on to the monster's autobiography before backing out through Frankenstein's conclusions to be left with Walton's last notes. That process cannot be filmed and so the very medium demands changes even before politics and ideology come into play.

The turning of novel into film also involves a change in the nature of the work's audience. David Punter has convincingly argued that the Gothic novel is pre-eminently a middle-class form in terms of authors and values as well as readership.[8] The films in question are middle-class in none of these senses, produced as they are by large businesses in search of mass audiences. That different site of production and area of distribution will again bear down on the work, pulling, stretching and clipping it to fit new needs and priorities.

Where this pulling, stretching and clipping appears most obviously is in the alterations in the third category mentioned earlier, namely the work's content, and I'd like to detail some of those in a moment. What needs emphasizing here is that the radical change in the class nature of producer and audience hacks away at the content of the original, so that the book is reduced to no more than an approximate skeleton, fleshed out in entirely and deliberately new ways. This makes it quite different from, for example, a BBC serial of a Jane Austen [1775–1817, English novelist] novel, where some attempt is made at a reasonably faithful reproduction of the text. It is therefore a traditional critical strategy in reviewing such serials to ask questions about how 'true' to the text, how 'accurate', is the portrayal of, say, Fitzwilliam Darcy or Emma Woodhouse [characters in novels by Jane Austen]. It is the failure to see this difference that makes one reviewer's querulous response to the 1931 film quite laughably beside the point :

> Mary Shelley's story has artistic interest as an essay in German horrific romanticism and I think that if *Frankenstein* had been produced by a historically-minded German the result would have been much more interesting . . . What is the object of taking Mary Shelley's story and then removing the whole point of it before starting to make the picture?[9]

The object, of course, is precisely to remove the whole point of it – and substitute other ones.

Other ones are necessary for several reasons – not least because there are no immutable fears in human nature to which horror stories always speak in the same terms. There is not, for all David Punter's strenuous arguing, 'some inner social and cultural dynamic which makes it necessary for those images to be kept alive';[10] rather, those images need to be repeatedly broken up and reconstituted if they are to continue to touch people, which is one of the reasons why horror films that are thirty or forty years old can often seem simply boring or preposterous to a later audience.

The Universal movie was calculated quite precisely to touch the audiences of 1931. At that time Universal was not one of the front-rank Hollywood studios; its rather cautious and unimaginative policies had left it some distance adrift of the giants of the industry at the end of the 1920s, namely Famous Players, Loews and First National.[11] But a way out of the second rank seemed to offer itself with the huge box office success of Universal's *Dracula*, starring Bela Lugosi [1882–1956, Hungarian actor], which opened in February 1931 and soon grossed half a million dollars. In April Universal bought the rights of Peggy Webling's *Frankenstein: An Adventure in the Macabre*. The play had run in London in 1930 and its title already suggests a tilting of the work away from Mary Shelley's complex scientific and political statement towards those conventional terror terms for which *Dracula* had indicated a market. *Frankenstein*, filmed in August and September 1931, was an even bigger profit-maker than *Dracula*. Costing a quarter of a million dollars to make, it eventually earned Universal twelve million dollars, was voted one of the films of 1931 by the *New York Times* and confirmed a fashion for horror movies that was soon to include Paramount's *Dr. Jekyll and Mr. Hyde* and Universal's *The Murders in the Rue Morgue*.

In looking at the content of this movie I'd like to confine my comments to those three areas where the shifts from the novel seem to me most important in terms of the ideological and political re-jigging that they betray; those areas are the Walton story, the nature of the monster and the ending.

The point about the Walton story is a simple one: it's gone. It's not there in the immediate source of the movie, namely Peggy Webling's play, where its disappearance is partly prompted by the need to cram a novel into the average duration of a play. But the fact is that to take away half of Mary Shelley's statement is to change it . . . the function of the Walton story within the text's meaning is to offer a different model of scientific and technological progress, one in which human survival is insured as long as that progress is under firm and effective popular control. Remove that narrative and the work collapses into Frankenstein's experience alone which can then be presented as a universal model, replete with the sort of reactionary moralizing about the dangers of meddling with the unknown and the delights of tranquillity which are implicit in that tale and made explicit at more than one point. The film can then more easily slide towards a wider statement about the perils of any kind of progress and change, feeding fears of the unknown that change brings and reinforcing those conservative values that stand in its way.

On the question of the nature of the monster, the most important revision here concerns the creature's brain. The film adds a new episode in which an extra character called Fritz, Frankenstein's assistant, is sent to a laboratory to steal a brain for the monster. In that laboratory are two such pickled organs, in large jars boldly labelled NORMAL BRAIN and ABNORMAL BRAIN. Before the theft, the audience hears an anatomy lecture from Professor Waldman in which he draws attention to various features of the normal brain, 'the most perfect specimen', and contrasts them with the abnormal brain whose defects drive its owner to a life of 'brutality, of violence and murder' because of 'degenerate characteristics'. Its original owner was, in fact, 'a criminal'. The lecture over, Fritz creeps in, grabs the normal brain and then lets it slip so that jar and contents are smashed on the floor. He is forced to take the abnormal brain instead.

The implications for the monster and his story are immense. A central part of Mary Shelley's thesis is to insist that the monster's eventual life of violence and revenge is the direct product of his social circumstances. The monster summarizes his own life in terms that the text endorses: 'Every where I see bliss, from which I alone am irrevocably excluded. I was benevolent and good; misery made me a fiend. Make me happy, and I shall again be virtuous' (*F* 1818, pp. 77–78). The film deletes this reading of the story through its insistence that the monster's behaviour is not a reaction to its experience but biologically determined, a result of nature, not nurture.

Most commentators on the film are bewildered by this change, one not found in Peggy Webling's play. It has been variously dismissed as an 'absurd and unnecessary sequence . . . a cumbersome attempt at establishing motivation', 'ridiculous' and 'the main weakness'.[12] If seen from Mary Shelley's stance, these comments are true; seen in terms of the film's ideological project, they miss the point. At one level in the text, Mary Shelley was concerned to suggest, in the imaginative terms of fiction, that Luddite violence was not the result of some brute characteristics of the nascent English working class but an understandable response to intolerable treatment. The Universal film, consciously or unconsciously, destroys the grounds for such a way of seeing with its radical political implications and instead sees violence as rooted in personal deficiencies, to be viewed with horror and to be labelled, literally, ABNORMAL and so sub-human. Bashing the monster ceases to be the problem but becomes instead the only way that the problem can be met and solved. So it is that Mary Shelley is stood on her head and *Frankenstein* is forced to produce new meanings for 1931.

This upending of Mary Shelley's book and its meaning explains two other profound changes in the monster's presentation that the film introduces. In the text, the monster spends Chapters 11 to 16 describing his life – a huge speech that is placed right in the centre of the novel and fills over twenty per cent of its pages. In the film the monster can't speak. Again, in the novel, the monster saves a child from drowning in Chapter 16; in the film, the monster drowns a child. Both reversals are of a piece with the Abnormal Brain scene and flow from it in that both deliberately seek to suppress audience sympathy for the monster. (Hence, when in the 1935 sequel *Bride of Frankenstein* the monster did speak, Boris Karloff [pseudonym of William Henry Pratt, 1887–1969, English-Canadian actor] protested that it made him seem 'more human' so that in the second sequel *Son of Frankenstein* in 1939 he is again wordless.) The changes sharpen a re-focusing which is itself part of the shift from novel to film: reading the book, we hear the monster at eloquent length but we don't see him except vaguely, in imagination, and so reader sympathy is easily evoked; watching the film, we hear nothing from him but instead we see a shambling goon with a forehead like a brick wall and a bolt through his neck, and so audience revulsion is promptly generated. Thus the novel makes him human while the film makes him sub-human, so that in the novel his saving of the drowning child is predictable while equally predictable is his drowning of the child in the film.

The way the film ends flows directly from the drowning of the child and so brings me to the third and last piece of ideological re-structuring in the Universal movie that I'd like to look at. In the novel, Frankenstein dies in his pursuit of the monster across the icy Arctic while the latter, in the final sentence, is 'borne away by the waves, and lost in darkness and distance.' In the film, the drowning of the child provokes the villagers to pursue the brute and trap it in an old windmill which is then burnt down; a brief, single-shot coda shows a recovered Frankenstein happily reunited with his fiancée Elizabeth. The politics of the mill-burning scene are overt: as the blaze engulfs the blades they form a gigantic fiery cross that deliberately suggests the Ku Klux Klan [secret organisation of white Southerners formed after the U.S. Civil War to fight Black emancipation and Northern domination], virulently active at the time, and so, as Tropp crudely puts it, 'points up the mob violence that does the monster in'.[13] Similarly, another observer sees the film ending 'with what [James] Whale [1896–1957, English director and set designer] called "the pagan sport of a mountain man-hunt"; at the finale, the film's sympathies are with the monster rather than with the lynch mob.'[14]

These may have been Whale's intentions but there is a wide gap between director's aims and the movie as distributed. In Whale's original version, in the drowning scene, the girl dies because the monster innocently tries to make her float on the water like the flowers they are playing with and then searches frantically for her when she sinks. But these moments were chopped from the print of the film put out for general release: there we simply see the monster reaching out towards the girl and then cut to a grief-stricken father carrying her corpse. Child rape and murder are the obvious assumptions, so that the immediate response of the community in organizing itself to eliminate the savage culprit comes across as a kind of ritual cleansing of that community, the prompt removal of an inhuman threat to civilized life which is comfortably justifiable within routine populist politics and at the same time provides the firm basis for and so receives its sanction from the conventionally romantic final scene of hero and heroine at last happy and free from danger. If Mary Shelley's monster alludes indirectly to working-class insurrection, one answer to that canvassed in the 1930s was counter-revolutionary mob violence.

Political readings of the film tend to see it either in simple reflectionist terms (Tropp, for example, regards the monster as 'a creature of the '30s shaped by shadowy forces beyond its control, wandering the countryside like some disfigured veteran or hideous tramp'[15] while another finds 'a world in which manipulations of the stock-market had recoiled on the manipulators; in which human creatures seemed to be abandoned by those who had called them into being and those who might have been thought responsible for their welfare'[16]) or as escapist – 'Large sections of the public, having difficulty in dealing with the Depression [the worldwide economic depression of the early 1930s which resulted in mass unemployment], were glad to spend some time in the company of a monster that could more easily be defeated.'[17] Readings of that sort can only be more or a lot less inspired speculation. I'd prefer to look within the film and see it as a *practice*, as an intervention in its world rather than just a picture of it or a retreat from it, a practice whose extent is marked out by the reconstruction of the text that I have indicated. Certainly it was released in the depths of the Depression, depths which can shock even when seen from Thatcherite Britain. The value of manufactured goods and services produced in the USA in 1929 had stood at 81 billion dollars and output at 119 (1923 = 100); as the film criss-crossed the nation in 1932, the value of goods and services had more than halved to 40 billion dollars and output was down to 64. There were 14 million unemployed. How the film reflects that catastrophe or seeks to escape from it is less important than what it says to it. . . . it is historically at precisely such moments of crisis that Frankenstein's monster tends to be summoned by ideology and have its arm brutally twisted till it blurts out the statements that ideology demands. What Universal's *Frankenstein* seeks to say specifically to the mass audience at whom it is aimed concerns above all mass activity in times of crisis: where that activity might be assertive and democratic and beneficial (the Walton story), it is removed and concealed; where it is violent and insurrectionary (the monster's story), it is systematically denigrated; and where it is traditional and reactionary (the mill-burning), it is ambiguously endorsed. The extent to which the film powerfully articulates those familiar stances of the dominant ideology in the 1930s is measured by its box-office success.[18] □

Concentrating on an analysis of *The Curse of Frankenstein*, Terence Fisher's first Frankenstein picture for Hammer Films, the fifth part of O'Flinn's essay reads as follows:

■ The fact that Frankenstein's monster is most urgently hailed at times of crisis perhaps accounts for the fact that, with the jokey exception of Universal's *Abbott and Costello Meet Frankenstein* in 1948, the English-speaking movie industry left the brute alone between 1945 (Universal's *House of Dracula*) and 1957 (Hammer's *The Curse of Frankenstein*) as the long post-war boom slowly built up. The Hammer film marked the end of the lengthiest break in Frankenstein pictures in the past fifty years and was the first attempt by a British studio to reproduce the story.

The relationships between, say, *Roderick Random* [novel by the Scottish writer Tobias Smollett (1721–1771), first published in 1748] and early capitalism are complex and highly mediated. The links between Hammer Films and late capitalism are less obscure; the executive producer of *The Curse of Frankenstein*, Michael Carreras, whose family founded Hammer Film Productions in 1947 and have run it for three generations, has put it simply enough: 'The best film is the one that makes money. Our job is to entertain and promote something that is really exploitable. Exploitation is the thing.'[19] Hammer's policy proceeded directly from this philosophy and has been well analyzed by David Pirie.[20] It specialized in stories that were already 'pre-sold' to the public by tradition or by radio or television so that public recognition of the product was not a problem – hence early films like *P.C. 49, The Man in Black, Robin Hood* and so on. At the same time, it sought for itself an area of the market left untouched by the dimpled complacencies of Rank and Ealing Studios. These two strands of policy combined to push it towards horror films, first with *The Quatermass Experiment* in 1955, a spin-off from the 1953 BBC serial *Quatermass*. The success of both serial and film prompted Hammer to explore the genre further, and the filming of *The Curse of Frankenstein* began in November 1956.

The result was a cultural phenomenon whose scale and importance has certainly been noted but whose significance has not really been investigated. *The Curse of Frankenstein* is, it has been claimed, 'the biggest grossing film in the history of the British cinema in relation to cost.'[21] When it opened in the West End in May 1957 it at once started breaking box-office records and it did the same across the USA that summer. One consequence was that the connections that Hammer had with the American market were rapidly reinforced: in September, for example, Columbia Pictures put Hammer under contract to make three films a year and by 1968 Hammer found itself a recipient of the Queen's Award to Industry after three years in which they had brought a total of £4.5 million in dollars into Britain – this at a time, of course, when most of the rest of the British film industry was in a state of vigorous collapse. In the decade and a half after the success of *The Curse of Frankenstein* Hammer made six sequels, all starring Peter Cushing [English actor, born in 1913] as the eponymous hero.

In looking at the first of this series, it's Cushing and the part he plays that I'd like to focus on, because it is there that the efforts of ideology in putting the myth to work for fresh purposes are most strenuous. At other points – the dropping of the Walton framework, for example – the film simply follows previous practices whose implications have been argued already. It is in the reconstruction of the protagonist that the Hammer film is distinctive, and here the [English] director Terence Fisher [1904–1980] was not encumbered by any sense of the original which indeed he had not read. Thus, although Fisher's script . . . was based on the novel, the way was clear for an alignment of the material that was not inhibited by considerations of accuracy, of being 'faithful to the text', but which was free to rework the elements towards those broad Hammer policies of exploitation and money-making.

The singularity of Cushing's role has been spotted by several observers without much attempt being made to see why this should be so.[22] The fact that the film is centred on creator rather than monster in this version is signposted by the way that Boris Karloff, the monster in the Universal movie, at once became a star while Colin Clive [pseudonym of Clive Greig, 1898–1937, British actor], who was Frankenstein, remained obscure; conversely, in the Hammer picture, it was Peter Cushing who featured in five of the six sequels whereas Christopher Lee [English actor, born in 1922] never took the part of the monster again.

Central to the specificity of Cushing's part is the way he makes Frankenstein unambiguously the villain of the story and this shift is produced by at least three major changes in his presentation. First and most obviously there are the crimes he commits which have no basis in the text or in previous film versions: to get a brain for his creature he murders a colleague, Professor Bernstein, and later on he sets up the killing of his servant Justine to conceal the fact that he has got her pregnant from his fiancée Elizabeth. Secondly there is a marked class mutation that takes a tendency that is apparent in earlier versions several stages further. Mary Shelley's hero is a student, the son of a magistrate; in the Universal movie he becomes the son of a baron; in the Hammer film for the first time he himself is styled Baron Frankenstein and is given decadent aristocratic trappings to go with his title – he becomes, in Pirie's eyes, 'a dandy'. And then thirdly there is the change in age: Mary Shelley's youthful student is turned into Peter Cushing's middle-aged professor. The relevance of that emerges if we remember that seventy per cent of the audience for horror movies in the 1950s were aged twelve to twenty-five, a fact of which the commercially alert Hammer were well aware. A film pitched largely at adolescents could evoke hostility towards the protagonist more easily by transforming him from one of their own kind into a standard adult authority figure.

In short, the ambiguity of earlier readings of the story is removed by these revisions and we are given a Frankenstein to hate – a Frankenstein who, as Martin Tropp points out, is the real monster, a villain who ends the film facing the guillotine and straightforwardly enacting Terence Fisher's own way of seeing: 'If my films reflect my own personal view of the world . . . it is in their showing of the ultimate victory of good over evil, in which I do believe.'[23] Peter Cushing's Baron Frankenstein is a lethal nutter, an archetypal mad scientist.

It is here that the break with the Universal version is sharpest. James Whale had worked specifically to avoid a mad scientist reading of the story and had written to actor Colin Clive insisting that Frankenstein is 'an intensely sane person . . . a sane and lovable person'.[24] And the one moment in Whale's film when this analysis wavers – namely Frankenstein's megalomaniac cry of 'Now I know what it feels like to be God' as his creature moves for the first time – was chopped by pious censors before anybody else got to see it.

What I'd like to argue is that close to the root of this transformation in the reading and reproduction of *Frankenstein* is a shift in the structure of fears within the dominant ideology. The possibility of working-class insurrection that had concerned Mary Shelley and terrified Universal was no longer a prime source of anxiety in 1956. To take one crude statistical indicator of working-class discontent: the number of working days lost or, rather, won in strikes in Britain in the 1940s and 1950s was the lowest in the twentieth century. But on the other hand the development of atomic and hydrogen bombs created a new and dire nightmare of the risk of world destruction flowing from a single, deranged individual – a cultural neurosis that the James Bond novels [by Ian Fleming, 1908–1964, English author of spy novels] and films, for instance, were to run and run again through the 1960s and beyond. To imagine a universal catastrophe initiated by one mad scientist was a fear that was simply unavailable to Mary Shelley granted the level of scientific capacities in 1818; indeed, the very word 'scientist' was not coined until 1834. *The Curse of Frankenstein*, by contrast, was made at a time when the processes of science seemed to threaten human survival. As David Pirie points out, six months before filming began, a headline in *The Times* on 21 May 1956 had read: 'Giant H-Bomb Dropped, Luminosity More Than 500 Suns.' Equally importantly, we need to remember events in the very week that filming began. The cameras turned for the first time on 19 November; two days earlier, the first Hungarian refugees had arrived in Britain driven out by the Russian tanks that smashed their revolution; a fortnight earlier, on 5 November, Anglo-French airborne troops had landed at Port Said at the depths of the fiasco of the Suez invasion.

The Curse of Frankenstein was therefore made at a unique and over-determined conjuncture in world history when, for the first time, both the technology and the crises existed to threaten the very survival of the planet. Once again Mary Shelley's novel was pulled off the shelf and ransacked for the terms of articulate cultural hysteria. In one sense, of course, the movie represents a flight from the politics of [Anthony] Eden [1897–1977, Conservative British prime minister (1955–1957)] and the Kremlin [Moscow residence of the Soviet government] into a spot of escapist Gothic knockabout; but to see it and then dismiss it as no more is to wipe out a series of factors including Fisher's ideology, Hammer's business sense, American investment and contemporary critical responses,[25] all of which mark out the seriousness of the project at one level. To put it baldly, at a time of genuine and multi-layered public fears, *The Curse of Frankenstein* addressed itself to a predominantly young audience and locates the source of anxiety in a deranged individual, focuses it down to the point where its basis is seen as one man's psychological problem. Wider systematic and social readings and other possibilities (the Walton story for one) are repressed as a structure whose values go unquestioned is presented as threatened by a loony rather than as being itself at the root of instability. Responsibility for imminent catastrophe is limited to a single intellectual standing outside both ordinary lives and the political establishment, so that the film can flow from and then feed back into a populist politics and a scrubby anti-intellectualism frustrated by its own impotence. *The Curse of Frankenstein* is the curse of blocked democracy looking for a scapegoat and being sidetracked from an analysis.[26] □

A kind of complementary update of O'Flinn's piece is represented by Thomas Frentz and Janice Rushing's co-authored essay, 'The Frankenstein Myth in Contemporary Cinema'. First published in 1994, this offers an insightful reading of three variations on the Frankenstein theme that came into our cinemas in the 1980s. Both individually and in combination, Ridley Scott's *Blade Runner* (1982), James Cameron's *The Terminator* (1984) and Sylvester Stallone's *Rocky IV* (1985) are read as symptomatic twentieth-century reproductions of Shelley's fable. According to Frentz and Rushing, the story lines and screen imagery of these three movies aptly encapsulate the quandaries of late-capitalist American consumer society as well as the general state of paranoia western society found itself in during the last decade before the end of the Cold War in 1989. Frentz and Rushing's approach differs from O'Flinn's in that it is inspired by Jungian psychology rather than the materialist axioms of Marxian historicism. Also, unlike O'Flinn, they are concerned not so much with what cultural recipients are able to 'know' and recognise, but with what they fail or refuse to acknowledge, that is, their cultural repressed or what Frentz and Rushing designate as mainstream culture's *doppelgänger* or 'shadow'. Like *Frankenstein*, the three films problematise the human 'love-hate relationship with the tools we have made',[27] the schizophrenic double bind of our simultaneous faith in and fear of technological progress. Against this background, the enduring topicality of the Frankenstein myth appears indicative of the persistent paranoia that not only informs but fuels contemporary western culture. As Rushing and Frentz explain, the Frankenstein myth 'expresses a process of increasing mechanization of the human and humanization of the machine, a process moving toward an ultimate end in which the machine is god and the human is reduced either to slavery or obsolescence'.[28] Guided by this central leitmotif of division and identification between humanity and its artificial offspring, Rushing and Frentz interpret the films as follows:

■ *Rocky IV.*[29] Beneath its ideological transparencies, *Rocky IV* suggests that people have extended themselves through and become dependent upon their tools to act for them and that technology is thus making over the human agent . . . in its own image, systematically restructuring its scene and emptying it of moral purpose. Although the robot in *Rocky IV* is not the main character, the film does chart the early stages of human obsolescence through increasing mechanization. As *Rocky IV* suggests, technology accomplishes the transformation of humans quite differently in the United States than it does in Russia. In America, technology is primarily for 'recreative' pleasure, and it already dominates the scene in the form of televisions, fast automobiles, cordless telephones, motorized kiddie cars, and household robots. Here, citizens experience the impact of technology from the outside in. Paulie, for example, is everyone's Ugly American. Soft, greedy, manipulative, and whiny, he typifies the consequences of recreational technology; unable to survive without his comics and his television, he grows fat on junk food which his 'female' robot . . . retrieves for him. 'She,' on the other hand, progressively takes on more human (i.e., stereotypically feminine) qualities as Paulie grows even more sedimented than he was. She learns to talk to him in terms of endearment, and Paulie explains to an astonished Creed, 'That's my girl. . . . She loves me.' As Paulie leaves for Russia, she nags him about taking his toothbrush. He responds with characteristic crudeness, 'When I get back, I'm gonna have her wires tied.'

Ever since Rocky won a moral victory in his Creed fight, he has walked a thin line in the sequels between moral integrity and Paulie's decadence, descending further into the temptations of wealth in each film, and requiring the rigors of spartan retraining for each redemption. By *Rocky IV*, his living situation is not only blatantly ostentatious but also obviously mechanized, and he is once again losing his edge. All of his interactions with his son emphasize a technologized scene: As Rocky arrives home early in the film, Rocky Jr. greets him through the lens of a video camera, warning him (with a bit too obvious childlike wisdom), 'Don't go too fast or you'll get out of focus.' As Rocky washes his Ferrari, the kid washes Paulie's robot, and their conversation is obscured by a radio turned up too loud. And when Rocky prepares to leave for Russia and tucks Junior in bed, father reminds son, 'Don't forget to feed your robot.' Even Adrian, previously the rock of good sense who protested the gadgetry the *nouveau riche* lifestyle brought her family, has succumbed and, by this fourth film, is patently dull and mechanical. When Rocky tells her he is going to Russia to fight Drago, she is confused. 'And for that [Rocky's choice to fight Drago], you're willing to lose everything?' she asks, indicating the comforts of home.

As another victim of recreational technology, Apollo Creed is a sadder case than Paulie or Adrian, for he has genuine talent. But his talent has been diluted by a different variant of recreational technology – the televised spectacle, the pseudo-event, the electric circus – which, although good for the image, extracts its pound of flesh from the person as moral agent.[30] By flattering appearance, pseudo-events break down human substance, hollow out the soul, and replace it with nothing but style. The opening act to Creed's exhibition match with Drago, with James Brown singing a telling 'Living in America,' is a carnival so overproduced and banal that Rocky and Adrian wince in recognition. It is a fitting scenic prelude for the tragedy to come; when empty posturing meets mechanized physical perfection, the outcome is quick, brutal, and final. Creed's death reveals the ultimate consequence for the human agent evacuated by technological recreation.

While American recreational technology erodes from the outside in, leaving purged vessels of stylized veneer, Russian technology 're-creates' the human agent from the inside out, perfecting nascent physical potential through blood doping [and] steroid ingestion . . . As Drago's publicist explains to the press: 'It's a matter of science, evolution, isn't it, gentlemen? Drago is the most perfectly trained athlete – ever . . . It's physically impossible for this little man [Rocky] to win. Drago is a look at the future.' David Edelstein writes of Drago: '. . . Rising up out of a pit for an exhibition match with Apollo Creed . . . he's like a socialist-realist Frankenstein's monster.'[31] Wearing a Nazi-like military uniform, backlighted, and shot from low angles through a smoky mist, Drago appears in the beginning of both fight scenes more as a futuristic *fascist* Frankenstein. Though Soviet technology leaves the agent cruel and 'hard,' rather than harmless and 'soft,' the cost of such physical consummation is the anesthetizing of the human spirit: feelings, creativity, compassion, self-awareness. Paulie may be a mushroom and Apollo Creed an image, but Drago is an automaton: dull, efficient, and relentless. His comments always resemble the vocalized print-out of a computer. 'You will lose,' he tells Creed before their fight. Looking down at a dying Creed, Drago remarks matter-of-factly, 'If he dies, he dies . . . I cannot be defeated. I defeat all men,' he intones after Creed's destruction. 'I must break you,' he tells Rocky moments before their own encounter. As the two slap gloves together in the obligatory prefight handshake, a metal clink resounds from Drago's fist; he is the mechanized 'dragon' of Russian recreational technology.

The refusal of the dreaming individual, or culture, to look at its own shadow is generally represented in the Frankenstein myth by humans who will not see the consequences of what they have created.[32] The prototype for this motif occurs in Shelley's novel when Victor Frankenstein is immediately repulsed as his handiwork opens his eyes. Frankenstein refuses to look at his creation, leaves the laboratory, and tries to forget him by going to sleep. 'Technology, then, allows us to ignore our own works. It is *license to forget*.'[33] Until the end of *Rocky IV*, all the characters (except Rocky, on occasion) similarly fail to notice the extent to which technology has drained them. Certainly, Paulie does not reflect on his own degeneracy. With his totally impassive face, it is not apparent that Drago sees anything clearly, much less that his own technocratic make-over has made him vulnerable by robbing him of 'heart.' And from the moment Creed first catches a glimpse of Drago (appropriately, as a televised image), he is so obsessed with planning his comeback that he pays no attention to Drago's re-created strength. When Rocky warns his aging friend, 'You don't want to hear this, but maybe the show is over,' Apollo protests vehemently. Prancing arrogantly in the prefight spectacle, and unaware of the irony, he says to himself, 'God, I feel born again!' as he enters into his own demise.

Blade Runner. Within the futuristic time frame of *Blade Runner* ([set in] 2019), technological agency has extended itself further toward its entelechial end [toward a full realisation of its potential].[34] In *Rocky IV*, the products of technical reason could significantly alter the human being, from without and within, but they still operated on the agent. In *Blade Runner*, agency as genetic engineering uses the DNA molecule to create synthetic agents (replicants) 'from scratch.' While it is true that these replicants share genetic substance with their human makers, their very consubstantiality makes them, paradoxically, more divided from each other. For, like an amoeba that replicates itself by splitting its cellular substance in two, the human agent has projected itself outward in space (in this film, the replicants, are placed *literally* in 'off-world' space) and now faces an *alter ego*: separate, nearly complete, and at the borderline of autonomy.

In *Blade Runner*, the question of who is in control, the humans or their agencies, has arrived at a perilous point. 'Commerce is our goal here at Tyrell,' the film's futuristic Dr. Frankenstein tells bounty hunter Rick Deckard, and Eldon Tyrell has certainly controlled the androids' genes to enhance their fitness as tools; the female 'pleasure models' are more beautiful, the combat officers more strategically intelligent, and the assassins stronger than their human counterparts. Tyrell is aware, however, that technical efficiency only provides freedom for other activities when concern is eliminated about malfunctions. Thus, he has cannily built a safeguard into his Nexus 6 series: they are not genetically programmed for emotion (presumably, the catalyst for the development of free will), and, just in case they do begin to generate emotion spontaneously, they are preprogrammed to 'die' after four years.

Nevertheless, human control is more elusive than Tyrell would like to admit; technology's vastly expanded influence is evident in the way it has restructured the scene in its own image. Technology is no longer *in* the scene; it *is* the scene. 'Nature' has virtually disappeared, and the line between outside and indoors seems insignificant, as light rarely penetrates the dark, smoky haze of either. . . . Michael Sragow writes, 'The city itself becomes a metaphor for a society that's lost organic growth. . . . The metropolis appears bloated yet constrained, like an overstuffed, glittering garbage can.'[35]

Technology has also redefined the relationship between humanity and its agencies. The real humans in *Blade Runner* make Paulie, Adrian, and Apollo Creed seem vibrant by contrast. The ever-present street people are alienated scavengers in a multilingual Tower of Babel. Although the city has the feel of stultifying overpopulation, no one seems to live near anyone else. (The wealthier by now have escaped to off-world suburbs.) Tyrell, a paranoid recluse, lives in an inaccessible penthouse high atop a grotesque, pretentious structure in downtown L.A., a fitting image for the perversion of the hierarchy of technical reason he has ascended. The police chief who forces Deckard back from retirement is a calloused bigot who refers to replicants as 'skin-jobs.' Deckard describes himself in an early voice over as 'Sushi, that's what my ex-wife called me. Cold fish.' The most poignant symbol of the humans' descent is J.F. Sebastian, the genetic engineer who works for Tyrell. Occupying an entire glum apartment building by himself, he manufactures 'friends' to keep him company, and perhaps also to ward off the knowledge that he is fast becoming extinct; at age 25, he has 'Methuselah Syndrome' ('accelerated decrepitude') and, like the desperate replicants, not long to live.

More human than human is the motto at Tyrell Corporation, and, indeed, the replicants display a much richer array of human qualities than do the people. Deckard's narration is [wearily self-reflective], but replicant leader Roy Batty speaks poetically and wonders about 'his own place between animals and angels, men and machines.'[36] Two of the replicants (Leon and Rachael) carry photographs, supposedly of family members, in order 'to give them the feeling (literally, the *impression*) that they have a human past. . . . For to have a past, whether your own or one you have created, is also to have a future'.[37] While the humans are too catatonic to suffer or to react angrily to the techno-commercial exploitation of their home, the replicants are furious at their enslavement. Whereas no human in the film cares about any other human, the replicants care passionately for each other; though murderous, they are more loyal to their own than are the human beings.

Unlike most critics,[38] we regard Rachael as the film's most sentient sign that the characteristics of creator and created have shifted places. Manufactured without a termination date, but implanted with memory chips from Tyrell's niece, she is the only character who does not know what she is, and whose self-definition changes in the course of the narrative from 'human' to 'replicant.' Rachael acts with mechanical indifference during the first half of the story, when she thinks she is human, as if she were imitating how the people around her seem to her. When she begins to suspect that she is a replicant, however, she drops her condescending facade and begins to act humanely. She shows initiative in escaping from Tyrell and questions Deckard intensely about her origins. After she shoots fellow replicant Leon in order to save Deckard, and Deckard tells her the shakes are 'part of the business,' she reflects tearfully on her ontological status: 'I'm not *in* the business. I *am* the business!' Her aesthetic sense is awakened as she begins to play the piano. And she forms a relationship with Deckard. Although she can be seen as acting in a traditionally feminine manner with him (to his 'Say you want me,' she replies, 'I want you'), this submissiveness, we believe, is more appropriately interpreted as the hesitant uncertainty that accompanies trying out each aspect of her 'new' identity as nonhuman.

As was the case in *Rocky IV*, the people in *Blade Runner* do not consciously see their own shadows walking among them. None of the 'average' people can tell the difference between a human and a replicant, and even the experts are sometimes fooled. Rachael wonders about this and asks Deckard if he has ever 'retired' a human by mistake. He answers 'no,' but his expression reveals that this is an obvious risk of the business. Rachael also asks whether Deckard thinks that the work at Tyrell is a benefit to the public. He answers: 'Replicants are like any other machine. They're either a benefit or a hazard. If they're a benefit, it's not my problem.' It is an answer that calls to mind the questionable Western assumption 'that technology is essentially neutral, a means to an end'.[39] But *Blade Runner*'s most near-sighted person, both literally and symbolically, is also the most 'rational.' Just as Victor Frankenstein failed to provide a place for his monster in society, Eldon Tyrell refuses to take moral responsibility for his creations. And just as Apollo Creed's pride veiled from him the dangers that technology posed for him, Tyrell is unable to see that what he calls his 'fail-safe device' is inadequate to protect him from his prodigies' revenge. His reason is impressive, but his eyesight is failing, and his *wisdom* is as artificial as the big-eyed owl that guards the entrance to his factory and home. . . . . . .

The Terminator.[40] The time traveler in this film, Kyle Reese, explains to Sarah Connor that the life he came from is 'one possible future' for humanity. Indeed, *The Terminator* represents most clearly the tragic consequences for humanity, should this shadow story ever be played out to its completion. In contrast to both *Rocky IV* and *Blade Runner*, in which technology is divided from but still dependent upon human agents, technology in *The Terminator* is fully autonomous.

In this post-nuclear context of 2029, technology has virtually completed its task of reconstructing the environment in its own image. Gargantuan [gigantic] tanks roll relentlessly through the 'scenery,' which, like that of *Blade Runner*, is another scrap heap of waste materials from the past. Unlike the scenery of *Blade Runner*, however, this landscape of discarded metal and human bones is all there is: no commercials lure the rich to off-world colonies, and no wooded mountains await the heroes' escape. Because their plight is so desperate, these future humans are no longer passive, as they were in *Rocky*, or dull and alienated, as they were in *Blade Runner*; they have awakened from their somnambulism [sleepwalking] and are fully aware that their shadows are alive, well, and threatening their pitiful existence. Unfortunately, it is almost too late for this newly found consciousness to do them any good. For their hunted condition has reduced them to the status of cornered animals. The brands they wear on their arms are signs that they have lost that most human of characteristics: the capacity to choose; as an endangered species, their only mode of intervention is to battle the machines.

At the outset, the people of *The Terminator*'s present are much like the average, contemporary Americans in *Rocky IV*: tuned into recreational technology and blissfully tuned out of the eventual consequences of their comfortable and convenient lifestyle. Sarah and her roommate Ginger use the requisite modern inventions: hair dryer, telephone answering machine, and scooter. Ginger's perpetual life-support system is a Sony Walkman, which she keeps connected even when making love. A revved-up dance bar is named the 'Tech Noir.' When the Terminator visits the present, however, the people who cross his path are instantly restricted to the choices of the people of the future: kill or be killed (and, for all but Sarah, the first 'choice' is purely academic). Sarah becomes as hunted as the future's guerrillas, her every *act* an automatic *reaction* to the Terminator's.

As separate beings who develop wills of their own, *Blade Runner*'s replicants were close to controlling their own destinies; they did not, however, possess the capacity to extend their immortality by reproducing their own kind. The computer network in *The Terminator*, only 10 years later, has found this key. This reproductive capacity breaks the umbilical cord that keeps technology dependent on its human parent and creates a seemingly unbridgeable generation gap. It also co-opts the most basic feminine form of creation: that of giving birth. In addition, since *Blade Runner*'s replicants were created in the image of a *human* maker, they were synthetic reproductions of the near-whole human agent, and, as the humans grew progressively more obsolete, the replicants grew more human than human. But the Terminator's roots are electric circuitry, itself generated by machines. He is created in the image of a *technological* maker and, as such, is a reproduction of a human part: that of technical reason. Whereas both Drago's and Roy's material substance was organic, the Terminator's is inorganic; he looks human on the outside, but is the most recent triumph in a series of sophisticated robots from the future. 'He's not a man. A machine. A terminator. Cyberdigm Systems Model 101,' Reese tells a disbelieving Sarah. 'The 600 series had rubber skin; we spotted them easy. But these are new. They look human. Sweat, bad breath, everything – very hard to spot.' He is, then, a more advanced incarnation than either Drago or the replicants of the entelechial end of this myth, which is the perfection of rational/technological *agency*, not of the whole human being.

We have already noted how technological agency progressively redefines the scene and the human agent with each advance in the myth. *The Terminator* represents the most perfected form yet of agency-determined *purpose*. Drago's purpose was the improvement of human efficiency; technology had not yet developed a separate intention. The replicants in *Blade Runner* did develop a purpose of their own (delaying their own mortality), but they were still dependent on their human makers to fulfil it. But *The Terminator*'s future computers have generated a purpose that they may act upon without human help. As Kyle 'reminisces' to Sarah: 'It was the machines – Defense Network Computers. New – powerful – hooked into everything. They say it got smart. A new order of intelligence. Then it saw all people as a threat, not just the ones on the other side. Decided our fate in a microsecond – extermination.' Presumably, the Defense Network Computers had been created as elaborate safeguards against nuclear holocaust. Their 'decision' to eliminate the human race by starting a war echoes Jung's prophecy in 1922 that 'fire-arms go off of themselves if only enough of them are together'[41] as well as Winner's warning that 'the foundations of technological society are less reliable than some had hoped'.[42] If humans have finally awakened to realize that the computers are now the master and humanity the slave, the humans must be exterminated lest they try to reclaim from technology the capacities they so blindly gave away. The Terminator's name captures well both his purpose and the fact that technology and humanity have exchanged places as agent and agency. 'Termination' is a term ordinarily not applied to human homicide but reserved for the cessation of mechanical functions, which have no purpose other than to serve as agencies for human intention. Since humans now serve no function for the machines, they might as well be liquidated.

When agency determines purpose rather than vice versa, however, purpose loses its customary association with morality, which is a 'flaw' in the perfection of agency. The Terminator is *rational*, for example, but not *reasonable*. 'You can't reason with him,' Kyle says, although he is the pure embodiment of technical reason. Furthermore, he has no need for community. Whereas Frankenstein's monster pleaded with his creator to make a place for him in human society, and *Blade Runner*'s replicants at least found society with each other, the Terminator has no such limitation and is unhampered by angst over any of his killings. 'He was just being systematic,' Kyle tells the police to explain why the Terminator killed all women with the name 'Sarah Connor' who preceded the Sarah Connor in the Los Angeles telephone directory. The metal skeleton that emerges from the ashes in the climactic battle scene with Sarah, free from all human bodily or communal constraints, seems a macabre caricature of the humanists' moral conception of a 'core self.'

As has been the case with other humans in this myth, the people of the present are so dependent on their technological devices that they do not see the Terminator for what he is. The film has a great deal of 'fun,' not only with the Terminator's masterful use of the humans' technology against them but with people dying while relying upon the latest mechanical gadgets. The Terminator's first act upon entering 1984 is to rip the heart out of a punker who refuses to give up his technology-inspired metallic clothes. His next victim is a local gun shop clerk, whose inventory would warm the heart of any *Soldier of Fortune* devotee. Ginger does not hear the Terminator enter her apartment (not that it would have saved her) because she is hooked up to her Walkman. Sarah gives away her whereabouts by leaving a message on her answering machine, which the Terminator is by now monitoring. In addition, it takes Sarah several near misses to see that the Terminator is somewhat unusual. And, even after the Terminator's inhuman survival of multiple shootings, the police try to convince Sarah he is just wearing a bulletproof vest. They tell her to 'get some sleep' (recalling Dr. Frankenstein's attempt to forget) as the Terminator crashes through the police department's doors in a muscle car.[43] □

The remainder of Frentz and Rushing's essay is dedicated to retrieving the promise of curative renewal that lies hidden within the dystopia of the Frankenstein myth. Rushing and Frentz conclude that, if only man could learn to confront and recognise the apocalyptic aspects of his technological progress, he might perhaps be able once and for all to defuse its annihilative potential. To overcome the haunting double bind of hubris and paranoia, contemporary society is required to follow the example of *Frankenstein*'s Robert Walton who eventually – when it is almost too late – comes to acknowledge that 'such a monster has, then, real existence!' (*F* 1831, p.202). Artificial intelligence is created in humanity's own image and fashioned after its own most cherished ideals. Hence, if the machine turns out vicious and gross, it only shows that there is something fundamentally wrong with humanity itself, something that only introspection and a return to spiritual meditation can cure. In Rushing and Frentz's words:

■ the Frankenstein myth advocates that the machine is currently a largely unseen malignancy which will indeed result in the degeneration or death of humanity in the future, but only if the prescription for remedy implanted within the myth itself is not heeded. Specifically, the myth suggests that the medicine for cultural psychic health lies within, as a form of *inner seeing* rather than *outer control*.[44] □

As the corresponding titles of the first and final chapters of this Guide suggest, a study on *Frankenstein* had better refrain from providing its readers with any kind of definitive conclusion. As amply demonstrated by the material introduced and discussed in this volume, Shelley's tale of artificial creation is sure to continue opening itself up to a never-ending revival in the imagination of both artists and critics, be they of a progressive or conservative persuasion, arrogant or timid. Uniquely combining a vision of immortality and human regeneration with a warning of apocalyptic decline and eternal damnation, the thematic ambivalence of *Frankenstein* remains unrivalled, alternately resounding with the human overreacher's cry of fearful triumph ('It's Alive!') and his robot's blunt annunciation of terminal destruction ('I'll Be Back!').

NOTES

INTRODUCTION

1 Most of these little-known texts are now available in Nora Crook's recent scholarly edition of *The Novels and Selected Works of Mary Shelley*, volumes 1–8 (London: Pickering, 1996).

2 Alan Rauch, 'The Monstrous Body of Knowledge in Mary Shelley's *Frankenstein*', *Studies in Romanticism*, 34 (1995), p. 227.

3 Frann Michel, 'Lesbian Panic and Mary Shelley's *Frankenstein*', *GLQ: Journal of Lesbian and Gay Studies*, 2:3 (1995), p. 237.

4 Jay Clayton, 'Concealed Circuits: Frankenstein's Monster, the Medusa, and the Cyborg', *Raritan*, 15:4 (1996), p. 56.

5 *Journals*, vol. 1, p. 70 (19 March 1815).

6 Chris Baldick, *In Frankenstein's Shadow: Myth, Monstrosity, and Nineteenth-Century Writing* (Oxford: Clarendon, 1987), p. 36.

7 William Veeder, *Mary Shelley and Frankenstein: The Fate of Androgyny* (University of Chicago Press, 1986), p. 4.

CHAPTER ONE

1 For a useful brief summary of early nineteenth-century debates concerning the 'principle of life' and the possibilities of animating lifeless matter see Marilyn Butler's introduction to *Mary Shelley. Frankenstein, or The Modern Prometheus. The 1818 Text* (Oxford University Press, 1993), especially 'The Shelleys and Radical Science', pp. xv–xxi.

2 Much has been written on *Frankenstein* as the first science fiction novel. See especially Brian Stableford, '*Frankenstein* and the Origins of Science Fiction', in David Seed, ed., *Anticipations: Essays on Early Science Fiction and Its Precursors* (Liverpool University Press, 1995), pp. 46–57, and Judith A. Spector, 'Science Fiction and the Sex War: A Womb of One's Own', *Literature and Psychology*, 31:1 (1981), pp. 21–32. Interesting also is the first chapter of Brian Aldiss, *Trillion Year Spree. The History of Science Fiction* (London: Paladin, 1986).

3 George Levine, 'The Ambiguous Heritage of *Frankenstein*' in G. Levine and U. C. Knoepflmacher, eds, *The Endurance of Frankenstein* (Berkeley: University of California Press, 1979), p. 7.

4 Fred Botting, 'Introduction', *Frankenstein* (Basingstoke: Macmillan, 1995), p. 4.

5 Christopher Small, *Ariel Like a Harpy: Shelley, Mary and 'Frankenstein'* (London: Gollancz, 1972), p. 25.

6 Small (1972), p. 24.

7 [John Croker], [review of] *Frankenstein, or The Modern Prometheus, Quarterly Review*, 18 (1818), p. 380.

8 Croker (1818), p. 383.

9 Croker (1818), p. 384.

10 Croker (1818), p. 385.

11 [Anonymous review of] *Frankenstein, or The Modern Prometheus, Gentleman's Magazine*, ND 88 (1818), p. 334.

12 [Sir Walter Scott], [review of] *Frankenstein, or The Modern Prometheus, Edinburgh Magazine*, NS 2 (March 1818), p. 249.

13 Scott (1818), p. 249.

14 Scott (1818), p. 253.

15 Percy Bysshe Shelley, 'On "Frankenstein"', *Athenaeum*, 10 November 1832, p. 730.

16 For selected extracts from these dramatisations, plus an informed critical commentary, see Stephen E. Forry, *Hideous Progenies: Dramatizations of Frankenstein from Mary Shelley to the Present* (Philadelphia: University of Pennsylvania Press, 1990).

17 [Anonymous], 'The Anniversary', *Knight's Quarterly Magazine*, 3 (1824), p. 197.

18 Levine (1979), pp. 3–4.

19 Small (1972), p. 15.

20 Edmund Burke, *A Philosophical Enquiry into the Origin of Our Ideas of the Sublime and Beautiful*, ed. J.T. Boulton (New York, 1958), part I, section XIV, p. 46.

21 M.A. Goldberg, 'Moral and Myth in Mrs Shelley's *Frankenstein*', *Keats-Shelley Journal*, 8 (1959), pp. 28–29.

22 Goldberg (1959), p. 29.

23 *The Works of Lord Byron*, ed. E.H. Coleridge (London, 1901), vol. 4, pp. 104–6, and *The Complete Works of Percy Bysshe Shelley*, ed. R. Ingpen and W.E. Peck (New York, 1926–9), vol. 1, p. 173.

24 William Godwin, *Enquiry concerning Political Justice*, ed. F.E.L. Priestley (Toronto, 1946), vol. 1, pp. 317, 311; vol. 2, pp. 325–6. See also vol. 1, p. 461, where Godwin insists that 'real knowledge is benevolent, not cruel and retaliating'.

25 Thomas Paine, *The Rights of Man* (New York, 1951), pp. 157–8.

26 Shelley (1926–9), vol. 1, p. 174.

27 Goldberg (1959), pp. 32–5.

28 R. Glynn Grylls, *Mary Shelley: A Biography* (London: Oxford University Press, 1938), p. 320.

29 Grylls (1938), ibid.

30 Sylva Norman, 'Mary Wollstonecraft Shelley', in Kenneth N. Cameron, ed., *Shelley and His Circle* (Cambridge, Massachusetts.: Oxford University Press, 1970), vol. 3, p. 409. Grylls and Norman share the same academic background, as Grylls's acknowledgement of indebtedness 'to Miss Sylva Norman for setting me on many tracks' reveals (Grylls [1938], p. viii).

31 Norman (1970), p. 408.

32 Norman (1970), ibid.

33 Muriel Spark, *Mary Shelley* (London: Constable, 1988), p. 154.

34 Levine (1979), p. 3.

35 George Levine and U.C. Knoepflmacher, 'Preface', *The Endurance of Frankenstein* (Berkeley: University of California Press, 1979), p. xii.

36 Levine and Knoepflmacher (1979), p. xiii.

37 Levine and Knoepflmacher (1979), p. xi.

38 Levine and Knoepflmacher (1979), ibid.

39 Levine and Knoepflmacher (1979), p. xii.

40 Botting (1995), p. 1.

41 Fred Botting, *Making Monstrous: Frankenstein, Criticism, Theory* (Manchester University Press, 1991), p. 4.

42 Botting (1991), p. 3.

CHAPTER TWO

1 Other biographical approaches to Mary Shelley's work include Walter E. Peck, 'The Biographical Element in the Novels of Mary Wollstonecraft Shelley', *PMLA*, 38 (1923), pp. 196–219, and William St Clair's more recent study, *The Godwins and the Shelleys: The Biography of a Family* (London and Boston: Faber and Faber, 1989).

2 In its reliance on Harold Bloom's psychoanalytically inspired concept of intertextuality Bronfen's approach resembles that of Sandra M. Gilbert and Susan Gubar in their chapter on *Frankenstein* in *The Madwoman in the Attic. The Woman Writer and the Nineteenth-Century Literary Imagination* (New Haven: Yale University Press, 1979). Gilbert and Gubar read the novel's many intertextual references to *Paradise Lost* as indicative of an oedipal father-daughter conflict between Mary Shelley and John Milton. In their view, 'Mary Wollstonecraft Godwin Shelley was the daughter and later the wife of some of Milton's keenest critics, so that Harold Bloom's useful conceit about the family romance of English literature is simply an accurate description of the reality of her life' (p. 221).

3 Elisabeth Bronfen, 'Rewriting the Family: Mary Shelley's "Frankenstein" in Its Biographical/Textual Context', in Stephen Bann, ed., *Frankenstein, Creation, Monstrosity* (London: Reaktion, 1994), p. 29. Once again, Bronfen's approach is reminiscent of Gilbert and Gubar's who suggest – in the inimitably exaggeratory style characteristic of their work – that 'endlessly studying her mother's works and her father's, Mary Shelley may be said to have "read" her family and to have been related to her reading, for books appear to have functioned as her

surrogate parents, pages and words standing in for flesh and blood' (*The Madwoman in the Attic*, p. 223).

4 Sigmund Freud, 'Family Romances', in *The Standard Edition of the Complete Psychological Works of Sigmund Freud*, ed. J. Strachey et al., 24 vols (London 1953–74), vol. 9, p. 237.

5 Freud (1953–74), vol. 9, p. 239.

6 Freud (1953–74), vol. 9, p. 241.

7 Harold Bloom, *The Anxiety of Influence: A Theory of Poetry* (New York: Oxford University Press, 1973).

8 Indeed, as Muriel Spark argues in *Mary Shelley* (London: Constable, 1988), while the parents Wollstonecraft and Godwin modified their theories as they put them into practice, the children Mary and Percy Shelley, initially at least, radicalized them. Repeatedly they lived by the books their parents wrote. As Spark notes: 'Mary was to return to her mother's work, as if to find in those pages a glimpse into part of her own nature; she was, moreover, justly proud of her parentage, and sitting on the rock with Shelley it pleased her to hear him talk about her mother's autobiographical romance' (p. 29). See also Anne K. Mellor, *Mary Shelley: Her Life, Her Fiction, Her Monsters* (New York: Routledge, 1988) and Emily W. Sunstein, *Mary Shelley: Romance and Reality* (Baltimore: Johns Hopkins University Press, 1991).

9 See Levine and Knoepflmacher (1979) and Botting (1991).

10 St Clair (1989) repeatedly documents how Percy Shelley copied Godwin in his activities, living out what both he and his wife had written. The parents' texts served as precedents and justification for the socially unconventional lifestyle of the children: 'It scarcely mattered that the books had been written at different times, in different circumstances, and to teach different lessons: it was enough that they had been written by Mary Wollstonecraft and William Godwin. If the books offered encouragement, the runaways were strengthened in their resolution. If they warned of suffering,

they were comforted to know that their own lives were conforming to pattern' (p. 366).

11 Spark (1988) notes that 'Mary formed the habit of taking her books to her mother's grave in St Pancras Churchyard, there to find some peace after her irksome household duties, and to pursue her studies in an atmosphere of communion with a mind greater than the second Mrs Godwin's' (p. 19). See also Gilbert and Gubar (1979), pp. 213–47.

12 Cited in St Clair (1989), p. 376.

13 Bronfen (1994), pp. 16–24.

14 As Margaret Homans argues in *Bearing the Word: Language and Female Experience in Nineteenth-Century Women's Writing* (University of Chicago Press, 1986), in the author's introduction, Shelley 'aims to bring the writing of the novel further within the fold of the conventional domestic life Shelley retrospectively substitutes for the radically disruptive life she in fact led' (p. 147); the introduction domesticating her 'hideous idea' serves as a trope for her desire to domesticate a monstrous family life.

15 St Clair (1989) documents the weeding of the Shelley archives of any embarrassing documents, as well as Shelley's attempt, in her publications on William Godwin and Percy Shelley, to sever all explicitly intellectual connections between her father and her husband (pp. 492ff.).

16 Spark (1988), p. 129.

17 Bronfen (1994), pp. 36–38.

18 In the introduction to his edition of the 1818 text James Rieger writes that *Frankenstein* 'virtually plagiarizes the diction, ideas, and symbolism of Shelley's "Mont Blanc" (p. xxiii). Percy's 'assistance' is claimed to have been crucial 'at every point in the book's manufacture . . . so that one hardly knows whether to regard him as editor or minor collaborator' ('Mary Shelley's Life and the Composition of *Frankenstein*' in *Mary Shelley's Frankenstein, or The Modern*

Prometheus (the 1818 Text) (Indianapolis: Bobbs-Merrill, 1974), p. xviii. See also E. B. Murray, 'Shelley's Contribution to Mary's *Frankenstein*', *Keats-Shelley Memorial Bulletin*, 29 (1978), pp. 50–68.

19 Mary Poovey, 'My Hideous Progeny: Mary Shelley and the Feminization of Romanticism', *PMLA*, 95 (1980), p. 332.

20 Poovey (1980), ibid.

21 Poovey (1980), p. 334.

22 James P. Carson, 'Bringing the Author Forward: *Frankenstein* through Mary Shelley's Letters', *Criticism*, 30:4 (1988), pp. 342–43.

23 Ellen Moers, 'Female Gothic', in *Literary Women* (Garden City, N. Y.: Doubleday, 1976), p. 94.

24 Carson is referring to Betty T. Bennett, ed., *The Letters of Mary Wollstonecraft Shelley*, 2 vols (Baltimore: Johns Hopkins University Press, 1980–88).

25 See Gilbert and Gubar (1979), pp. 187–247. Disputing Gilbert and Gubar's position, Fred V. Randel argues that Mary Shelley engages in the Bloomian struggle and wins, 'outperforming an illustrious male tradition at its own game' ('Frankenstein, Feminism, and the Intertextuality of Mountains,' *Studies in Romanticism*, 24 [1985], p. 529). William Veeder, in a psychobiographical critique of the conventional oedipal model, regards the artistic productions of the Shelleys as negotiating strategies, or ways of dealing with their psychical investment in personal and literary relationships; see *Mary Shelley & Frankenstein: The Fate of Androgyny* (University of Chicago Press, 1986). My own attempt to place Shelley's authorial struggles within the context of an incipient critique of individualism follows the general lines of, while it draws on different evidence from, the argument of Gayatri Chakravorty Spivak in 'Three Women's Texts and a Critique of Imperialism', *Critical Inquiry*, 12 (1985), pp. 243–61.

26 Peggy Kamuf, 'Writing Like a Woman', in S. McConnell-Ginet, R. Borker and N. Furman, eds, *Women and Language in Literature and Society* (New York: Praeger, 1980), p. 286. In her critique of Anglo-American feminism, Toril Moi makes a similar point about how the notion of the integrated self is part of patriarchal ideology: 'In this humanist ideology the self is the sole author of history and of the literary text: the humanist creator is potent, phallic and male – God in relation to his world, the author in relation to his text' (*Sexual/Textual Politics: Feminist Literary Theory* [London: Methuen, 1985], p. 8).

27 *Letters*, vol. 2, p. 22 (5 January 1818).

28 Mary Poovey, *The Proper Lady and the Woman Writer: Ideology as Style in the Works of Mary Wollstonecraft, Mary Shelley, and Jane Austen* (University of Chicago Press, 1984), pp. xvii and 4.

29 For the late eighteenth-century 'feminization of discourse' or even 'feminization of human nature itself', see Terry Eagleton, *The Rape of Clarissa: Writing, Sexuality and Class Struggle in Samuel Richardson* (Oxford: Basil Blackwell, 1982), pp. 13 and 95, and Terry Castle, 'The Female Thermometer', *Representations*, 17 (1987), pp. 13–15.

30 *Letters*, vol. 2, p. 17 (9 November 1827).

31 *Letters*, vol. 2, p. 4 (12 September 1827).

32 Carson (1988), p. 432.

33 *Letters*, vol. 2, p. 48 (20 June 1828). Stéphanie du Crest de Saint-Aubin, Comtesse de Genlis was the author of *Mémoires Inédits de Madame la Comtesse de Genlis* (Paris and London: Colburn, 1825). One is reminded here of Virginia Woolf's reaction to a new novel by 'Mr. A.': 'after reading a chapter or two a shadow seemed to lie across the page. It was a straight dark bar, a shadow shaped something like the letter "I". . . . One began to be tired of "I"' (*A Room of One's Own* [Harmondsworth: Penguin, 1975], p. 98).

34 Carson (1988), pp. 435–8.

35 Poovey (1980), p. 339.

36 Carson (1988), p. 450.

37 *Letters*, vol. 1, p.254 (27 August 1822).

38 Carson (1988), pp.445–8.

39 *The Journals of Mary Shelley*, ed. by P.R. Feldman and D. Scott-Kilvert (Oxford University Press, 1987), vol. 2, p.554. Quoted in James O'Rourke, '"Nothing More Unnatural": Mary Shelley's Revision of Rousseau', *ELH*, 56:3 (1989), p.566.

40 Like Shelley herself, Rousseau lost his mother in early infancy.

41 See U.C. Knoepflmacher, 'Thoughts on the Aggression of Daughters', Levine and Knoepflmacher (1979), pp.88–119.

42 *Journals*, vol. 2, p.555.

43 Mary Shelley, 'Rousseau', in *Lives of the Most Eminent Literary And Scientific Men Of France* (London: Longman and Taylor, 1839), vol. 2, pp.130–31. The volume is part of the Reverend Dionysius Lardner's *Cabinet Cyclopedia*, and the Rousseau essay occupies pp.111–74 of this volume.

44 'Rousseau', p.132.

45 'Rousseau', pp.132–3.

46 'Rousseau', pp.134–5.

47 'Rousseau', p.135.

48 Mary Wollstonecraft, *A Vindication of the Rights of Woman*, ed. by C.H. Poston (New York: Norton, 1975), p.14.

49 Jean Jacques Rousseau, 'A Discourse on the Origin of Inequality among Men' in *The Social Contract and Discourses*, trans. G.D.H. Cole; revised and augmented by J.H. Brumfitt and J.C. Hall (New York: Dutton, 1973), p.41.

50 *Paradise Lost*, 8.287–91.

51 Rousseau, 'A Discourse on the Origin of Inequality among Men', p.50.

52 It is beyond the scope of this essay to offer an extensive interpretation of the *Second Discourse*. Rousseau's account in the *Second Discourse* of the origin of a social instinct can be found in the Pleiade edition (Paris: Gallimard, 1964), p.169, or in Cole's translation, p.81.

53 Rousseau, 'A Discourse on the Origin of Inequality', p.66.

54 Rousseau, 'A Discourse on the Origin of Inequality', p.108.

55 Knoepflmacher (1979), p.106.

56 George Levine, 'Frankenstein and Realism,' in *The Realistic Imagination: English Fiction from Frankenstein to Lady Chatterley* (University of Chicago Press), p.26.

57 *Journals*, vol. 1, p.70 (19 March 1815). Ellen Moers discusses this entry in *Literary Women* (1974).

58 William Godwin, *An Enquiry Concerning Political Justice*, ed. F.E.L. Priestley (University of Toronto Press, 1946), vol. 2, p.526.

59 'Rousseau', pp.172–3.

60 'Rousseau', p.174.

61 Journals, vol. 2, p.555.

62 Journals, vol. 2, p.553.

63 Journals, vol. 2, p.557.

64 Journals, vol. 2, p.559.

65 'Rousseau', p.131.

66 Jean Jacques Rousseau, *The Confessions*, tr. by J.M. Cohen (Middlesex: Penguin, 1953), pp.605–6.

67 Journals, vol. 2, p.555.

68 Journals, vol. 2, p.557.

69 'Rousseau', p.126.

70 O'Rourke (1989), pp.544–59.

71 See also Mellor (1988) who points out that 'in identifying Victor Frankenstein with Prometheus, Mary Shelley was alluding to both versions of the Prometheus myth: Prometheus *plasticator* and Prometheus *pyrphoros*. In the first version, known to Mary Shelley through Ovid's *Metamorphoses* which she read in 1815, Prometheus created man from clay . . . In the alternate, more famous version of the myth, Prometheus is the fire-stealer, the god who defied Jupiter's tyrannical oppression of humanity by giving fire to man and was then punished by having his liver eaten by vultures until he divulged his secret foreknowledge of Jupiter's downfall. By the third century A.D., these two versions had fused; the fire stolen by Prometheus became the fire of life with which he animated his man of clay' (p.71).

72 Theodore Ziolkowski, 'Science, Frankenstein, and Myth', *Sewanee Review*, 89:1 (1981), pp.44–8.

CHAPTER THREE

1 See J.M. Hill, 'Frankenstein and the Physiognomy of Desire', American Imago, 32 (1975), pp. 335–58; Gordon D. Hirsch, 'The Monster Was a Lady: On the Psychology of Mary Shelley's Frankenstein', Hartford Studies in Literature, 7 (1975), pp. 116–53; Gerhard Joseph, 'Frankenstein's Dream: The Child as Father of the Monster', Hartford Studies in Literature, 7 (1975), pp. 97–115; Morton Kaplan and Robert Kloss, 'Fantasy of Paternity and the Doppelgänger: Mary Shelley's Frankenstein', in The Unspoken Motive: A Guide to Psychoanalytic Literary Criticism (New York: Free Press, 1973), pp. 119–45; and Marc A. Rubenstein, '"My Accursed Origin": The Search for the Mother in Frankenstein', Studies in Romanticism, 15 (1976), pp. 165–94. See also Rosemary Jackson, 'Narcissism and Beyond: A Psychoanalytic Reading of Frankenstein and Fantasies of the Double', in Aspects of Fantasy. Selected Essays from the Second International Conference on the Fantastic in Literature and Film, ed. by W. Coyle (Westport/Connecticut and London: Greenwood, 1986), pp. 43–53. Other interpretations largely or partly indebted to psychoanalytic criticism include Massao Miyoshi, The Divided Self: A Perspective on the Literature Of the Victorians (New York Univ. Press, 1969), pp. 79–89; William A. Walling, Mary Shelley (New York: Twayne, 1972); John A. Dussinger, 'Kinship and Guilt in Mary Shelley's Frankenstein', Studies in the Novel, 8 (1976), pp. 238–55; and Martin Tropp, Mary Shelley's Monster (Boston: Houghton, 1976).

2 Botting (1991), p. 93.

3 See Rubinstein (1976), p. 176.

4 Both the mother and Elizabeth are orphans, one 'adopted' by Frankenstein's father, the other by Frankenstein as his 'more than sister' (F 1831, p. 35). The mother, on her deathbed, urges the Frankenstein-Elizabeth union, and after the mother's death Elizabeth assumes the maternal role in the household. It is noteworthy that the first Gothic tale mentioned in the Introduction is 'the History of the Inconstant Lover, who, when he thought to clasp the bride to whom be had pledged his vows, found himself in the arms of the pale ghost of her whom he had deserted' (F 1831, p. 7). If Elizabeth is the mother's corpse, Justine is a miniature of the mother, the incriminating object the Creature plants on Justine's person.

5 See Peter Brooks, '"Godlike Science/Unhallowed Arts": Language, Nature, and Monstrosity', in Levine and Knoepflmacher (1979), p. 213.

6 Most of my definitions of psychoanalytic terminology are taken from Feminism and Psychoanalysis. A Critical Dictionary, ed. by E. Wright (Oxford: Blackwell, 1992).

7 Hill (1975), p. 350.

8 George Levine, 'Frankenstein and the Tradition of Realism', Novel, 7 (1973), p. 25.

9 Levine (1979), p. 15.

10 See Harold Bloom, 'Frankenstein, or The Modern Prometheus', in The Ringers in the Tower: Studies in Romantic Tradition (University of Chicago Press, 1971), pp. 121–2. On Mary Shelley's psyche see Hirsch (1975), Rubenstein (1976), Moers (1977), Knoepflmacher (1979), and Susan Harris Smith, 'Frankenstein: Mary Shelley's Psychic Divisiveness', Women and Literature, 5 (1977), pp. 42–53.

11 Compare Poovey (1980), p. 337.

12 Jacques Derrida, Positions (Chicago University Press, 1981 [1972]), p. 27. Quoted in Jonathan Culler, On Deconstruction. Theory and Criticism after Structuralism (London: Routledge, 1983), p. 97.

13 On the traditional daemon see Paul Sherwin, Precious Bane: Collins and the Miltonic Legacy (Austin: University of Texas Press, 1977), pp. 67–75.

14 Paul Sherwin, 'Frankenstein: Creation as Catastrophe', PMLA, 96 (1981), pp. 883–91.

15 Botting (1991), p. 136.

16 Joseph (1975), p. 100.

17 Tropp (1976), p. 31.

18 Botting (1991), pp. 90–91.

19 See, for example, Hill (1975), p. 350.

20 Hill (1975), pp. 335–6.

21 Hill (1975), p. 338.

22 Kaplan and Kloss (1973), p. 6.

23 Robert Wexelblatt, 'The Ambivalence of *Frankenstein*', *Arizona Quarterly*, 36 (1980), p. 105.

24 Kaplan and Kloss (1973), p. 136.

25 Wexelblatt (1980), p. 107.

26 Tropp (1976), p. 20.

27 Kaplan and Kloss (1973) argue that art has therapeutic functions (p. 144).

28 Hill (1973), p. 338 [Botting's emphasis].

29 Botting (1991), pp. 94–98.

30 In 'Science Fiction and the Sex War: A Womb of One's Own', Judith Spector explains why – despite its roots in early nineteenth-century women's writing – science fiction developed into an almost exclusively male genre: 'In the . . . claiming of science fiction as a genre for, by, and about men of action, male authors have had some assistance from Freudian and Jungian Psychology. Freud enables us to see the creation of culture and art as a masculine compensatory activity in lieu of woman's physical procreative function; Jung declares that Logos or intellect is man's true function, and leaves Eros and its concomitant procreative activities to women. Understood prescriptively, both Freud and Jung send Mary Shelley and other women writers back to their nurseries to fulfill themselves through anatomy and Eros and to avoid the terrible guilt which might ensue should they pursue intellectual creativity to the exclusion of all else.' Spector adds that 'as soon as women are relegated to physical procreativity, men are free to claim intellectual creativity as their equal opposite right' (*Literature and Psychology*, 31:1 [1981], p. 22).

31 Devon Hodges, '*Frankenstein* and the Feminine Subversion of the Novel', *Tulsa Studies in Women's Literature*, 2:2 (1983), pp. 158–59.

32 Hodges (1983), p. 156.

33 Hodges (1983), p. 162.

CHAPTER FOUR

1 Barbara Johnson, 'My Monster/My Self', *Diacritics*, 12:2 (1982), p. 2.

2 Ellen Moers, *Literary Women* (London: Allen, 1977), p. 92.

3 Johnson (1982), p. 6.

4 Mary Jacobus, 'Is There a Woman in This Text?', *New Literary History*, 14 (1982–83), p. 138.

5 Gilbert and Gubar (1979), p. 232.

6 Gilbert and Gubar (1979), p. 237.

7 Gilbert and Gubar (1979), p. 249.

8 Johnson (1982), p. 7.

9 Johnson (1982), p. 9.

10 Brian Easlea, *Fathering the Unthinkable: Masculinity, Scientists and the Nuclear Arms Race* (London: Pluto, 1983), p. 36.

11 Angela Carter, *The Sadeian Woman. An Exercise in Cultural History* (London: Virago, 1979), p. 5.

12 Mary Shelley thus heralds a tradition of literary utopias and dystopias that depict single-sex societies, a tradition most recently appropriated by feminist writers to celebrate exclusively female societies. For an analysis of the strengths and weaknesses of such feminist utopian writing, in which female societies are reproduced by parthenogenesis [nonsexual reproduction], see my 'On Feminist Utopias', *Women's Studies*, (1982): pp. 241–62. Leading examples of this genre include Charlotte Perkins Gilman's *Herland*, Sally Miller Gearhart's *The Wanderground*, Joanna Russ's *The Female Man*, James Tiptree, Jr.'s 'Houston, Houston Do You Read?' and Suzy McKee Charnas's trilogy *The Vampire Tragedy*.

13 On the gender division of nineteenth-century European culture, see Jean Elshtain, *Public Man, Private Woman: Women in Social and Political Thought* (Oxford: Robertson, 1981) and E. Hellerstein et al., *Victorian Women: A Documentary Account of Women's Lives in Nineteenth-Century England, France, and the United States* (Stanford University

Press, 1981). For a study of sex roles in *Frankenstein*, see Kate Ellis, 'Monsters in the Family: Mary Shelley and the Bourgeois Family', in Levine and Knoepflmacher (1979), pp. 123–42, and Anca Vlasopolos, '*Frankenstein*'s Hidden Skeleton: The Psycho-Politics of Oppression', *Science-Fiction Studies*, 10 (1983): pp. 125–36. William Veeder, in his insightful but occasionally reductive psychological study of Mary and Percy Shelley and Frankenstein, *Mary Shelley and Frankenstein: The Fate of Androgyny* (University of Chicago Press, 1986), wishes to define masculinity and femininity as the complementary halves of an ideally balanced androgynous or agapic [free of sexual division] personality that is destroyed or bifurcated by erotic self-love; his book traces the reasons why Shelley's fictional characters realise or fail to achieve her androgynous ideal. While he is right to argue that Shelley believed in balancing 'masculine' and 'feminine' characteristics, he consistently defines as innate psychological characteristics those patterns of learned behaviour (masculinity, femininity) that I prefer to see as socially constructed gender roles. His readings thus unintentionally reinforce an oppressive biological determinism and sex-stereotyping, even as they call attention to the dangers of extreme masculine and feminine behaviours.

14 Henry Fuseli, *The Nightmare*, first version, 1781 (The Detroit Institute of Art). This famous painting was widely reproduced throughout the early nineteenth century and was of particular interest to Shelley, who knew of her mother's early passionate love for Fuseli. For further details see Peter Tomory, *The Life and Art of Henry Fuseli* (London, 1972), and the *Catalogue Raisonnée* by Gert Schiff, *Johann Heinrich Fussli* (Zurich, 1973). Gerhard Joseph (1975) was the first to note the allusion to Fuseli's painting. Veeder (1986, pp. 192–3) denies the association on the grounds that Elizabeth's hair half-covers her face; in

this regard, it may be significant that Fuseli's woman's face is half-covered in shadow.

15 Paul Cantor has discussed Frankenstein's rejections both of normal sexuality and of the bourgeois lifestyle in *Creature and Creator: Myth-Making and English Romanticism* (New York: Cambridge University Press, 1984), pp. 109–15.

16 *Letters*, vol. 1, p. 303.

17 Veeder (1986) has emphasised the homosexual bond between Frankenstein and his monster (pp. 89–92). Eve Kosofsky Sedgwick arrives at this conclusion from a different direction. In her *Between Men: English Literature and Male Homosocial Desire* (New York: Columbia University Press, 1985), she observes in passing that *Frankenstein*, like William Godwin's *Caleb Williams*, is 'about one or more males who not only is persecuted by, but considers himself transparent to and often under the compulsion of, another male. If we follow Freud [in the case of Dr. Schreber] in hypothesising that such a sense of persecution represents the fearful, phantasmic rejection by recasting of an original homosexual (or even merely homosocial) desire, then it would make sense to think of this group of novels as embodying strongly homophobic mechanisms' (pp. 91–2).

18 While I largely agree with Mary Poovey's intelligent and sensitive analysis of Frankenstein's egotistic desire (in *The Proper Lady and the Woman Writer,* pp. 123–33), I do not share her view that the nature we see in the novel is 'fatal to human beings and human relationships'. Poovey fails to distinguish between Frankenstein's view of nature and the author's and between the first and second editions of the novel in this regard.

19 On Mary Shelley's subversive representation of the traditionally masculinized Alps as female, see Fred Randel, '*Frankenstein*, Feminism, and the Intertextuality of Mountains', *Studies in Romanticism*, 13 (1984), pp. 515–33.

20 Carol Gilligan, *In a Different Voice:*

Psychological Theory and Women's Development (Cambridge, Massachusetts: Harvard University Press, 1982), p. 174.

21 See Nancy Chodorow, *The Reproduction of Mothering: Psychoanalysis and the Sociology of Gender* (Berkeley and Los Angeles: University of California Press, 1978), and Dorothy Dinnerstein, *The Mermaid and the Minotaur: Sexual Arrangements and Human Malaise* (New York: Harper and Row, 1976). See also Nancy Friday, *My Mother/My Self: The Daughter's Search for Identity* (New York: Dell, 1977).

22 Anne K. Mellor, 'Possessing Nature: The Female in *Frankenstein*', in *Romanticism and Feminism*, ed. by A. K. Mellor (Bloomington and Indianapolis: Indiana University Press, 1988), pp. 220–30.

23 Gilbert and Gubar (1979), p. 224.

24 Gilbert and Gubar (1979), pp. 219–20.

25 Leslie Tannenbaum, 'From Filthy Type to Truth: Miltonic Myth in Frankenstein,' *Keats-Shelley Journal*, 26 (1977), pp. 101–13.

26 Gilbert and Gubar, (1979), p. 221. I classify the Gilbert-Gubar view of Frankenstein as a 'cultural feminist' interpretation, in that they tend to see male/female relations as static; that is, they assume that all men are by nature oppressors and that women have no options except 'despairing acquiescence' (a phrase that Gilbert and Gubar apply to Mary Shelley) or sullen resistance. Cultural documents such as novels become, when seen from this perspective, merely reflections of this static confrontation of men and women. Gilbert and Gubar also tend to see literature as existing in isolation from society. Milton's supposed 'misogyny' thus becomes merely a proof that be was a bad man, and Mary Shelley's failure to protest this misogyny becomes a sign of her cowardice. In contrast, a Marxian interpretation of social relationships sees the forms of male oppression and of female resistance and self-assertion as

evolving in response to changes in the social relations of production. As applied to literature, a Marxian perspective enables us to see Milton's and Mary Shelley's views of male/female relationship as conditioned by the social realities of their times. But a Marxian perspective also allows us to seek in literary texts signs of the emergent claims of women to full human freedom, and I detect such signs in the writings both of Milton and of Mary Shelley.

27 My sense that Frankenstein encodes a powerfully subversive vision of human social relations is shared by at least two of the contributors to *The Endurance of Frankenstein*, Levine's and Knoepflmacher's valuable collection of critical essays on the book: see Kate Ellis, 'Monsters in the Garden: Mary Shelley and the Bourgeois Family', pp. 123–42, and Peter Dale Scott, 'Vital Artifice: Mary, Percy, and the Psychopolitical Integrity of *Frankenstein*', pp. 172–202. At least one other critic also shares my belief that Mary Shelley saw Milton as primarily a proponent of human liberation: Milton A. Mays, '*Frankenstein*, Mary Shelley's Black Theodicy', *Southern Humanities Review*, 3 (Spring 1969), pp. 146–53.

28 Burton Hatlen, 'Milton, Mary Shelley, and Patriarchy', *Bucknell Review* 28 (1983), pp. 19–21.

29 Joseph Wittreich, ed., *The Romantics on Milton*, (Cleveland, Ohio: Case Western Reserve University Press, 1970), p. 20.

30 Wittreich (1970), ibid.

31 William Godwin, *An Enquiry Concerning Political Justice*, ed. by I. Kramnick (Baltimore: Penguin, 1976), p. 309.

32 Wollstonecraft (1975), pp. 20–21.

33 Wittreich (1970), p. 538.

34 Wittreich (1970), ibid.

35 Knoepflmacher (1979), pp. 88–119.

36 *Paradise Lost*, 10.743–5.

37 Tannenbaum (1977), p. 110.

38 For some useful comments on *Frankenstein* as a dramatisation of the

struggle between wilful egoism and human sympathy, see Robert Kiely, *The Romantic Novel in England* (Cambridge, Massachusetts.: Harvard University Press, 1972), esp. pp. 166ff.

39 Hatlen (1983), pp. 22–35.

40 Hatlen (1983), p. 35.

41 Hatlen (1983), pp. 36–40.

42 These are Henry Weekes's pièta-like sepulchral monument of the Shelleys, now on display at Christchurch Priory in Dorset, and Louis-Edouard Fournier's painting *The Funeral of Shelley* (1889).

43 James Rieger, 'Mary Shelley's Life and the Composition of *Frankenstein*', in *Mary Shelley's Frankenstein, or The Modern Prometheus* (the 1818 Text) (Indianapolis: Bobbs-Merrill, 1974), p. xxiii.

44 From the first, this figure – variously named Ygor, Fritz, and Dr. Praetorius – has been a staple of stage and screen adaptations of the novel. See Albert J. Lavalley, 'The Stage and Film Children of *Frankenstein*', in Levine and Knoepflmacher (1979), pp. 243–89.

45 Rieger (1974), p. xviii.

46 Rieger (1974), p. v.

47 Rieger here refers to his practice of interpolating the autograph variants from the Thomas copy into the text rather than relegating them to footnotes or an appendix.

48 Rieger (1974), p. xliv.

49 Jacobus (1982–83), p. 138.

50 Jacobus's essay – which forcefully interrogates the text's modus operandi, its participation in a structure that inevitably sacrifices the woman – opens the way for such a discussion, shifting the potential direction for feminist inquiry to the problematic representation of masculine 'theory'.

51 Homans (1986), p. 117.

52 Bette London, 'Mary Shelley, *Frankenstein*, and the Spectacle of Masculinity', *PMLA*, 108:2 (1993), pp. 256–58.

53 London (1993), p. 264.

54 Johnson (1982), p. 3.

55 This view of the novel's gender is generally shared even by feminist critics who do not explicitly engage a theory of female autobiography. Veeder (1986), somewhat reductively, questions this tendency: 'Feminist readings can, however, go too far. . . . Mother can achieve such prominence that father is cast into shadow' (p. 125).

56 This interpretation of *Frankenstein*'s secret is an inversion of Johnson's paradigm: 'It is thus indeed perhaps the very hiddenness of the question of femininity in *Frankenstein* that somehow proclaims the painful message not of female monstrousness but of female contradictions. For it is the fact of self-contradiction that is so vigorously repressed in women' (1982, p. 9). [In *Between Men: English Literature and Male Homosocial Desire* (1985)] Sedgwick sees *Frankenstein*'s 'tableau of two men chasing one another across a landscape' as emblematic of what she calls 'The Age of Frankenstein'. Sedgwick argues that it is 'importantly undecidable in this tableau, as in many others like it in Gothic novels, whether the two men represent two consciousnesses or only one; and it is importantly undecidable whether this bond . . . is murderous or amorous.' For her, texts like *Frankenstein* crystallise 'this paranoid, i.e. specifically homophobic, tableau': 'What I have argued most distinctively and rhetorically marks The Age of Frankenstein is the absolute omnipresence of this homophobic, paranoid tableau, *in the absence of* a widely available sense of a possible homosexual role or culture, and *in the absence of* any felt specificity of male homosexual desire in the culture at large' (pp. ix–x). This analysis of homophobia, however, has not received sustained attention in the *Frankenstein* scholarship. A reading that emphasises masculine contradiction in the novel might link the hysteria- and paranoia-oriented perspectives Sedgwick distinguishes as 'feminocentric' and 'masculocentric'.

57 In my thinking on male subjectivity, I have benefited from the ongoing theoretical work of Kaja Silverman (in

particular, 'Fassbinder and Lacan: A Reconsideration of Gaze, Look, and Image', *Camera Obscura*, 19 [1989], pp. 54–8). Until recently, discussions of masculinity and spectacle have been most vigorously pursued in film studies; see, for example, Steve Neale, 'Masculinity as Spectacle: Reflections on Men and Mainstream Cinema', *Screen*, 24:6 (1983), pp. 2–16.

58 Hodges (1983) makes an analogous point: 'On viewing the animated creature, Frankenstein becomes "discomposed" and his disrupted state appears in the language of the passages following his act of creation: "I started from my sleep with horror; a cold dew covered my forehead, my teeth chattered, and every limb became convulsed . . ."' (p. 159). Hodges reads *Frankenstein*'s thematic and stylistic refusal of coherence as emblematic of 'the feminine subversion of the novel'.

59 Nancy Vickers, 'Diana Described: Scattered Woman and Scattered Rhyme', in *Writing and Sexual Difference*, ed. by E. Abel (Chicago University Press, 1982), pp. 95–110, and 'The Mistress and the Masterpiece', in *The Poetics of Gender*, ed. by N.K. Miller (New York: Columbia University Press, 1986), pp. 19–41. See also Patricia Parker, *Literary Fat Ladies: Rhetoric, Gender, Property* (London: Methuen, 1987).

60 John Mullan offers a valuable discussion of male hysteria in 'Hypochondria and Hysteria: Sensibility and the Physicians', in *Sentiment and Sociability: The Language of Feeling in the Eighteenth Century* (Oxford University Press, 1988), pp. 201–40. Frankenstein would seem to meet all the conditions Mullan summarizes as activating the condition: 'Specifically, hypochondria is seen to be visited upon those for whom refinement, study, or "imagination" involves solitude or retreat, the meditation which excludes all but the subjects of its fixation, the "lucubration" which implies cloistered nocturnal reflection and the writing which comes out of it' (pp. 210–11).

61 See, for example, Frankenstein's complaint on his survival of Clerval's murder: 'Of what materials was I made, that I could thus resist so many shocks, which, like the turning of the wheel, continually renewed the torture' (*F* 1818, p. 149). Freed from literal imprisonment, Frankenstein re-creates the dungeon in his own psyche, in a world circumscribed by the inextinguishable figures of interchangeable men: 'and although the sun shone upon me, as upon the happy and gay of heart, I saw around me nothing but a dense and frightful darkness, penetrated by no light but the glimmer of two eyes that glared upon me. Sometimes they were the expressive eyes of Henry, languishing in death . . . sometimes it was the watery clouded eyes of the monster, as I first saw them in my chamber at Ingolstadt' (*F* 1818, p. 154). In most stage and film versions of the novel, Frankenstein is called not Victor but Henry (Clerval's given name), a substitution that may suggest another novelistically motivated slippage in masculine identity.

62 Veeder (1986), the critic perhaps most concerned with *Frankenstein*'s explorations of masculinity, reads these signs as emblematic of Victor's impotence and effeminacy (p. 122); such a reading, however, relegates these signs to psychological abnormality, foreclosing what might be a more complex exploration of the contradictions that structure the articulation of 'normal' masculinity.

63 See D.A. Miller, 'Cage aux Folles: Sensation and Gender in Wilkie Collins's *The Woman in White*', *Representations*, 14 (1981), pp. 107–36.

64 London (1993), pp. 260–5.

65 Colleen Hobbs, 'Reading the Symptoms: An Exploration of Repression and Hysteria in Mary Shelley's *Frankenstein*', *Studies in the Novel*, 25:2 (1993), p. 156.

66 Hobbs (1993), p. 165.

67 Hobbs (1993), ibid.

CHAPTER FIVE

1 Botting (1991), p. 140. See also Fred Botting, 'Reflections of Excess: *Frankenstein*, the French Revolution and Monstrosity', in Alison Yarrington and Kelvin Everest, eds., *Reflections of Revolution: Images of Romanticism* (London and New York: Routledge, 1993), pp. 26–38.

2 Ronald Paulson, 'Gothic Fiction and the French Revolution', *ELH*, 48:3 (1981), p. 552.

3 Paulson (1981), p. 545.

4 Paulson (1981), ibid.

5 Paulson (1981), ibid.

6 Journals, vol. 2, p. 555.

7 Lee Sterrenburg, 'Mary Shelley's Monster: Politics and Psyche in *Frankenstein*', in Levine and Knoepflmacher (1979), p. 144.

8 Sterrenburg (1979), p. 145.

9 On the rise and duration of the reaction against Godwin see B. Sprague Allen, 'The Reaction Against William Godwin', *Modern Philology*, 4:5 (September 1918), pp. 57–75, and Ford K. Brown, *The Life of William Godwin* (London 1926), pp. 151ff.

10 The use of anti-Jacobin imagery against domestic liberals is discussed in Gerald Newman, 'Anti-French Propaganda and British Liberal Nationalism in the Early Nineteenth Century: Suggestions Toward a General Interpretation', *Victorian Studies*, 17:4 (June 1975), pp. 385–418.

11 Edmund Burke, *Letter to a Noble Lord* (1796), in *The Works and Correspondences of the Right Honourable Edmund Burke*, new edition (London 1852), vol. 5, p. 241.

12 Cited by Brown (1926), p. 155.

13 Brown (1926), ibid.

14 *Anti-Jacobin Review*, 5 (1800), p. 427.

15 *Anti-Jacobin Review*, 3 (1799), pp. 98–9.

16 *Tait's Magazine* (March 1837), reprinted in *The Collected Works of Thomas de Quincey*, ed. David Masson (Edinburgh 1890), vol. 3, p. 25.

17 Godwin, *Enquiry Concerning the Principles of Political Justice*, ed. H.S. Salt (London 1890), pp. 126–7.

18 See especially Gerald McNiece's chapter 'The Literature of Revolution', *Shelley and the Revolutionary Idea* (Cambridge, Massachusetts 1969), pp. 10–41.

19 Burke (1852), vol. 5, p. 216.

20 Burke, *Reflections on the Revolution in France*, ed. Connor C. O'Brien (Harmondsworth: Penguin, 1968), p. 333.

21 Burke (1968), p. 339.

22 Burke (1968), p. 248.

23 Paulson (1981), p. 546.

24 Thomas Jefferson Hogg, *The Life of Percy Bysshe Shelley*, ed. by H. Wolfe (London 1933), vol. 1, p. 367. See also W.E. Peck, 'Shelley and Abbé Barruel', *PMLA*, 35:1 (1921): pp. 347–53, as well as McNiece (1969), pp. 22–24, and Peter Dale Scott (1979), pp. 176–7.

25 Abbé Barruel, *Memoirs Illustrating the History of Jacobinism*, tr. by R. Clifford (London 1798), vol. 3, p. 414.

26 Barruel (1798), vol. 1, p. viii.

27 Sterrenburg (1979), pp. 146–71.

28 Alexander Hamilton, *Outlines of the Theory and Practice of Midwifery*, new ed. (Edinburgh: Charles Elliot, 1787), p. 188.

29 Hamilton, *The Family Female Physician: or, a Treatise on the Management of Female Complaints, and of Children in Early Infancy* (Worcester, Massachusetts: Isaiah Thomas, 1793), pp. 161–2.

30 Hamilton (1787), p. 189.

31 Michel Foucault, *The History of Sexuality. Volume I: An Introduction*, tr. by R. Hurley (New York: Pantheon, 1978), p. 42.

32 James A. Blondel, *The Strength of Imagination in Pregnant Women Examin'd: And the Opinion that Marks and Deformations in Children Arise from Thence, Demonstrated to be a Vulgar Error* (London: Peele, 1727), pp. 10–11.

33 Ambroise Paré, *Of the Generation of Man, in The Works of that Famous Chirugeon Ambrose Parry*, tr. by T. Johnson (London: Clark, 1678), p. 596.

34 The implicit rivalry between the father and these surrogate images is indicated in the story, attributed to Saint Jerome, of how Hippocrates saved a

noblewoman from being punished as an adulteress, for giving birth to a child of dark complexion when she and her husband were both white. It is said that he had observed a picture hanging in the woman's chamber, 'exactly resembling the Infant, and which he found she had been often very intently viewing' (Daniel Turner, *De Morbis Cutaneis. A Treatise of Diseases Incident to the Skin. In Two Parts* [London: Bonwicke, 1723], p. 169).

35 Aristotle [pseud.], *Aristotle's Compleat and Experienc'd Midwife: In Two Parts*, 7th ed. (London, 1740?), p. 28.

36 Blondel (1727), p. i, and *The Power of the Mother's Imagination over the Foetus Examin'd* (London: Brotherton, 1729), p. xi.

37 Blondel (1729), p. 2.

38 Aristotle [pseud.], *Aristotle's Compleat Master-Piece, In Three Parts; Displaying the Secrets of Nature in the Generation of Man*, 13th ed. (London: Felding, 1766), p. 40.

39 Homans (1986), p. 103.

40 The citation includes autograph variants from the Thomas copy of 1823.

41 In a more extensive study of the medical discourse on sexuality informing *Frankenstein*, it would be valuable to explore, as Veeder (1986) has insightfully suggested, the ways in which contemporary descriptions of the physiological effects of masturbation provide an additional explanation for Victor's increasing nervousness and possible insanity. The major works in this area are the frequently reprinted anonymous book *Onania; or the Heinous Sin of Self-Pollution, and all its Frightful Consequences, in Both Sexes, Considered* (1707–8) and S. A. Tissot's *Onanism* (London 1766). For secondary literature on this subject, see E. H. Hare, 'Masturbatory Insanity: The History of an Idea', *Journal of the History of Medical Science*, 108 (1962): pp. 1–25; R. H. MacDonald, 'The Frightful Consequences of Onanism', *Journal of the History of Ideas*, 28 (1967), pp. 423–31, and G. S. Rousseau, 'Nymphomania, Bienville and the Rise of Erotic

Sensibility' in *Sexuality in Eighteenth-Century Britain*, ed. by P. G. Boucé (Totowa: Barnes and Noble, 1982), pp. 95–119.

42 It is worth noting that during the eighteenth century accounts of monstrous births begin to appear with greater frequency in the proceedings of the Royal Academy. The subject matter of this genre of medical discourse . . . can be gleaned from a listing of the titles of some of these cases: 'A Foetus of Thirteen Years'; 'Fatal Accident: Woman Carry'd a Child Sixteen Years'; 'Account of a Monstrous Boy'; 'Account of a monstrous child born of a woman under sentence of transportation'; 'An account of a monstrous foetus resembling an hooded monkey'; . . . 'Part of a letter concerning a child of monstrous size'; . . . 'Part of a letter Concerning a child born with the jaundice upon it, received from its father's imagination, and of the mother taking the same distemper from her husband the next time of being with child' . . . It is clear that when Victor Frankenstein decided to give a scientific account of his own 'monstrous birth', a child that took two years to create, he was not writing in a vacuum, but was contributing to an already well-established genre of scientific inquiry.

43 Wollstonecraft, *Vindication of the Rights of Woman*, ed. by M. Brody (Harmondsworth: Penguin, 1975), p. 247.

44 Veeder (1986), p. 31. This argument was originally made by Poovey (1984) who suggests that the development of Shelley's career reveals 'the way that a certain kind of literary self-expression could accommodate a woman's unorthodox desires to the paradigm of the Proper Lady' (p. 116).

45 Rubinstein (1976), p. 179.

46 Alan Bewell, 'An Issue of Monstrous Desire: *Frankenstein* and Ostetrics', *Yale Journal of Criticism*, 2 (1988), pp. 106–20.

47 Chris Baldick, *In Frankenstein's Shadow: Myth, Monstrosity, and Nineteenth-Century Writing* (Oxford: Clarendon, 1987), p. 10.

48 Alan Rauch, 'The Monstrous Body of Knowledge in Mary Shelley's *Frankenstein*', *Studies in Romanticism*, 34 (1995), p. 253.

49 Rauch (1995), pp. 252 and 231.

50 Rauch (1995), p. 237.

51 Rauch (1995), p. 238.

CHAPTER SIX

1 Sterrenburg (1979), p. 166.

2 Ray Hammond, *The Modern Frankenstein: Fiction Becomes Fact* (Poole: Blandford, 1986), pp. 14–15.

3 These details are taken from W. H. Lyles, *Mary Shelley: An Annotated Bibliography* (New York and London: Garland, 1975), and Peter Haining, ed., *The Frankenstein File* (London 1977).

4 See in particular Tony Bennett, *Formalism and Marxism* (London: Methuen, 1979), chapters 7, 8, and 9, Catherine Belsey, *Critical Practice* (London: Methuen, 1980), chapters 2 and 6, and Terry Eagleton, *Walter Benjamin: Or Towards a Revolutionary Criticism* (London: Verso, 1981), part 2, chapter 3.

5 D. W. Harding, 'The Character of Literature from Blake to Byron' in Boris Ford, ed., *The Pelican Guide to English Literature*, vol. 5: *From Blake to Byron* (Harmondsworth: Penguin, 1957), p. 45.

6 Paul O'Flinn, 'Production and Reproduction: The Case of *Frankenstein*', *Literature and History*, 9:2 (1983), pp. 194–5.

7 O'Flinn (1983), p. 195.

8 See the concluding chapter, 'Towards a Theory of the Gothic' in David Punter, *The Literature of Terror. A History of Gothic Fictions from 1765 to the Present Day* (London: Addison-Wesley, 1980).

9 *New Statesman* (30 January 1932), p. 120.

10 Punter (1980), p. 424.

11 Information from J. Douglas Gomery, 'Writing the History of the American Film Industry: Warner Brothers and Sound', *Screen*, 17:1 (Spring 1976). Facts about the making of the Universal *Frankenstein* in this section are derived from Haining (1977), Levine and Knoepflmacher (1979), Paul M. Jensen, *Boris Karloff and His Films* (New Jersey 1974) and Donald F. Glut, *Classic Movie Monsters* (New Jersey 1978).

12 See, respectively, Tropp (1976), pp. 87 and 90, David Pirie, *A Heritage of Horror. The English Gothic Cinema 1946–1972* (London 1973), p. 69, and Jensen (1974), p. 30.

13 Tropp (1976), p. 97.

14 Jensen (1974), p. 41.

15 Tropp (1976), p. 93.

16 S. S. Prawer, *Caligari's Children: The Film as Tale of Terror* (Oxford 1980), p. 22.

17 Jensen (1974), p. 44.

18 O'Flinn (1983), pp. 202–7.

19 Quoted in Prawer (1980), p. 241.

20 See Pirie (1973), p. 26.

21 Allan Eyles, Robert Adkinson and Nicholas Fry, eds., *The House of Horror: The Story of Hammer Films* (London 1973), p. 16.

22 See, for example, Pirie (1973), pp. 69ff., Tropp (1976), pp. 125ff., Donald Glut, 'Peter Cushing: Doctor Frankenstein I Presume' in Haining (1977), and Albert J. LaValley, 'The Stage and Film Children of Frankenstein: A Survey' in Levine and Knoepflmacher (1979).

23 Quoted in Eyles *et al.* (1973), p. 15.

24 Quoted in Jensen (1974), p. 35.

25 *The Tribune*, for example, found the movie 'depressing' and 'degrading', and for C. A. Lejeune in *The Observer* it was 'among the half-dozen most repulsive films I have encountered'. The inadequacy of a dismissal of horror stories as merely escapist has recently been powerfully argued by Rosemary Jackson, *Fantasy: The Literature of Subversion* (London: Methuen, 1981).

26 O'Flinn (1983), pp. 207–9.

27 Thomas S. Frentz and Janice H. Rushing, 'The Frankenstein Myth in Contemporary Cinema' in *Critical Questions. Invention, Creativity, and the Criticism of Discourse and Media*, ed. by W. Nothstine, C. Blair and G. A. Copeland (New York: St Martin's Press, 1994), p. 116.

28 Frentz and Rushing (1994), p.162,

29 Because science fiction is pre-eminently concerned with contexts that are removed in time and/or place from the present, stories that comment on the present stage of the human/technology relationship often occur outside that genre. *Rocky IV* is included here for this reason.

30 See D.J. Boorstin, *The Image or What Happened to the American Dream* (New York: Atheneum, 1962).

31 David Edelstein, 'Going for the Biff-Bam-Bang', *Voice* (10 December 1985), p.67.

32 See Christopher Small, *Mary Shelley's Frankenstein* (University of Pittsburgh Press, 1972), p.164.

33 L. Winner, *Autonomous Technology: Technics-out-of-Control as a Theme in Political Thought* (Cambridge: Massachusetts Institute of Technology Press, 1977), p.315.

34 *Blade Runner* is based on Philip K. Dick's novel, *Do Androids Dream of Electric Sheep?* (New York: Signet, 1969). However, as Peter Fitting has pointed out, the novel and the film suggest significantly different conclusions concerning the humanity/technology relationship; our comments are thus confined to the film ('Futurecop: The Neutralization of Revolt in *Blade Runner*', *Science-Fiction Studies*, 14 (1987), pp.340–54).

35 Michael Sragow, '*Blade Runner:* Stalking the Alienated Android', *Rolling Stone* (5 August 1982), p.33.

36 Harlan Kennedy, '21st-Century Nervous Breakdown', *Film Comment* (July-August 1982), p.65.

37 D. Desser, '*Blade Runner:* Science Fiction & Transcendence', *Literature Film Quarterly*, 13 (1985), p.175.

38 See Desser (1985) and P. Kael, 'Baby, The Rain Must Fall', *The New Yorker* (12 July 1982), pp.82–5.

39 Winner (1977), p.25.

40 *The Terminator* takes place within two time frames, the future (2029) and the present (1984). Since the robot is constructed in the future and sent to the present, our comments concerning the state of technology are relevant to both time frames.

41 C. G. Jung, *The Portable Jung*, ed. by J. Campbell, tr. by R.F.C. Hull (New York: Viking, 1971), p.465.

42 Winner (1977), pp.295–6.

43 Frentz and Rushing (1994), pp.166–74.

44 Frentz and Rushing (1994), p.178.

SELECT BIBLIOGRAPHY

Recent editions of Shelley's work

Bennett, Betty T., ed. *The Letters of Mary Wollstonecraft Shelley*. Baltimore: Johns Hopkins University Press, 1980–1988.

Butler, Marilyn, ed. *Mary Shelley. Frankenstein, or The Modern Prometheus. The 1818 Text*. Oxford University Press, 1993.

Crook, Nora *et al.*, eds. *The Novels and Selected Works of Mary Shelley*. Volumes 1–8. London: Pickering, 1996.

Feldman, Paula R. and Diana Scott-Kilvert, eds. *The Journals of Mary Shelley*. Oxford University Press, 1987.

Hindle, Maurice, ed. *Mary Shelley. Frankenstein, or The Modern Prometheus*. London: Penguin, 1985.

Smith, Johanna M., ed. *Mary Shelley. Frankenstein*. Boston and New York: Bedford Books of St Martin's Press, 1992.

Biographical criticism

Bronfen, Elisabeth. 'Rewriting the Family: Mary Shelley's "Frankenstein" in Its Biographical/Textual Context'. In Bann 1994, pp. 16–38.

Church, Richard. *Mary Shelley*. London: Howe, 1928.

Clubbe, John. 'Mary Shelley as Autobiographer: The Evidence of the 1831 Introduction to *Frankenstein*'. *Wordsworth Circle*, 12 (1981), pp. 102–6.

Dunn, Jane. *Moon in Eclipse: A Life of Mary Shelley*. London: Weidenfeld and Nicolson, 1978.

Grylls, R. Glynn. *Mary Shelley: A Biography*. London: Oxford University Press, 1938.

Norman, Sylva. 'Mary Wollstonecraft Shelley'. In Kenneth N. Cameron, ed. *Shelley and His Circle*. Volume 3. Cambridge, Massachusetts: Oxford University Press, 1970, pp. 397–422.

Peck, Walter E. 'The Biographical Element in the Novels of Mary Wollstonecraft Shelley'. *PMLA*, 38 (1923), pp. 196–219.

Spark, Muriel. *Mary Shelley*. London: Constable, 1988.

St Clair, William. *The Godwins and the Shelleys: The Biography of a Family*. London and Boston: Faber and Faber, 1989.

Sunstein, Emily W. *Mary Shelley: Romance and Reality*. Baltimore: Johns Hopkins University Press, 1991.

Weissman, Judith. 'A Reading of Frankenstein as the Complaint of a Political Wife'. *Colby Library Quarterly*, 12 (1976): pp. 171–80.

Criticism on *Frankenstein*

[Anon.]. [review of] *Frankenstein, or The Modern Prometheus. Gentleman's Magazine*, ND 88 (1818), pp. 334–5.

[Anon.]. 'The Anniversary'. *Knight's Quarterly Magazine*, 3 (1824), pp. 195–9.

Baldick, Chris. *In Frankenstein's Shadow: Myth, Monstrosity, and Nineteenth-Century Writing*. Oxford: Clarendon, 1987.

Bann, Stephen, ed. *Frankenstein, Creation and Monstrosity*. London: Reaktion, 1994.

Bewell, Alan. 'An Issue of Monstrous Desire: *Frankenstein* and Obstetrics'. *Yale Journal of Criticism*, 2 (1988), pp. 105–28.

Bloom, Harold, ed. *Mary Shelley's Frankenstein*. New York and Philadelphia: Chelsea House, 1987.

Botting, Fred, ed. *Frankenstein*. Basingstoke: Macmillan, 1995.

Botting, Fred. 'Reflections of Excess: *Frankenstein*, the French Revolution and Monstrosity'. In Alison Yarrington and Kelvin Everest, eds. *Reflections of Revolution: Images of Romanticism*. London and New York: Routledge, 1993, pp. 26–38.

Botting, Fred. *Making Monstrous: Frankenstein, Criticism, Theory*. Manchester University Press, 1991.

Brooks, Peter. '"Godlike Science/Unhallowed Arts": Language, Nature, and Monstrosity'. In Levine and Knoepflmacher 1979, pp. 205–20.

Carson, James P. 'Bringing the Author Forward: *Frankenstein* through Mary Shelley's Letters'. *Criticism*, 30:4 (1988), pp. 431–53.

Clayton, Jay. 'Concealed Circuits: Frankenstein's Monster, the Medusa, and the Cyborg'. *Raritan*, 15:4 (1996), pp. 53–69.

Cottom, Daniel. '*Frankenstein* and the Monster of Representation'. *SubStance*, 28 (1981), pp. 60–71.

[Croker, John]. [review of] *Frankenstein, or The Modern Prometheus*. *Quarterly Review*, 18 (1818), pp. 379–85.

Cross, Ashley J. '"Indelible Impressions": Gender and Language in Mary Shelley's *Frankenstein*'. *Women's Studies*, 27 (1998), pp. 547–80.

Dickerson, Vanessa D. 'The Ghost of a Self: Female Identity in Mary Shelley's *Frankenstein*'. Journal of Popular Culture, 27:3 (1993), pp. 79–91.

Dunn, Richard. 'Narrative Distance in *Frankenstein*'. *Studies in the Novel*, 6:4 (1974), pp. 408–17.

Dussinger, John A. 'Kinship and Guilt in Mary Shelley's *Frankenstein*'. *Studies in the Novel*, 8 (1976), pp. 38–55.

Fisch, Audrey A., Anne K. Mellor and Esther H. Schor, eds. *The Other Mary Shelley: Beyond Frankenstein*. Oxford University Press, 1993.

Forry, Stephen E. *Hideous Progenies: Dramatizations of Frankenstein from Mary Shelley to the Present*. Philadelphia: University of Pennsylvania Press, 1990.

Frentz, Thomas S. and Janice H. Rushing. 'The Frankenstein Myth in Contemporary Cinema'. In William Nothstine, Carole Blair and Gary A. Copeland, eds. *Critical Questions. Invention, Creativity, and the Criticism of Discourse and Media*. New York: St Martin's Press, 1994, pp. 155–82.

Friedman, Lester D. 'Sporting with Life: *Frankenstein* and the Responsibility of Medical Research'. *Medical Heritage*, 1:3 (1985), pp. 181–5.

Frost, R.J. '"It's Alive!" *Frankenstein*: the Film, the Feminist Novel and Science Fiction'. *Foundation*, 67 (1996), pp. 75–94.

Gilbert, Sandra M. and Susan Gubar. *The Madwoman in the Attic. The Woman Writer and the Nineteenth-Century Literary Imagination*. New Haven: Yale University Press, 1979.

Goldberg, M.A. 'Moral and Myth in Mrs Shelley's *Frankenstein*'. *Keats-Shelley Journal*, 8 (1959), pp. 27–38.

Goldner, Ellen J. 'Monstrous Body, Tortured Soul: *Frankenstein* at the Juncture between Discourses'. In Lee Quinby, ed. *Genealogy and Literature*. Minneapolis and London: University of Minnesota Press, 1995, pp. 28–47.

Hatlen, Burton. 'Milton, Mary Shelley, and Patriarchy'. *Bucknell Review*, 28 (1983), pp. 19–47.

Heffernan, James A.W. 'Looking at the Monster: *Frankenstein* and Film'. *Critical Inquiry*, 24:1 (1997), pp. 133–58.

Hill, J.M. '*Frankenstein* and the Physiognomy of Desire'. *American Imago*, 32:4 (1975), pp. 335–58.

Hirsch, Gordon D. 'The Monster Was a Lady: On the Psychology of Mary Shelley's *Frankenstein*'. *Hartford Studies in Literature*, 7 (1975), pp. 116–53.

Hobbs, Colleen. 'Reading the Symptoms: An Exploration of Repression and Hysteria in Mary Shelley's *Frankenstein*'. *Studies in the Novel*, 25:2 (1993), pp. 152–69.

Hodges, Devon. '*Frankenstein* and the Feminine Subversion of the Novel'. *Tulsa Studies in Women's Literature*, 2:2 (1983), pp. 155–64.

Hogle, Jerrold E. 'Otherness in *Frankenstein*: The Confinement/Autonomy of Fabrication'. *Structuralist Review*, 2 (1980), pp. 20–48. [Reprinted in Botting 1995, pp. 206–34.]

Homans, Margaret. *Bearing the Word: Language and Female Experience in Nineteenth-Century Women's Writing*. University of Chicago Press, 1986.

Jackson, Rosemary. 'Narcissism and Beyond: A Psychoanalytic Reading of *Frankenstein* and Fantasies of the Double'. In William Coyle, ed. *Aspects of Fantasy. Selected Essays from the Second International Conference on the Fantastic in Literature and Film*. Westport, Connecticut and London: Greenwood, 1986, pp. 43–53.

Johnson, Barbara. 'My Monster/My Self'. *Diacritics*, 12:2 (1982), pp. 2–10. [Reprinted in Bloom 1987, pp. 55–66.]

Joseph, Gerhard. 'Frankenstein's Dream: The Child as Father of the Monster'. *Hartford Studies in Literature*, 7 (1975), pp. 97–115.

Kaplan, Morton. 'Fantasy of Paternity and the *Doppelgänger*: Mary Shelley's *Frankenstein*'. In M. Kaplan and Robert Kloss, eds. *The Unspoken Motive: A Guide to Psychoanalytic Literary Criticism*. New York: Free Press, 1973, pp. 119–45.

Kranzler, Laura. 'Frankenstein and the Technological Future'. *Foundation*, 44 (1988–89), pp. 42–9.

LaValley, Albert J. 'The Stage and Film Children of Frankenstein'. In Levine and Knoepflmacher 1979, pp. 243–89.

Levine, George. 'The Ambiguous Heritage of *Frankenstein*'. In Levine and Knoepflmacher 1979, pp. 3–30.

Levine, George and U.C. Knoepflmacher, eds. *The Endurance of Frankenstein*. Berkeley: University of California Press, 1979.

Lew, Joseph W. 'The Deceptive Other: Mary Shelley's Critique of Orientalism in *Frankenstein*'. *Studies in Romanticism*, 30:2 (1991), pp. 255–83.

London, Bette. 'Mary Shelley, *Frankenstein*, and the Spectacle of Masculinity'. *PMLA*, 108:2 (1993), pp. 253–67.

Mays, Milton A. '*Frankenstein:* Mary Shelley's Black Theodicy'. *Southern Humanities Review*, 3 (Spring 1969), pp. 146–53.

Mellor, Anne K. *Mary Shelley: Her Life, Her Fiction, Her Monsters.* New York: Routledge, 1988.

Mellor, Anne K. 'Possessing Nature: The Female in *Frankenstein*'. In A. K. Mellor, ed. *Romanticism and Feminism.* Bloomington and Indianapolis: Indiana University Press, 1988, pp. 220–32.

Michel, Frann. 'Lesbian Panic and Mary Shelley's *Frankenstein*'. *GLQ: Journal of Lesbian and Gay Studies*, 2:3 (1995), pp. 237–52.

Michie, Elsie B. 'Production Replaces Creation: Market Forces and *Frankenstein* as Critique of Romanticism'. *Nineteenth-Century Contexts*, 12:1 (1988), pp. 27–33.

Moers, Ellen. *Literary Women.* London: Allen, 1977. ['Female Gothic', reprinted in Levine and Knoepflmacher 1979, pp. 77–87.]

Murray, E. B. 'Shelley's Contribution to Mary's *Frankenstein*'. *Keats-Shelley Memorial Bulletin*, 29 (1978), pp. 50–68.

Newman, Beth. 'Narratives of Seduction and the Seductions of Narrative: The Frame Structure of *Frankenstein*'. *ELH*, 53:1 (1986), pp. 141–63.

O'Flinn, Paul. 'Production and Reproduction: The Case of *Frankenstein*'. *Literature and History*, 9:2 (1983), pp. 194–213. [Reprinted in Botting 1995, pp. 21–47.]

Oost, Regina B. 'Marketing *Frankenstein:* The Shelleys' Enigmatic Preface'. *English Language Notes*, 35:1 (1997), pp. 26–35.

O'Rourke, James. '"Nothing More Unnatural": Mary Shelley's Revision of Rousseau'. *ELH*, 56:3 (1989), pp. 543–69.

Pollin, Burton R. 'Philosophical and Literary Sources of *Frankenstein*'. *Comparative Literature*, 17:2 (1965), pp. 97–108.

Poovey, Mary. *The Proper Lady and the Woman Writer: Ideology as Style in the Works of Mary Wollstonecraft, Mary Shelley, and Jane Austen.* University of Chicago Press, 1984.

Poovey, Mary. 'My Hideous Progeny: Mary Shelley and the Feminization of Romanticism'. *PMLA* 95 (1980), pp. 332–47. [Reprinted in Bloom 1987, pp. 81–106.]

Power, Henriette L. 'The Text as Trap: The Problem of Difference in Mary Shelley's *Frankenstein*'. *Nineteenth-Century Contexts* 12:1 (1988), pp. 85–103.

Randel, Fred V. '*Frankenstein*, Feminism, and the Intertextuality of Mountains'. *Studies in Romanticism*, 24 (1985), pp. 515–32.

Rauch, Alan. 'The Monstrous Body of Knowledge in Mary Shelley's *Frankenstein*'. *Studies in Romanticism* 34 (1995), pp. 227–53.

Rieger, James. 'Mary Shelley's Life and the Composition of *Frankenstein*'. In *Mary Shelley. Frankenstein; or, The Modern Prometheus* (the 1818 Text). Ed. J. Rieger. Indianapolis: Bobbs-Merrill, 1974, pp. xi–xxxvii.

Rubinstein, Marc A. '"My Accursed Origin": The Search for the Mother in *Frankenstein*'. *Studies in Romanticism*, 15 (1976), pp.165–94.

[Scott, Sir Walter]. [review of] *Frankenstein, or The Modern Prometheus*. *Edinburgh Magazine*, NS 2 (March 1818), pp.249–53.

Shelley, Percy B. 'On "Frankenstein"'. *Athenaeum* (10 November 1832), p.730.

Sherwin, Paul. '*Frankenstein*: Creation as Catastrophe'. *PMLA* 96 (1981), pp.883–903. [Reprinted in Bloom 1987, pp.27–54.]

Small, Christopher. *Ariel Like a Harpy: Shelley, Mary and 'Frankenstein'*. London: Gollancz, 1972.

Smith, Susan H. '*Frankenstein*: Mary Shelley's Psychic Divisiveness'. *Women and Literature*, 5 (1977), pp.42–53.

Stableford, Brian. '*Frankenstein* and the Origins of Science Fiction'. In David Seed, ed. *Anticipations: Essays on Early Science Fiction and Its Precursors*. Liverpool University Press, 1995, pp.46–57.

Sterrenburg, Lee. 'Mary Shelley's Monster: Politics and Psyche in *Frankenstein*'. In Levine and Knoepflmacher 1979, pp.143–71.

Swingle, L.J. 'Frankenstein's Monster and Its Romantic Relatives: Problems of Knowledge in English Romanticism'. *Texas Studies in Literature and Language*, 15:1 (1973), pp.51–65.

Tannenbaum, Leslie. 'From Filthy Type to Truth: Miltonic Myth in *Frankenstein*'. *Keats-Shelley Journal*, 26 (1977), pp.101–13.

Thornburg, Mary K.P. *The Monster in the Mirror. Gender and the Sentimental/Gothic Myth in Frankenstein*. Ann Arbor, Michigan: UMI Research Press, 1987.

Veeder, William. *Mary Shelley and Frankenstein: The Fate of Androgyny*. University of Chicago Press, 1986.

Vine, Steven. 'Filthy Types: *Frankenstein*, Figuration, Femininity'. *Critical Survey*, 8:3 (1996), pp.246–58.

Vine, Steven. 'Hellish Sport: Irony in *Frankenstein*'. *Q/W/E/R/T/Y*, 3 (1993), pp.105–14.

Vlasopolos, Anca. '*Frankenstein*'s Hidden Skeleton: The Psycho-Politics of Oppression'. *Science-Fiction Studies*, 10:2 (1983), pp.125–36.

Walling, William A. *Mary Shelley*. New York: Twayne, 1972.

Zakharieva, Bouriana. 'Frankenstein of the Nineties: The Composite Body'. *Canadian Review of Comparative Literature*, 23:3 (1996), pp.739–52.

Ziolkowski, Theodore. 'Science, Frankenstein, and Myth'. *Sewanee Review*, 89:1 (1981), pp.34–56.

Related criticism

Aldiss, Brian W. *Trillion Year Spree. The History of Science Fiction*. London: Paladin, 1986.

Cantor, Paul. *Creature and Creator: Myth-Making and English Romanticism*. Cambridge University Press, 1984.

Easlea, Brian. *Fathering the Unthinkable: Masculinity, Scientists and the Nuclear Arms Race*. London: Pluto, 1983.

Hammond, Ray. *The Modern Frankenstein: Fiction Becomes Fact*. Poole: Blandford, 1986.

Hume, Robert D. 'Gothic vs. Romantic: A Revaluation of the Gothic Novel'. *PMLA*, 84 (1969), pp.282–90.

Jacobus, Mary. 'Is There a Woman in This Text?' *New Literary History*, 14 (1982–83), pp.117–41.

Jackson, Rosemary. *Fantasy: The Literature of Subversion*. London and New York: Methuen, 1981.

Kiely, Robert. *The Romantic Novel in England*. Cambridge: Harvard University Press, 1972.

Marshall, Tim. *Murdering to Dissect. Grave-Robbing, Frankenstein and the Anatomy Literature*. Manchester University Press, 1995.

Miyoshi, Masao. *The Divided Self: A Perspective on the Literature of the Victorians*. New York: New York University Press, 1969.

Moretti, Franco. *Signs Taken for Wonders: Essays in the Sociology of Literary Forms*. London: Verso, 1983.

Musselwhite, David E. *Partings Welded Together: Politics and Desire in the Nineteenth-Century English Novel*. London: Methuen, 1987.

Paulson, Ronald. 'Gothic Fiction and the French Revolution'. *ELH*, 48:3 (1981), pp.532–54.

Platzner, Robert L. 'Gothic vs. Romantic: A Rejoinder'. *PMLA*, 86 (1971), pp.266–74.

Punter, David. *The Literature of Terror: A History of Gothic Fiction from 1765 to the Present Day*. London: Longman, 1980.

Sedgwick, Eve K. *Between Men: English Literature and Male Homosocial Desire*. New York: Columbia University Press, 1985.

Spector, Judith A. 'Science Fiction and the Sex War: A Womb of One's Own'. *Literature and Psychology*, 31:1 (1981), pp.21–32.

Spivak, Gayatri C. 'Three Women's Texts and a Critique of Imperialism'. *Critical Inquiry*, 12:1 (1985), pp.243–61. [Reprinted in Botting 1995, pp.235–60.]

ACKNOWLEDGEMENTS

The editor and publisher wish to thank the following for their permission to reprint copyright material: *Yale Journal of Criticism* (for material from 'An Issue of Monstrous Desire: *Frankenstein* and Obstetrics'); Manchester University Press (for material from *Making Monstrous: Frankenstein, Criticism, Theory*); Reaktion (for material from 'Rewriting the Family: Mary Shelley's "Frankenstein" in Its Biographical/Textual Context', in *Frankenstein, Creation and Monstrosity*); *Criticism* (for material from 'Bringing the Author Forward: *Frankenstein* through Mary Shelley's Letters'); St Martin's Press (for material from 'The Frankenstein Myth in Contemporary Cinema', in *Critical Questions. Invention, Creativity, and the Criticism of Discourse and Media*); *Keats-Shelley Journal* (for material from 'Moral and Myth in Mrs Shelley's *Frankenstein*'); *Bucknell Review* (for material from 'Milton, Mary Shelley, and Patriarchy'); *PMLA* (for material from 'Mary Shelley, *Frankenstein*, and the Spectacle of Masculinity', and '*Frankenstein*: Creation as Catastrophe'); Indiana University Press (for material from 'Possessing Nature: The Female in *Frankenstein*', in *Romanticism and Feminism*); *Literature and History* (for material from 'Production and Reproduction: The Case of *Frankenstein*'); *ELH* (for material from '"Nothing More Unnatural": Mary Shelley's Revision of Rousseau'); University of California Press (for material from 'Mary Shelley's Monster: Politics and Psyche in *Frankenstein*', in *The Endurance of Frankenstein*); *Sewanee Review* (for material from 'Science, Frankenstein, and Myth').

There are instances where we have been unable to trace or contact copyright holders before our printing deadline. If notified, the publisher will be pleased to acknowledge the use of copyright material.

Berthold Schoene-Harwood lectures in Literature and Cultural History at Liverpool John Moores University. His research interests concern post-coloniality, Scottish literature and literary representations of masculinity. He is the author of *The Making of Orcadia. Narrative Identity in the Prose Work of George Mackay Brown* (Peter Lang, 1995) and *Writing Men. Literary Masculinities from Frankenstein to the New Man* (Edinburgh University Press, 2000).

INDEX